An OPUS book

Change in British So...

A. H. Halsey is Professor of Social and Administrative Studies at Oxford University and a fellow of Nuffield College. His many publications include *Power and Ideology in Education* (with J. Karabel) and *Origins and Destinations* (with A. F. Heath and J. M. Ridge).

CHANGE IN BRITISH SOCIETY

A. H. HALSEY

Fourth Edition

Oxford   New York
OXFORD UNIVERSITY PRESS

Oxford University Press, Walton Street, Oxford OX2 6DP

Oxford New York
Athens Auckland Bangkok Bombay
Calcutta Cape Town Dar es Salaam Delhi
Florence Hong Kong Istanbul Karachi
Kuala Lumpur Madras Madrid Melbourne
Mexico City Nairobi Paris Singapore
Taipei Tokyo Toronto

and associated companies in
Berlin Ibadan

Oxford is a trade mark of Oxford University Press

First published by Oxford University Press 1978
Second edition 1981
Third edition 1986
Fourth edition issued as an Oxford University Press paperback 1995

British Library Cataloguing in Publication Data
Data available

Library of Congress Cataloging in Publication Data
Halsey, A. H.
Change in British society/A. H. Halsey.—4th ed.
p. cm.
"An OPUS book"—Half t.p.
Includes bibliographical references and index.
1. Social change—Great Britain—History—20th century. 2. Great
Britain—Social conditions—20th century. 3. Great Britain—
Economic conditions—20th century. I. Title.
HN390.H3 1995 303.4'0941—dc20 94-27131

ISBN 0-19-289236-3

10 9 8 7 6 5 4 3

Typeset by Best-set Typesetter Ltd
Printed in Great Britain by
Biddles Ltd
Guildford and King's Lynn

For Norman Dennis

True friend and exemplary citizen

ACKNOWLEDGEMENTS

My thanks are due to the *Oxford Review of Education* for allowing me to incorporate part of my article 'Authority, Bureaucracy, and Education' from Vol. 3, No. 3, 1977; to the *Listener* for permission to reprint part of my essay on Liverpool, first published there on 24 February 1983; and to HMSO for allowing me to use tables from the *Report* of the Royal Commission on the Distribution of Income and Wealth; and from *Social Trends*. Thanks also to the *British Journal of Sociology*, for permission to republish part of my article 'A Turning of the Tide', from Vol. 40, Sept. 1989.

PREFACE TO THE FOURTH EDITION

This book has its origins in my Reith Lectures of 1977. A second edition was published in 1981 in response to an invitation from the Open University to revise it as a set book for the Social Sciences Foundation Course. In a third edition it became possible to take advantage of the experience of students in using the book as a general introduction to the social sciences. Few authors have the enlightening, if painful, experience of learning directly about the difficulties they impose on their readers by unclarity or other faults of composition. I am grateful to the Open University tutors and their students for their detailed candour in criticizing my earlier versions. I am especially grateful to Andy Northedge, whose introduction, signpostings, and summaries written for the students about the book have been an invaluable guide in my rewriting.

Professor Stuart Hall and John Clark also put me in their particular debt by their own contributions to the Open University foundation course. Their expositions obliged me to be clearer about my theoretical and political position.

A third edition also gave me the opportunity to take account of social change in the 1980s. In the previous six years a new concept was bequeathed to social science—Thatcherism. It became clear that in the mid-1970s the post-war period came to an end. The Berlin Wall fell in 1989 and the Soviet Union disintegrated. The whole system of the 'Second World' ended. Margaret Thatcher's period as Prime Minister and leader of the Conservative party also ended in 1991. In the period of John Major's premiership, and the leadership of the Labour Party by John Smith in 1992 and Tony Blair from 1994, it has become increasingly clear that Britain has to find its place in post-Maastricht Europe and to revise the Welfare State at home. My intention is to give meaning to these remarks, to provide a comprehensive introduction to the information needed in order to form a view of the direction of twentieth-century social history in Britain, and to offer a sociological interpretation of that history. In a short concluding chapter I have deliberately trespassed beyond sociology to a moral and political interpretation. This I have done mainly in the hope that the reader may thereby be helped and encouraged to form his or her own view and to appreciate both the separation of and the link between the social sciences and social action.

The Current State of British Sociology

When the editors of the *British Journal of Sociology* asked me in 1989 to put together an issue on the current state of British sociology, my first thought was that there is much to be said against it. The point of sociology, after all, is to do it, not to talk about it. This assertion is not simply intended, however, as a doctrinal declaration of empiricism or as a rejection of what is usually called social theory. There is and must be continuing labour on the difficult epistemological and methodological problems concerning the nature of the social sciences. Some of the literature is of high intellectual quality: most of it is essential foundation for empirical enquiry. But agreement at that level is not in sight, whereas technical improvement in research design, data collection, and data analysis cannot be denied. And in between is the core of the research life of the discipline which, through constant professional practice, gradually establishes a corpus of well-defined theoretical problems, tested theories, and attested applications. That position must be always defended and must indeed stand as a redoubt of professional commitment at a time when dispute grumbles and rumbles on over the place of sociology in British intellectual and academic life.

Recent times have not been propitious. A full description of hostile circumstance would include the niggardliness of governmental support for sociological teaching and independent research, the ill-balanced 'client to contractor' policy of Whitehall departments, the centralization of the Economic and Social Research Council (ESRC) on meagerly budgeted programmes from 'initiatives', the utilitarian bias of business support, the declining trickle of graduate studentships, and the remorseless chill of received opinion about sociology. Contemporary sociologists are unloved in a cold climate. Their faith is assailed by adversity and they are obliged to seek their salvation through works.

A recent comment on sociology as an undergraduate subject deserves to be recorded. Martin Albrow in his 1986 presidential address to the British Sociological Association said:

It ought to be clear by now that I make no apology for sociology at degree level. On the contrary, there is every reason to believe that in the current climate, where the narrowest and most vocational possible construction is placed on higher education by government, sociology has a leading role to play in asserting the breadth of a humane education. We can have allies in every sector of the colleges, polytechnics or universities—where support is needed for sustaining a truly humane conception of higher education—and such a conception is still cherished in fields as diverse as medicine, philosophy, management, art and law. The huge extension of so-called service teaching is ample testimony to this.[1]

A Generation Ago

Albrow's view of the nature of sociology offers illuminating contrast with the view taken by W. G. Runciman a generation ago. In 1965 Runciman essayed an answer to the then frequently asked question: why do sociologists write such bad prose?[2] He dismissed some other fashionable explanations and went on to put forward his own in terms of the nature of the subject. Jargon, was, he argued, like treason, only so labelled if it failed. Successful sociology had the rare misfortune of being likely to be assigned to some more specialized discipline or else to be taken over by historians, novelists, or political commentators into the general language of the educated.

Runciman's dependent variable, jargon, is by definition, an unlikely candidate as a fundamental component of a humane education. Yet the technical language of sociology is much less often pilloried today, and many sociological words like charisma or anomie, about which Runciman wondered, have been absorbed into the common language without losing their sociologi-

cal association. What is interesting is that the assumption which
Runciman was able to make, viz. that of all the disciplines sociology was the only one whose most successful achievements
were in constant danger of being classified as something else, is
now probably untenable. The autonomy of the subject internationally seems to be established. In Britain, however, its official unpopularity is greater while its penetration into medicine,
law, history, and management studies is deeper. The problem
seems to have become peculiarly British.

In the mid-1960s it was apparent to Runciman, first, that 'an
almost limitless diversity of topics is covered by writers called
"sociologists"', and second, that the best writers on the same
topics were not normally described as sociologists (and were
much less frequently accused of jargon). It was true then that
sociology, as the academic study of collective human behaviour,
claimed virtually all of history and psychology as its province.
Why then, asked Runciman, are not all books on these subjects
published as 'sociology' books? If Professor David Riesman's
Lonely Crowd was a work of sociology then why wasn't Matthew
Arnold's *Culture and Anarchy* or R. H. Tawney's *Equality* or
H. L. A. Hart's *The Concept of Law* (which Hart himself had
described as 'an essay in descriptive sociology')?

The answer, according to Runciman, was that the best sociologists were likely to be labelled something else and the sad
inference was that sociology was a self-defeating enterprise. Its
successes passed to other academic empires and its failures remained its own residual heartland. But now, towards the end of
the century, it may be claimed, or at least more plausibly argued,
that sociology overseas is successful in defending its conquests
and that where it has withdrawn, for example from its vitalizing
intrusions into political science, it has either secured its captives
or left an acknowledged mark on the territories it temporarily
occupied. It would now be strongly disputed that successful
sociologists are awarded other disciplinary titles or that sociological explanation can only travel to foreign academic jurisdic-
tions on pain of applying for naturalization. To be sure, a
contemporary appraisal could scarcely fail to note opposition

and hostility but it would no longer assume automatic self-destruction.

Explanation of these melancholy phenomena is itself a sociological challenge. For sociology, like industrialism, came early to British culture, struck root but never fully flowered in a soil which remains stubbornly inhospitable. The long story remains to be told. The short one is drear.

We can lay no claim to offer a systematic history of recent British sociology. There is none such. Such a history might well be anticipated as a challenging task for a sociological historian in the closing years of the twentieth century. It might well take off from Philip Abrams's account of nineteenth-century origins.[3] Some of its elements exist in the occasional remarks of Perry Anderson,[4] Joe Banks's essays on the British Sociological Association,[5] my personal account of the first professional post-war generation of British sociologists,[6] Martin Bulmer's collection of essays on the twentieth-century history of research,[7] and Norman Dennis's pungent comment on the influence of Marxism and the Frankfurt school in the 1960s and 1970s.[8] A further step, and a large one, may be anticipated when Ralf Dahrendorf writes his history of the London School of Economics. These sources relate the background of British sociology up to *circa* 1960. A generation later, I would change Runciman's question and further pursue the problem. Jargon apart, it seems to me that the language of sociology has gained in power over the past two decades. A battery of concepts is now available as an integrated vocabulary for the analysis of collective human life by users who are more concerned with its utility than with its derivation, its aesthetic, or its possible destination.

There is now relatively unhampered exchange of words across the range of the social sciences. Let me offer four examples. First, Amartya Sen's distinction between provisions and entitlements is used adroitly by Ralf Dahrendorf to analyse modern forms of conflict and thereby integrate it with T. H. Marshall's distinction between citizenship and social class. Our view of economy (provisions, class) and polity (entitlements, citizenship) thus becomes more powerfully sophisticated.[9]

Second, a trifold distinction between voice, exit, and loyalty, invented by the political scientist Albert Hirschman, can add further to our capacity in sociology to speak about the boundary between economics and politics. Exit generalizes an option in market provision and voice an option in political entitlement. And all three words are useful in sociologists' analysis of co-operation and conflict between spouses over participation in the formal economy and the household division of labour. Third, Brian Barry points out that 'the paradigm of socialism is the prisoner's dilemma'.[10] This use of the language of rational choice theory is then used effectively in contemporary debate over the efficiency respectively of collective and individual market solutions to the provision of goods and exposes the ideological obfuscation which identifies self-interest with individual choice and self-sacrifice with socialism.

Fourth, to take an example of the transfer of concepts across a generation of sociologists as well as from one special sociology to another, we find Heath, Jowell, and Curtice using both the Parsonian distinction between instrumental and expressive behaviour and the statistical distinction between absolute and relative rates to clarify debate about the patterns of voting in the British electorate. This fourth illustration is worth elaborating. Heath and his colleagues[11] distinguish two theories—the expressive and the instrumental—which inform the study of electoral behaviour. The expressive theory holds that social structure determines party support, thus making parties prisoners of circumstance and agency impotent. On this view the future of politics in Britain is ineluctably fixed by the decline of the working class and the rise of non-manual employment. Class cohesion has also weakened and political loyalty increasingly lies elsewhere. The instrumental theory, by contrast, gives causal priority to attitudes as the determinants of votes but treats them as 'givens'. Thus parties should and do shift their policies rationally to maximize support, and citizens, similarly rationally, weigh the issues and policies against their own preferences and vote accordingly. Strictly applied, this theory would predict a Conservative and Labour convergence at the centre of attitudinal gravity (which means, for example, that the Conservatives after 1983 should have modified their policies of privatization and opposition to nuclear disarmament).

Neither theory fits the facts either before or since 1983. To demonstrate their deficiencies, Heath deploys both a refinement of class theory and the method of measurement of relative voting rates to argue that class cohesion has not diminished and to show the limits of changes in social structure as constraints on electoral choice. He then formulates an interactionist theory which incorporates the strength of both of the theories it displaces. In consequence, it can be properly claimed not only that the sociological lexicon is more comprehensive but also that the electorate and the parties are offered significant new enlightenment. Advances of this kind in theory, technique, and application are the mark of a sociology which has matured its capacity to serve both the profession and the society that supports it.

My point in all four examples is a double one. The theories and methods of sociology are becoming a flexible language for the understanding and potentially the changing of the world. That language is increasingly internationalized and interdisciplinary. It flows internationally into as well as out of the formal discipline of sociology. What matters is its intellectual power, not its subject origins. Only in the highly resistant culture of Britain can this development be trivialized into one of detecting and dismissing jargon.

Advance and Adversity

How then can we account for this emerging state of affairs, for disciplinary progress and institutional frailty? The explanation of academic advance internationally is, I believe, primarily endogenous—the profession has learnt from its labours. The establishment of the discipline on the other hand is weak in Britain because of both exogenous and endogenous forces. Internally it had spectacularly over-rapid growth in the 1960s and externally a definition as the equivalent of 'folk devil' in political culture inducing 'moral panic' among the conviction politicians of economic liberalism in the 1980s. University expansion in the 1960s coincided with unanticipated (though not at all unprecedented) student disorder. Sociology and sociologists were identified with disruption and dissent, by some as cause and by others as effect. In either case the hostility consequently created was most intense precisely among the supporters of neo-conservative politics. The heavy bill of Malcolm Bradbury's *The History Man* continues to be exacted long after its characters among tutors and taught have disappeared from the campus.

Sociology as cause of conflict was implausible as an explanation. Consequences do not precede their causes. Student protest and turbulence is spasmodically as old as the European university.

Moreover, other and powerful forces were at work: impatience with the feeble achievements of social democratic politics, disillusion from the increased visibility of the chasm between international ideals and the inhumanity of war, guilt from First World plenitude and Third World penury, frustration among a uniquely indulged generation struggling to come to terms with the gap between the romantic expectations of undergraduate life and the boring, competitive realities of preparation for professional and managerial careers. Sociologists were twice unblessed. They were urgently invited to forsake the vocation of sociology for the avocation of politics and they were simultaneously blamed for their incapacity to explain the changing world which had itself created their profession. Add to these circumstantial distortions the logistic difficulty of staffing the explosion of university posts—at least twenty chairs were created in Britain during the 1962–7 quinquennium—and a parvenu profession, at once passionate in its mission and tenuous in its tenure, was suddenly instated.

Parsonian orthodoxy collapsed as much for external political as for internal intellectual reasons. Cold war and civil commotion denied explanations of order in terms of ultimate values just as the First World War had exploded Hobhousian idealistic belief in societies as evolving progressively towards civilized harmony. But the cognitive turmoil was amplified by the fragility of the orthodoxy which preceded it.

A robust period of functionalist consensus can easily be over-stated. As Giddens has argued,[12] Parsons's *Structure of Social Action* (1936) was never fully accepted in the post-war years as a synthesis of European sociological thought from the earlier years of the century. Giddens is right to insist that Marxism remained influential in Europe, that Weber's theory of action was misrepresented in Parsons, that structural functionalism was inadequate in its treatment of motivation or human agency, and that the problem of subjectivism and objectivism remained un-solved. His own attempt to bridge this fundamental gap by a theory of structuration is in hot current contention. But the point about the recent history of the sociological theory is that the frailty of structural functionalism was catastrophically ex-posed by the political upheavals of the 1960s. It was a major casualty of the chaotic warfare that ensued and sociology itself was desperately wounded.

Intellectual development in the substance of sociology was also driven by these external forces. Most prominent was a resurgent Marxism, structurally biased like Parsonianism, but with its all too easy offer not only to provide the theory and praxis of future history but also to translate private discontent into public issues. Less noticed, but in Britain at least no less important, was an inheritance from the liberal tradition of a different form of historicism. Evolutionary theory and the Whig version of history could be readily attached as a dismissive label to the British legacy from the first Chair of Sociology held from 1907 at the London School of Economics by L. T. Hobhouse.

Nor was historicism of either stripe the only disaster. The nineteenth-century controversy concerning the scientific status of sociology—the battle between natural and cultural science models—confounded the confusion in the shape of the Frankfurt School of Critical Sociology. Meanwhile the rapid social change which encourages sociological thought also tends to promote moral relativism and did so, especially in the 1970s, in the form of yet another competing enterprise—ethnomethodology. Phenomenology had long held a respected if relatively subsidiary place in sociological thought in Europe and America. Its resurgence as ethnomethodology and symbolic interactionism added a further dimension to the bewildering chaos of sociological perspectives struggling to escape not only from evolutionism but also from the consensual varieties of functionalism that had become such dominant imports from the Parsonian school.

It cannot be pretended that theoretical consensus has since been restored. Yet despite all these distractions, displacements, and disputes the claim can still be made that, as a discipline of skills for the pursuit of empirical knowledge, the subject has advanced in the 1970s and 1980s and that British sociologists have participated. For one thing the older Marxist orthodoxy has been shattered. Some of the confrontation and demolition has gone on within the Marxist camp, allowing the re-entry of humanism, the granting of serious explanatory status to 'agency' as against 'structure', and the rediscovery of revisionist possi-bilities in Marx's own writings. Freed from the strait-jacket of its original deterministic theory of history and its conception of class derived from the theory of surplus value, Marxist insight has become available for profitable use at many points in the explanation of human collective behaviour—in the workplace, the family, the school, and the relations between men and women.

But above all, I would suggest, progress within the discipline is owed to positivism. I mean, of course, not the positivism of Auguste Comte but the positivism which is best expressed in the methodological views of Karl Popper. Paradoxically it is this steady drive towards explanation patiently sought through the rigorous empirical testing of theories—a painstaking and often pedestrian enterprise so derided and despised by the active spir-its of 1968—that has gradually secured for sociology the foun-dations of its claims to autonomy. A further and related healing influence is less often remarked. Popper's teaching was rooted just as deeply in morals as in method. *The Open Society* argued for freedom and justice just as passionately as *The Poverty of Historicism* made the case for the logic of discovery most likely to realize such a society. A concept of the good life, civic and cognitive, informs the work as a whole. If Utopian vision can for a moment be stripped of its associations with either impractical dreaming or tyrannical government, then the open society is a Utopia that describes the aspirations of many of the founding fathers of sociology and their contemporary descendants.

This generalization applies equally to sociology itself as an intellectual movement. To be sure, the reflection of a fragmented conception of their subject leaves British sociologists weak in numbers and dispersed in precarious academic organizations, often under confusing titles. And the maintenance of analytic competence through the proper training of students, especially in the empirical and quantitative techniques, requires urgent effort.[13] None the less the task in Britain now is to build the edifice on footings established by our predecessors, to emulate the impressive constructions of our colleagues in the USA, Germany, Japan, and Scandinavia, and so to serve a nation starved of the sociology it needs more urgently than its global competitors.[14]

I have acknowledged my many debts to friends and colleagues in previous prefaces. The debts are now greater: I must thank David Coleman for bringing my demography up to date in Chapter 5, and I must particularly thank Sue Dyson for her secretarial labours.

A.H.H.

Nuffield College, Oxford
May 1994

CONTENTS

LIST OF FIGURES AND TABLES

1 TO KNOW OURSELVES

Britain has changed immensely in the twentieth century. The vast majority of its people have had no direct experience of Victorian society. The tiny minority of $\frac{1}{3}$ million who are over 95 began their lives in a society without radio, the Labour party, plastics, or airlines. They have survived into a world without trams or Sunday suits and with television, computers, the Open University, the closed shop, and the nuclear bomb. Yet it is, in a similar range of trivial and serious senses, the same country. Fish and chips and Sheffield Wednesday and Cambridge and the monarchy are still parts of the social continuity which is Britain.

I want to describe these changes and continuities, and even to explain them. The explanations will be limited and partial, partly because there could be no full explanation without careful comparison with other countries, and more fundamentally because a comprehensive and accepted theory of social change does not exist. By the end of the book I hope to have moved towards a convincing interpretation. But on the way it will become evident that social scientists do not agree as to what causes changes and continuity or even what are the significant features, changing or unchanging, which require either notice or explanation. Accordingly I shall be arguing along the way about the disagreements between sociologists, as well as about the society they wish to explain. And the argument will also raise the question of how far people have it in their power to determine for themselves change in the society in which they live.

The question of the power of people to influence and control their own destiny, whether alone or in concert with others as members of classes or countries or races or religions or historical periods, has been dominated in our time by the philosophical battle between liberalism and Marxism. It might mistakenly be assumed that the battle ended in 1989 with the fall of the Berlin Wall. It might, even more parochially, be assumed that the British mind was made up when Mrs Thatcher came to power in 1979. But states of mind are not that simple and to know ourselves turns out to be a more complex process. On most of the issues of continuity and change, my own position is opposed to both orthodox or 'main-stream' Marxism and to orthodox or economic liberalism. Both these doctrines, in my view, give too much weight to 'structure' as against 'agency'—Marxism conceiving of class struggle and economic liberals discovering the market to be the engine of social change. In arguing otherwise I shall find myself closer to those liberals or socialists who look to democratic institutions as vehicles of change, and closer to the earlier writings of Karl Marx in which he insisted not only that people 'make their own history' but also 'under circumstances directly encountered, given and transmitted from the past'.

Britain is, of course, a Western European capitalist society which has evolved into a capitalist Welfare State governed politically by parliamentary democracy. Its commitment to both state welfare and a free market results in conflicts and accommodations which are to be found in all the Western countries. The present shape of the international world, with its aggressive multinational capitalism, its underdeveloped Africa, rapidly developing Pacific rim and China, and its uneasy search for integration both within the European Community and with Eastern Europe, the aftermath of the Soviet Union, the Balkans and the Middle East, make up a mosaic of order and disorder. But Britain's past is also distinctive. First it has had a millennium of territorial integrity, which culminated in the nineteenth century in a far-flung empire. Second it has a preindustrial as well as an industrial past which, while bequeathing it a continuous structure of inequality, has also profoundly marked and modified the class structure which is basic to capitalist development. The analysis of persistent inequality in British society requires therefore a more complex analysis than that which is afforded by a simple class theory. British nationalism and the social hierarchy are intertwined.

Third, and most fundamentally, British culture is deeply individualistic. It is no accident that Hume and Locke are its philosophers rather than Hegel or Marx. The deeply embedded cultural assumption is that ultimate values are individual, that society is in no sense superior to the sum of the people who make it up; that collectivism can only be instrumental and that the state is best when minimal. Not that ordinary British men and women or their politicians have ever had much taste for such abstractions: it is just that individualism is built into 'custom and practice', into local work places and community organizations, into all commonsensical explanations of why people do what they do.

Inequality has lived through centuries of this culture. The ruling minority has survived all the transformations from medieval to modern society by a long series of concessions and assimilations to successive demands of the excluded and underprivileged, always provided that incorporation has accepted the limitation of not seriously challenging established privileges and rights of property. Those who have aspired to challenge the existing order of inequality, whether as 'left' revolutionaries or as 'right' reactionaries, have been successfully excluded and with remarkably little bloodshed. British violence has been characteristically naval rather than military.

Yet the question of social disorder has never and could never be finally solved. Conflicting interests whether from without or within must always threaten any establishment. So finally that question must be raised in the context of present conditions. The new Conservatism which gained power in 1979 set out, at least rhetorically, to revitalize the movement towards an order of economic liberalism which made its first bid for dominance in the first half of the nineteenth century. Most twentieth-century observers (of the Left and the Right) had believed this type of conservatism to be buried by the evolved consensus of traditional conservative, political liberal, and ethical socialist forces. Although Margaret Thatcher was deposed by her party in 1991, 'Thatcherism' was still a doctrine and an interpretation of the Welfare State, of government and people, of popular capitalism, citizenship, and dependency which remains central to political argument and which informs attitudes to Maastricht and local town halls as well as to Westminster and Whitehall. So we live, as the Chinese say, in interesting times.

Continuity and change

Given that change is the central theme of the book, we could start by putting the problem in biological terms. You and I are the same in that we belong to the same species—*Homo sapiens*—which has existed on earth for something like two million years. We are therefore the product of roughly 100,000 generations. But these reproductions have never been exact replications. The complexity of genetic transmission is so great that it is a reasonable guess that no two persons alive (identical twins excepted) carry the same genes. So you and I are both alike and different.

Moreover our sameness and difference are more than genetic. We are creatures of cultural as well as genetic reproduction. Culture is the sum of the skills by which we live, which are passed down the generations by means other than genetic trans-mission—our language, science, religion, art, and practical knowledge, as well as our material artefacts and social organiz-ations. These too exhibit continuity and change in interaction with genetic evolution. Just as you and I share differentially a genetic inheritance, so too we are variant products of a common human culture.

As to continuity and change, we must appreciate that the country experienced by Britons now was made and continues to be modified for them by forces beyond their own encounters—by its geology, topography, latitude and longitude, and by the activity of their ancestors, labouring incessantly down the ages to master their environment. The unfinished result is their cul-tural inheritance. Whether they see it as a 'green and pleasant land', or as the cradle of 'dark, Satanic mills', or both, what they see and, indeed, how they learn to see it, is rooted in a long process of human history and cultural evolution.

Much of all this we must simply take for granted, appealing to what every mythical schoolboy knows, for example, that the Phoenicians dug tin in the mines of Cornwall, that Derby, given its name, must have been founded by the Danes, or that 30.8 per cent of the inhabitants of Wales were Welsh-speaking in 1921. The lessons of history are no doubt numberless but, quite apart from sifting them out of the lessons of historians, they do not foreclose the future. A story about Scotland can illustrate both points. Edward Gibbon, writing in the eighteenth century, noted that the Romans failed to conquer northern Scotland.

The native Caledonians preserved in the northern extremity of the island their wild independence, for which they were not less indebted to their poverty than to their valour. Their incursions were frequently repelled and chastised; but their country was never subdued. The masters of the fairest and most wealthy climates of the globe turned with contempt from gloomy hills assailed by the winter tempest, from lakes concealed in a blue mist, and from cold and lonely heaths, over which the deer of the forest were chased by a troop of naked Barbarians.[1]

If we are listening here to a faithful echo of the Roman voice, we are bound to remark that the Romans could not have anticipated Gibbon's Scottish contemporaries like David Hume, or John Millar,[2] or Adam Smith,[3] who made their universities the leading centres of European thought in their day; and, if we are listening to Gibbon's amiable prejudices, we can at least remark that he could not have anticipated North Sea oil.

When sociologists or historians consider continuity and change they must also start from the commonplace generalization that man is to be distinguished from the brutes, not so much by his desire for a better life as by the range of his conception of what that life might be, and the complexity of the language in which he is able to express his hope. Our period in the twentieth century can be thought of as one of unprecedented advance in the capacity of mankind to realize dreams—at least in that one-third of the world to which Britain belongs where, in the past generation, the natural sciences have been harnessed to spectacular new dominance over nature. The power of productive systems, whether for peace or war, has transformed the significance of the age-old debate over the ends towards which society may be directed. Such clichés of political discussion as 'the revolution of rising expectations' point to that significance. Dreams have come to earth and ends are secularized. An aerial view of the island shows the motorway and the church spire as the ubiquitous monuments of human aspiration. But the spires point to other-worldly vision, and were built over centuries of a passing civilization in which the attainment of bliss was seen to belong to the next world. The road, by contrast, seems to hold out the promise of satisfaction, tomorrow if not today, but *on this earth* as it busily connects factory to town to suburb to coastal resort. So, for example, in the older world, poverty was accepted as inevitable, and morality was addressed to the endurance of it and its relief. In the twentieth century, the moral objective has switched from endurance to protest, and from relief to abolition. Equality is to be realized among men, not only found before God. Liberty is for the lords of the earth, not the angels in heaven.

There are, of course, those who prophesy that these dreams come true will shortly turn into living nightmares. The twentieth century in Britain and throughout the so-called first and second worlds of industrial capitalism and communism, is thought by some critics to be an interlude of materialist fantasy. Global environmental pollution threatens to destroy life on the planet. The earthly paradise is a miasma and the modern secular '-isms' doomed to fail. So the late Mr Muggeridge, with a journalist's genius for self-caricature, expresses the traditionalist opposition to modernity when he tells us that if he were Pope he would form an underground church, organized to survive through the new Dark Ages we are about to enter, until the time when the world can again be given the eternal verities hitherto preserved, albeit imperfectly and with gross infidelity, by the Catholic Church.[4]

So ends remain in question and this must not be forgotten even though my purpose in this book is to consider means, that is, the changes in social organization of the past fifty years through which people in Britain have co-operated and argued in pursuit of their interests. Sociology cannot prescribe ends, but it can help us to argue about them more intelligently by describing accurately the social conditions under which people act, and the intended and unintended consequences of their actions.

Older studies of continuity, and particularly the study of national character by cultural anthropologists and historians, were posited essentially on the existence of a modal personality in each nation. The last such anthropological book on Britain (actually more narrowly focused on England) was Geoffrey Gorer's *Exploring English Character* (1953). Such works are out of fashion now: but one of them is especially remarkable. Writing as a German for Germans, Wilhelm Dibelius tells us that he conceived of his book on *England* during the First World War out of an 'overwhelming sense of a people giving its best in fighting an enemy which it did not know'.[5] He wrote in a spirit of high European liberalism, and evoked the essential manners and outlook of the British with the clarity—perhaps false clarity—which can sometimes appear from off the coast of Dover of what is held in common, but unnoticed, between the natives.

He was neither the first nor the last observer to insist on the extraordinary combination of solidarity and hierarchy in British society. And his basic explanation is the long-established, always dominant, force of English aristocracy. 'To the great surprise of the Continental student of England', says Dibelius, 'this matter-of-fact, practical, and conservative English character appears wherever the Anglo-Saxon is met with: the differentiation between different geographical sub-types of the race is astonishingly small.' He then goes on to put stress on the early establishment of royal absolutism in England by the Norman kings. Real variations from the type appear in Britain only outside England and the Norman sphere of influence.

Thus, the Scot was affected neither by Norman centralization, nor by a civilization based upon the Anglican Church. So, under Calvinist influences, he developed a profound habit of thought, and a one-sidedly religious character, while the wildness of his nature, half-English and half-Celtic, never fully submitted to the surface polish of an Anglo-Saxon court. The Irish, even after the loss of their language, went their own way. Visionary dreamers, capable of swift, passionate excitement, prone to swift weariness and disillusionment, and richly endowed with artistic gifts,they also have their full share of the peasant inheritance of coarse materialism, and at the centre of their inner life, in the sphere of religion and national feeling, are capable of an amazing endurance, that centuries of disappointment proved powerless to break.

In England itself, Dibelius insists that there was a homogeneous national character, even across classes. 'Apart from Scotland, English national life contrasted with the rich variations of the Continent, presents a picture of drab uniformity, fatally congenial to the creation of a featureless and spineless urban population.'[6]

These sketches of national character are amusing: they may even be true. They speak to us of stubborn historical persistence and uniformity. But what of conflict and change?

Continuity normally presupposes consensus. Change typically results from conflict. We must, therefore, explore the sources of consensus and conflict. How are differences between classes, sexes, generations, and ethnic groups to be depicted, how have they been changing, and how controlled? The answers are to be found, I think, in the relation between means and ends.The means are social organizations and movements, and these we shall consider in the following chapters. The ends are the ideals which dominate modern social thought—what I have referred to as the dreams of the modern age.

Continuity is no accident. Social customs, like personal habit, economize human effort. They store knowledge, pre-arrange decisions, save us the trouble of weighing every choice afresh. In this way the world is ordered; but, in the same way, control in the interest of the status quo is more or less powerfully embodied in any society. Maintenance of that control then depends on a stable environment of which one important element is external security. In this respect British history is distinctive by contrast with the history of the European continent. The towns and villages of the island have peaceable traditions over many centuries. The last battle on British soil took place at Culloden in 1746; every other European country has known violent and bitter warfare with foreigners on its own territory. Britain has exported its bloodshed. But above all, continuity is a matter of social control and this brings with it its puzzles. For example, many have noted and praised Britain as a land of tolerance and liberty, while at the same time wondering at its capacity to resist the claims of egalitarian movements without resort to overt force.

The issue of freedom and control was raised in a moment of dramatic debate when the Russian leader Gorbachev visited London in 1984 and was challenged by the Conservative MP Norman St John-Stevas about the persecution of Christians in the Soviet Union. Gorbachev replied by asking whether Britain was not persecuting its three-and-a-quarter million unemployed. Questions of liberty and equality can be put or evaded in ways which reveal alternative assumptions about human priorities and social controls.

Personal knowledge

Any number of questions can be put about persistence and change. My answers will be those of a sociologist. This you may immediately find an imprisonment of method, especially if I add that just by living and learning to the point of reading this book, you already know practically all the sociology that is to be known. But that is a misleading truth—a play on the verb 'to know'. Sixth-form boys and girls setting out on an A level science course are frequently told that they already know 95 per cent of all known physics. It is true: but the other 5 per cent transforms the meaning and the power of knowing.

Yet personal knowledge is by no means to be disregarded as a traditional and commonly shared method of cultural understanding. An immense store of information about a country is lodged in the minds and memories of its inhabitants. The collective store, including as it does visual, auditary, olfactory, and tactile knowledge, is vastly greater than that of any conceivable data set stored from a survey into a computer file. Any British native has accordingly acquired by nurture a formidable battery of, so to say, tests of significance which he or she may readily apply to the findings of sociological research.

To elaborate the point I will cite my own version of this accumulation of personal knowledge: for it happens that in the early 1980s I tried to sketch the condition of Britain by making a series of excursions out of Oxford and London with the object of preparing a series of talks for the BBC. The idea was to use personal knowledge. I tried to eschew official statistics, Blue Books, or analyses of British social structure. I could not be wholly successful, for professional knowledge inevitably becomes personal. Nevertheless, in anyone of middle age, memory is more than adequate to a mere 160 minutes of talk; and the journeys could easily be contrived to lift the dust from stored recollections. So I planned my excursions to repeat my own biography, and thus to construct one slender strand in British experience from the early 1920s to the 1980s.

The professional sociologist will shudder at the imperfections of such a method. The encounters of the traveller are not random: a sample cannot be a scientific basis for assertion about a population without specified probabilities of representing it. Indeed, the people to whom I talked were not even a sample in any scientific sense. I did not choose them in relation to the British population. They were chosen for me by my passage through the restricted circumstances of the street, the railway compartment, or the pub, to which the traveller is confined: or if they were private contacts they were my friends and acquaintances and thus a refraction of public life through the peculiar network of my personal associates.

On the other hand, personal knowledge, however unsystematically, covers a vastly larger territory than any specialized professional knowledge. A man may be no architect, but buildings evoke periods and people he has never known. A woman may be no paediatrician yet spend half her life tending children: people may be innocent of theology but can scarcely avoid coming to terms with life and death. In any case I was committed on this occasion to the method of personal encounter and encouraged in it by awareness of my predecessors. The genre is well known and thoroughly understood. Journeying through the island is a tradition. Every child learns the phrase 'from Land's End to John o' Groats'. There is a large library of books where the author has projected his personal knowledge on to the national screen and called it England. Daniel Defoe, William Cobbett, and J. B. Priestley are only a few famous names in a multitude. George Orwell justified them all in the introductory section of his *The Lion and the Unicorn* to which he gave the subtitle 'England your England'.

above all, it is *your* civilisation, it is *you*. However much you hate or laugh at it, you will never be happy away from it for any length of time. The suet puddings and the red pillar boxes have entered into your soul. Good or evil, it is yours, you belong to it, and this side of the grave you will never get away from the marks that it has given you.[7]

I pondered this passage before setting out on my summer travels, knowing that I was a patriot and fearing that I was a sentimentalist. So I asked myself in advance what fragments in my memory would put a stamp of interpretation on the journeys I was preparing to make. Slowly the confused recollections ordered themselves into four themes as personal perceptions of my country and my compatriots. You might care to compare them with your own as a prelude to reading the sociological analysis in the chapters which follow.

The first is an age-old tension between urban and rural life. I was born among the dirty brick, smoky streets, little men in baggy trousers, and shapeless women with shopping baskets that made up Kentish Town in the early 1920s. Then I was transported to Lyddington in Rutland. A railway journey from the grandiose grime of Gothic St Pancras through the more domestic Victorian elegance of Kettering Station, with its neat platforms and its decorated iron stanchions, gave way finally to a horse-and-cart ride across the Welland Valley into a rural world of medieval sleepiness. Stone and thatch, huge skies, vast woods, and unending open fields were my first memories of the English countryside.

None the less, I retained a cockney snobbishness towards the 'country bumpkin'. When I first read the *Communist Manifesto of 1848* the phrase which leapt out of that strident pamphlet of vulgarized Marxism was 'the idiocy of rural life'. Marx gave historical credit to the bourgeoisie for our escape from rural stagnation. I had to give the credit to the London Midland and Scottish Railway, which gave railway servants periodic free passes to go anywhere in the country. We always went back to St Pancras. The tension never ceased, and I came to accept it as not only a private experience but as an integral part of the national psyche. In the end it gave me two patriotisms, the one of the soil, the other of the Cenotaph.

The second theme was a kaleidoscope in memory of continuous variation of colour, sound, and smell. England is a Jacob's coat of a country. The black splendour of Liverpool Town Hall, white hawthorn everywhere in the spring, the red mud of Devon, the golden stone of villages scattered from Banbury to Peterborough, and the innumerable greens encircling and shrouding all human settlements.

The ear of the traveller too is assailed by a great variety of sound if only from what is called common speech. Shaw's *Pygmalion* is not a caricature. A man from Sunderland has only to say 'good morning' to distinguish his origins from the Newcastle man twelve miles away. I remember the two languages which I learned in order to survive the day in a grammar school and the evening in the village street. Scents also linger, persistently pervading my recollections. Coal fires, crushed grass, road tarmac, and pigsties. I can still smell the clammy stink of urine and stale vegetables in the kitchens at the wrong end of the street by contrast with the odour of the carbolic soap and boot polish of the respectable families.

Then, third, there was the hierarchy. A sociologist may refine it into abstractions, but no one could grow up in England without acquiring a deep personal-cum-anthropological knowledge of class and status. Two memories are enough to evoke it. On one occasion in the 1930s the tram from Kentish Town was slow. My mother, the latest baby, my sister, my brother, and I rushed into the vault of St Pancras Station and bundled with our impedimenta into the corridor of a first-class carriage, seconds before the train drew out. A large, florid-faced man in a pinstriped suit flung open a compartment door to demand of my mother whether she had a first-class ticket. Some years later I was youth hostelling through Bath, and idling beside the entrance to a hotel in one of the stately crescents of classical architecture, when I heard the female version of the same arrogant voice demanding coffee at the reception desk. A mumbling, apologetic, but stubborn West Country voice replied that the kitchens were closed: the lady stormed out with the disdainful judgement of English metropolitan snobbery, 'these damned provinces'.

Fourth, and finally, there is the sense of tension between change and changelessness in English society. The London townscape has been transformed in my lifetime—invaded by the international architecture of Corbusier and modern brutalism. New towns appear and old industrial development falls into decay. But underneath lies the never defeated countryside, and English sentiment refuses to give up its rural nostalgia. The Victorian hierarchy has virtually collapsed and generations of 'class abatement' have changed poverty from the common experience of the working class into the misfortunes of the old, the sick, children on meagre income support, and the deprived areas. Yet the House of Lords, the public schools, the phoney farms of the millionaires, and the shabby back streets of Toxteth and Brixton remain.

Sociological knowledge: positivism

How then can we proceed from personal to sociological questions and answers? One approach, borrowing from the natural sciences, is to strive for objectivity and value-neutrality: to study ourselves as objects, to record the pattern and regularities of our behaviour and to explain what we observe by theories which are tested to ensure that they 'fit the facts'. This is the method called positivism. At the risk of caricature we can appreciate its force by imaging ourselves as visitors from some other planet, as Martian anthropologists, possessed of belief in science and of the intelligence to use it, but without the understanding which enables us to interpret our neighbour through the fact of our own humanity. What would the interplanetary visitor see? Even without human understanding, his computer picture would reveal order rather than chaos, regularity rather than randomness. A guarded boundary of British society would be as clear to him as the physical coastline. He would notice that there are two ways of entering this society, either through the wombs of mothers and the records of the Registrar of Births, Marriages, and Deaths, or from other countries overseas and via the desk of the immigration officer. Exit is similarly marked and rule-bound. Births, deaths, and migrations are governed not only by physical laws, but also by social mechanisms: there are both legitimate and illegitimate births and deaths. Further inspection, again unaided by any kind of human empathy, would reveal patterns and continuities of relations inside the boundary. Our Martian would quickly conceptualize pair-bonding in what we call marriage, cohabitation, courtship, and friendship, class structure in the social relations of production, scientific organizations in the social relations of discovery, status systems in the relations of dominance and submission, and so on. Without doubt, considerable inhuman sense could be made of British society and its history.

Sociological knowledge: humanism

But why not seek for human rather than inhuman sense? Why cannot men and women be the subject rather than the object of social science? Various modern schools of sociological thought take this humanistic view. Whatever their difference (denoted by such labels as phenomenological, ethnomethodological, idealist, existentialist, etc.) they agree on defining sociology as a way of interpreting the meanings created by people in their relations with one another. Society is to be understood through these meanings. Men and women are conceived as active makers of society; their intentions move the world.

On this view our own social knowledge is both less and more than Martian. Less, because human involvement makes us creatures of our time and place, hampering us with preconceptions and prejudices, and restricting the range of our imagination. More, and it is a crucial more, because we can turn understanding to the service of scholarship. You might, therefore, think of the social sciences as striving simultaneously both to understand so as to interpret human activity, and also to achieve Martian objectivity so as to remove from it adulterating passion. This, at all events, is the intellectual posture I will adopt in my attempt to interpret recent generations of British social experience.

This is a considerable task. A single book could not hope to reproduce more than the most minute fraction of the social action and perception of a single hour in British society. Moreover, the fact that to understand other human beings is an indispensable tool to sociological explanation also constitutes a peculiar handicap in exposition because it makes sociologists of us all. Words like 'class' or 'status' are common to 'folk sociology' as well as to professional sociology, but their meanings differ (and, in the case of this particular pair of words, are usually reversed as between a newspaper and a learned article). Hence the struggle to rescue scholarship and science from gossip, which the physicist has largely won, is much harder for the social scientist, for the paradoxical reason that he more readily 'knows' and is known to the 'object' of his study.

The posture I have described as proper to sociologists, its difficulty apart, is not the only possible one for understanding society; nor is it either confined to or always adopted by sociologists. Much of our collective self-knowledge comes from fiction or books and essays in persuasion. It is arguable whether we learn more about the social circumstances of childhood at the beginning of the present century from Arthur Morrison's *A Child of the Jago*, or from Charles Booth's *London Survey* of that time. Yet there can be no doubt that accuracy of perspective is more likely to be obtained by use of the sociological method. The novel seeks drama before balance. As it happens, both of the works cited are excellent examples of their genre. But the Jago was the worst of slums, and therefore Morrison's novel tells us about childhood in that environment only, while Booth's *Survey* not only described but quantified the population living in a much wider range of environments. From him we receive a quantified description not only of the 'lowest class of occasional labourers, loafers and semi-criminals', but also of 'the very poor' and 'the poor', those on 'regular standard earnings', 'higher-class labour', and so on. Booth estimated the lowest class to number 11,000 out of 900,000. But this was the class, the lumpenproletariat so heartily detested by Marx, which has constantly attracted the attention and caught the imagination of research workers, reformers, and journalists. The resulting descriptions make good copy, but they tempt romantic minds to identify the working class as a whole with a distinctive and unrepresentative segment of it.

Structure and agency

Whether or not a sociology can combine positivist and humanist approaches, it will still have essential features distinguishing it from other kinds of writing about social life. If I again ask a native of our chosen country—'Who are you?'—he or she might reply with the title of one of Graham Greene's entertainments, *England Made Me*. The sociologist would then ask, 'How?' Or he might quote Sir Harry Smith's mother who took leave of him saying 'If you ever meet your enemy, remember you are born a true Englishman.'[8] The sociologist would want to ask who, apart from a traditional matriarch, advances a definition of the true Englishman, what other definitions are available, from whom, and who knows them, follows them, or defies them. Sociology is about social relations—relations of individuals and groups in work and in play, war and peace, transient encounters and enduring bonds. Sociologists seek regularity and pattern in these relations. Hence they summarize them in abstractions as relations of production and reproduction, of kinship and affinity, of authority and freedom, power and advantage. They assume that the social world is not a universe of random changes and exchanges but, on the contrary, that the successful study of social relations will yield general rules governing their persistence and their rupture—rules which are by no means necessarily known to the social actors themselves.

Now I realize I have already taken us into deep water. To go further would be to navigate those oceans in which are to be found the question of free will, and whether there are laws of social motion, historical necessities, propelling us towards a determined fate.

Sociologists are no more agreed on this issue than are philosophers. There have been deterministic theories of many kinds to which humanistic sociology is opposed. Structural Marxism is one such theory—that the history of man and society is ultimately determined by the mode of production. But there are non-Marxist determinisms attributing guiding force to climate or race or culture. And there is Marxist humanism as well as the voluntaristic humanism usually associated with liberal traditions of thought. In other words there remains unresolved debate as to whether and to what degree human beings are made by or make their own history. The debate over 'structure' and 'agency' is tied to any interpretation of the problem of continuity and change. The dispute cuts across that between Marxists and non-Marxists. I cannot promise to settle it in this book. Indeed I doubt whether it can be resolved by social science. What will emerge from an attempt at objectivity of method is my belief that men and women have been relatively more constrained by 'structure' in the past than their age-old aspiration to 'agency' need be in the future.

The search for objectivity through social science has another characteristic feature. Sociology, as I have said, is essentially a set of propositions about social relations, about characteristic tendencies and variations in social conditions and social consciousness. Sociological reference is thus to the role, not to the person. Even references to groups should normally be taken as statements about a structure of relations rather than an aggregate of people. For example, if we speak of the British working class, it is more often than not misleading to take this to mean a summary label for the enumeration of men and women in manual employment in Britain at a point of time. So the sociologist Colin Crouch is faithful to his calling when he begins a book with a firm reminder to the reader that 'class is treated here as an analytical relationship rather than as the identification of empirical groups of persons'. And he goes on to point out that where this usage is carried to its logical conclusion, as in the writings of Marxists like Poulantzas, human beings are seen 'as simply the "bearers" of structural variables'.[9] At first reading, this may seem a weird distortion of language. Certainly it runs risks. It can lead to what is called the over-socialized conception of man which, in its crude form, portrays people as mere social puppets so that the Britons we study in this book are depicted as nothing but the expression of, say, bureaucratization, or class conflict, or secularization. But the method is justified precisely to distinguish and analyse such social forces. That is what sociology is. It does not set out to describe and explain some total 'human condition'. It narrows the beam to intensify the light: and the world it thus illuminates is far from being the whole world.

Liberty, equality, and fraternity

Our task, then, is to use sociology to explain cultural continuity and social change. The sociological method intrinsically draws our attention to structures of social relations. One way to keep 'agency' in view is to phrase questions in terms of the ideals sought by people through social action. Three ends or ideals have dominated European thought since the eighteenth century and the transition out of agrarian into industrial society. In the popular slogan of the French Revolution they are liberty, equality, and fraternity. They are the dreams of radicals and reformers. They are, so to say, courts of appeal before which policy and practice appear as plaintiffs or defendants in an evolving trial of promise and performance. As society develops, it is through various combinations of these three ideals that scholars abstractly, and ordinary people concretely, assess the quality of that development. And in this complex interplay of social action and reflections upon it, we can discern two contending traditions of reform—the one liberal, evolutionist, and giving highest priority to liberty; the other socialist, revolutionary, critical, and giving highest priority to equality. What is most clearly evident from the British experience, in my opinion, is an unresolved problem of fraternity or basis for social order beneath the clash of egalitarian and libertarian argument. This argument is central to political debate. Fraternity, for all its relevance, is somehow left to moralists and theologians.

To the contemporary ear fraternity is an unsatisfactory concept if only because of its male connotation. I shall therefore revise the terminology in the last chapter. Meanwhile, accepting its historical meaning, as I understand it, fraternity is sociologically prior to liberty and equality. All three principles are difficult to define. All three have a subjective as well as an objective aspect: they are all, in other words, both abstractions about the experience of people in their dealings with others as well as phenomena which can be observed by our Martian visitor as behaviour. But the priority of fraternity is that it is the principle which defines the *group* within which certain social *values* are to be applied. These values are essentially those of recognizing a common humanity: quintessentially they consist for each individual in recognizing the value of life for the other and the common fate of death for all. But the totality of social morality covers many more features of social life. Social moralities may be restricted with respect to either the group within which they are applied or in the extent that others are treated as equivalent to self. The moral community is bounded by these restrictions. Primitive man, characteristically, made linguistic distinctions at the boundary of the tribe to exclude the outsider from access to the humanity attributed to the insider. Every case of racism or sexism, or class or status distinction is to some greater or lesser extent such a restriction. The subjective feeling of fraternity is that of brotherhood: the objective behaviour is that of altruism. But this brotherhood may be exclusive or universal. The mark of the world religions is that they discovered and proclaimed the species as the only group boundary. As St Paul put it in the famous letter to the Ephesians (4: 25), 'We are members one of another.' The code of conduct enjoined by universal fraternalism is expressed most graphically in the story of the Samaritan. Sociologically, then, we mean by fraternity that, objectively, a collectivity in which the fraternal principle operates is one in which the members are integrated in their relations to one another by a set of distributional rules in which all are implicated and in which all share. Yet a fraternal society need be neither liberal nor egalitarian. Fraternity may be linked to liberty in that the liberty in question may be held to be a right for, and an obligation upon all. Fraternity may be linked to equality in that the values to be distinguished are held, in some sense, to be everyone's equal due. But liberty and equality can operate as social principles only within the bounds set by fraternity.

Equality, by contrast with fraternity, occupies an extensive place in sociological writing. There is broad agreement that society always and everywhere, though it constitutes a powerful apparatus of survival for its members, is also a structure of inequality. But sociologists differ as to the origin and development of inequality, and therefore draw different conclusions as to how it persists, and to what extent it can be modified, if not eliminated.

The sources of inequality are of two fundamental kinds. On the one hand, individuals have *interests* in life. If we assume, as we must, that there is scarcity in the means available to satisfy wants, desires, or appetites, then interests potentially imply conflict. On the other hand, human beings are, whatever else they are, *evaluating* animals: they have preferences; they distinguish between better or worse in all things, and thus continually judge themselves and others with respect to all human attributes and behave accordingly towards each other. There are, to be sure, fashionable movements of moral relativism, including postmodernism and deconstruction, which deny superiority (élitism) and assert only cultural difference. In reality, however, there are hierarchies of virtue, taste, sexual attractiveness, occupational skill, artistic talent, sporting prowess, and so on. Social relations reflect these as invidious comparisons, deference and disrespect, admiration and contempt. Evaluation, given scarcity, also implies conflict.

Sociological thought tends to divide according to the emphasis put on interest as distinct from evaluation, in explaining the social origins of inequality. We shall elaborate this division as class (interest) and status (evaluation) analysis in Chapters 2 and 3. The fact that both interests and evaluations are created and maintained by society itself is not in question. Nor is the fact of scarcity. The capacity of human beings to consume or hoard is unlimited, and the thirst for honour and power may be insatiable. As Thomas Hobbes said:

Felicity is a continuall progresse of desire, from one object to the other; the attaining of the former being still but the way to the later . . . So that in the first place, I put as the general inclination of all mankind, a perpetual and restlesse desire of Power after power, that ceaseth onely in Death . . . because he cannot assure the power and means to live well, which he hath present, without the acquisition of more . . . and when that is done, there succeedeth a new desire; in some, of Fame from new Conquest; in others, of ease and sensuall pleasure; in others of admiration, or being flattered for excellence in some art, or other ability of the mind.[10]

If this is so, then the problem would appear to be not so much how conflict arises, but how civil society exists at all.

Marxism, liberalism, and social order

In this division of sociological thought, Marxists start from the primacy of interests, and liberals start from the primacy of evaluations. Their accounts of social change differ accordingly. For Marx and his followers, both continuity and change are systematically built into the history of all societies in the form of a class struggle. The social relations of people are fundamentally determined by their attachment to the means whereby they wrest a living from nature—that is, the productive system of their day. The ensuing principle of distribution is exploitation. The consequent view of British history in our time is of class struggles

against inequality. There is no national or international fraternity, only class solidarity and such liberty as is consistent with
maintaining the dominance of a capitalist class—a dominance
which necessarily imposes unequal rewards and opportunities.

For liberals, by contrast, the maintenance of civil society, as
well as its improvement, operates through tastes, preferences,
and human values. Society changes through the inventive activity of individuals seeking to satisfy their preferences. The
principle of distribution on this view is competition. The liberal
version of historical experience emphasizes the expansion of
liberty through the development of free economic and political
activity. Expansion is the watchword, whether in markets, or
education, or culture. Expansion gradually assimilates every
man into the material and cultural privileges previously enjoyed
by a minority. Expansion also equalizes, but by granting new
opportunities, not by curtailing existing freedoms. Fraternity
consists essentially in this universal offer of new opportunity.

Of course both Marxism and liberalism have complexities and
internal debates within them: both are dynamic traditions of
thought, transcending the simple characterization I give to them
in this introduction. Both recognize both interests and evaluations. Moreover, for all its ideology of individualism, economic
liberalism as distinct from political liberalism is tied to the concept of class because of its emphasis and support for market
relations. Nevertheless, it is a distinctive Marxist assertion that
social ideas and attitudes are controlled by the ruling class.
Order is maintained, at least in the short run, by monolithic
control. For the liberal, on the other hand, society is pluralistic
and status groups, family, school, church, and voluntary organizations can play independent roles as bearers of socializing or
civilizing influence. Socialization is the key in liberal thought
about order and continuity. Economic liberalism, with its
emphasis on market relations, makes strong, if tacit, assumptions that the family is capable of maintaining a stable moral
order.

So we inherit two fundamentally opposed theories of history.
One gave Eastern Europe a seventy-year experiment with state

communism. The other has been tested in our own time and in Western Europe. They are both, of course, children of the same historic European convulsion, but our immediate concern is with Britain. For Britons, the triad of social aspirations descends in popular imagination from the slogans carried across Europe by French revolutionary soldiers after the fall of the *ancien régime*. But a competent Chinese historian would pay scant attention to what he would see as the trivial tribal boundaries of European states. He would note that these political proclamations were to be heard in Manchester as well as in Paris in the 1790s—that is to say, in the heartland of the economic as distinct from the political territory of Western Europe which was modernizing itself in the late eighteenth and early nineteenth centuries.

Professor Hobsbawm, adopting on this occasion an impeccably Chinese view, has graphically described all this in his book *The Age of Revolution*. The old society of hierarchy, order, duty, and reciprocity was to be replaced by one of democratic fellowship in a society of free men associating together on equal terms. True that two of the three principles—equality and freedom—could be shown in some ways to oppose and in more ways to limit each other in the actual social relations of people. These oppositions and limits have absorbed the attention of social scientists down to our own day. We still find them ranged from the aggressive libertarianism of Milton Friedman,[11] through the gentler accommodations to egalitarianism of Isaiah Berlin,[12] or the 'new liberty' to which Ralf Dahrendorf has devoted his recent writing,[13] on through the argued egalitarian liberalism of John Rawls,[14] to the radical egalitarianism of R. H. Tawney.[15]

Liberalism has to face the problem of social order as an immediate problem of reconciling equality with freedom. Since the mid-1970s that reconciliation has become more difficult and the spectre of a Hobbesian disorder of 'every man's hand against every other man's' is raised by economic decline. Thatcherite economic and social policies divide the nation in class and sectional conflict over a smaller 'national cake'. Before 1979 the liberal solution was to increase the size of the cake; to promote economic growth and rely on prosperity to 'trickle down' from the rich to the poor.

Economic growth, of which Britain was the leader in the first half of the nineteenth century, might still appear to offer a way out of the Hobbesian tragedy. And modern political promises to enlarge and spread material abundance seem to reassert that promise. But it cannot be so. As Professor Hirsch argued, there are social limits to growth.[16]

We can see these limits if we follow Hirsch and distinguish two economies: one in *material* goods, and the other in *positional* goods. Material goods like tea or mugs can be expanded in their supply practically without limit. But positional goods are in more or less fixed supply. If we have a monarchy, only one of us can be queen: only 49 per cent can enjoy superior amenities. There is a range of positional goods such as old masters, sub-urban houses, and the Wardenship of Nuffield College which are fixed or scarce in some socially imposed sense or spoilt if more extensively used. The market for them is a zero-sum game—if you win I lose—or even a negative sum game, in that people consume resources in mutually cancelling efforts to gain market advantage. Hirsch's thesis is, then, a restatement of the Hobbesian problem applied to the special conditions of modern Britain, where economic liberalism, as he puts it, is 'the victim of its own success'. He argues that affluence presents a new form of the old problem of reconciling limited means to unlimited ends. 'The liberal capitalist order', he says, 'was associated with what can now be seen as transient inaugural conditions. First, full participation was confined to a minority—the minority that had reached material affluence before liberal capitalism had set the masses on the path of material growth.' But the story of Britain in the twentieth century, as in other industrial countries, is un-doubtedly one of gradually increasing demand for full partici-pation in the 'good life'.[17] And so it becomes increasingly clear that the economic liberalism which encourages self-interest (or liberty) runs against the no less pressing need for a social moral-ity of obligation, if markets are to be free and efficient. As Emile

Durkheim argued, 'There is more to the contract than the contract.'

Here again, then, is the problem of fraternity. Its origins lie in the intrinsic character of scarcity as an essential feature of society which also gives rise to a perennial problem of inequality in the distribution of power, and advantage. Scarcity will always bring us back to the problem of fraternity. In present-day discussion, the characteristic and confused expression of this problem is a familiar and widely expressed fear of the fragility of our social order. In that form it appears as the comprehensive proposition that British society faces imminent disaster. The proposition is that Britain has declined, is declining, and will shortly collapse. There are many versions of it short of apocalyptic prophecy with which no sociologist is equipped to deal. The secular versions point to the threats to institutions which are necessary to ensure our survival, banal as it may be to say so. Thus Britons must produce and the economy is held to be faltering. And Britons must reproduce, yet it is widely argued that their institutions of kinship and upbringing are in increasing disarray.

Some Conservative politicians tended to describe British conditions in the 1980s in terms of the eleventh hour at which the country must turn back, or give itself up to socialist tyranny. Mrs Thatcher's government was swept to power in 1979 and was returned in 1983 and 1987 on precisely this rhetorical tide. Even the Labour party, the main bearer of political cheerfulness in our time, tended to see North Sea oil as a last chance to modernize the British economy and society. No industrial technology is without a scientist to forecast its demise: no political party, Labour, Conservative, Liberal, or Communist, is without a political scientist to predict its break-up and the end of parliamentary institutions. Nor do anticipations of mortality stop at the economy and the state. The institutions of reproduction, that is, the family and the school, have collected to themselves a chorus of equally gloomy forecast over the past generation: and with them, according to many intellectuals, go the foundations of authority and the maintenance of cultural standards.

Here is Lord David Cecil's expression of the thesis: he is looking back in 1973 to the death of his grandfather, Lord Salisbury, in 1903.

My grandfather died that evening, as the sun was setting.

This sunset, as subsequently historians have not failed to point out, was symbolic; and not just of my grandfather's death. To the contemporary observer his career had remained to its close a success story. He died still a revered national figure, with his party in power and his policies apparently successful: he had been Prime Minister of England at the Diamond Jubilee of 1897, which celebrated the highest point of dominion and glory ever attained by the English. In fact Fate, in a spirit of irony which my grandfather would have appreciated, if grimly, had designed these triumphs as though to provide a contrasting prelude to a period of spectacular catastrophe, which entailed, incidentally, the decline of most of what my grandfather had stood for: British greatness, aristocratic government, individual liberty and international peace. Within fifty years of his death, British greatness had dwindled, aristocratic government had disappeared, individual liberty had lost its prestige and England had been involved in the two greatest wars in the history of mankind.[18]

Can all these authorities be wrong? Certainly it would be imprudent to ignore them. I want, therefore, to set out the main lines of argument in contemporary writing, and thus to arrive, if I can, at a more secure base for agreeing or disagreeing with what I take to be the dominant theme of current conventional wisdom.

Conclusion

The main lines of argument are concerned with the ends of liberty, equality, and fraternity, and they run between the two traditions of social thought to which I have referred, Marxism and liberalism. The fundamental question, as I understand it, is whether or to what extent these values can be realized in any society: and the approach to an answer is by examining twentieth-century experience of the basic institutions of one country, Britain. I have tried to illustrate the sociological method in this introductory chapter, emphasizing its focus on structures of social relations, its concern to explain both continuity and change, and its two opposed theories of history which are rooted in alternative liberal and Marxist views of the place of interests and evaluations as springs of human action.

The arrangement of the chapters which follow is guided by these themes. We begin, in Chapter 2, with the economy, asking first what is the outcome of work and how its fruits are distributed within the nation. Both economic growth and unequal distribution will be found as the main features of our description. With the facts of affluence and inequality before us, we can then ask how far inequality can be explained in terms of the class structure which has evolved in Britain as it developed from an agrarian to an advanced industrial nation.

We shall conclude from this analysis that not all inequality can be accounted for as a consequence of class. Accordingly, in Chapter 3, we shall turn to the history of status as distinct from class in Britain so as to refine our conception of stratification and to rest our explanation of inequality on a broader base.

Then, in Chapter 4, we can carry our class and status analysis further to include the power of organization or 'party' and in this way further strengthen our understanding of the changing distribution of power and advantage through economic, social, and political processes. Thus we shall have related the ends of liberty and equality to the means through which they have been sought in the institutions and organizations of class, status, and party.

At this point we will have completed our survey of Britain as a productive system—productive, that is, of material and psychic values—and we can turn, in the following Chapters 5 and 6, to the reproduction of the society and its culture through the family and education. These matters, from yet another point of view, confront us with the problem of explaining continuity and change over recent generations.

Finally, in Chapter 7, we shall attempt a composite picture of the changing state of British society, asking how liberty, equality, and fraternity interact as the underlying principles of the social order, how these interactions of consensus and conflict strengthen or weaken the integration of the United Kingdom, and what view we are to take of the widespread opinion that Britain is in decline. The answers to these questions will in turn guide our views on the further questions of policies for the future. The claim, and the aim, throughout the argument is that sociological analysis is an aid to more sophisticated analysis. But it cannot carry us to final views beyond political or moral challenge. I have not hesitated to end, in Chapter 8, with a brief statement of my own preferences. It is for you to decide whether and how far my interpretations are consistent with the arguments leading to them. More important is the hope that you may thereby arrive more confidently at your own.

2 A CLASS-RIDDEN PROSPERITY

Our aim is to understand continuity and change. In this chapter
we focus our attention on class. Class, though much disputed in
its contemporary meaning,[1] remains a key concept in analysing
British history. If, as is now clear, the postwar period came to
an end in the mid-1970s, giving way to a new period of
deindustrialization, national economic decline, and Thatcherism
as a strategy of attempted revival by policies of economic liberalism, then our new period must be one of increased class conflict. In the long and the short run class persists in continually
changing forms.

'A class-ridden society'; that is the common judgement on
Britain made by social observers, whether delivered as praise or
condemnation. I heard this exact phrase from two foreign acquaintances, revisiting the island in the 1980s. Both sociologists,
but the one a Russian Communist, and the other an American
liberal. The Russian spoke of the continuing hegemony of a
capitalist class with its power legally based on concentrated
ownership of property and its control operating both through
the direct employment of labour and through the state apparatus of budgetary manipulation of the level of employment,
definition of welfare spending, domination of the mass media
and, in the last resort, disposition of the means of violence
through the armed forces and the police. He gave me, in short,
a brief recital of Marxist orthodoxy in which every significant
feature of social structure and the distribution of life-chances
rested fundamentally on the present sovereignty and approaching overthrow of a capitalist class.

The American used the phrase with a tone and in a context
which changed its meaning. Under the leadership of Mrs

Thatcher at that time the country was seeking to renew its economic growth by greater efficiency in private industry, which required thorough reform of outdated class attitudes among both managers and employees. Nevertheless, class was still the outstanding feature of British society: neither the élite Establishment nor the attitudes of lower-class people had really changed. That, he added, is the reason why Britain still has the highest-quality television in the world: adaptations of Hardy's novels or Robert Graves's *I Claudius* would be impossible in mainstream America; and so would the Reith Lectures. Nowhere else in the Western world does the élite retain the confidence both to indulge its own cultural tastes and also to believe that these should be offered to or imposed didactically upon the mass of the population. The American upper class just doesn't have that status any more. He gave me, in short, a nostalgic anglophile expression of the liberalism which regrets what it sees as the inevitable sacrifice of quality when democracy is triumphant. Here then is the large theme for this second chapter. Why is it that, though Britain has become a rich country, social inequality is a continuing feature of its internal life as it approaches the twenty-first century?

A vocabulary of social inequality

In looking for an answer to this question, and noting the different words used by my American and Russian colleagues, we shall be carried to the centre of the debate about Britain among sociologists. Quite apart from the contrasting explanations of my visitors, their terminology is confusing. It includes references to upper, lower, capitalist, and working classes, to élites, the Establishment, status, mass, and power. My first task, therefore, is to assemble a clear vocabulary from modern sociological writing. It is a vocabulary which differs from common speech and derives mainly from the German sociologist, Max Weber, who may be said to have stood on the shoulders of Marx in order to reach a refinement of the language of stratification in general and of class in particular.

When sociologists speak of a structure of inequality they refer to the ways in which power and advantage form a stratified system of relations. By power they mean the resources which individuals or groups use to have their will, irrespective of the will of others. A board of directors can close a plant: a union can strike. By advantage, they mean control over things which are valued and scarce, such as the wealth of a millionaire, or the skill of a surgeon. Power and advantage are convertible. Together they define the character of strata and the relations between them in a stratification system. This system has three dimensions or forms of organization through which power and advantage are distributed.

The three dimensions are class, status, and party. Classes—for example, professional people or factory workers—are formed socially out of the division of labour. They make up more or less cohesive and socially conscious groups from those occupational groups and their families which share similar work and market situations. Status is formed out of the no less fundamental tendency of human beings to attach positive and negative values to human attributes, and to distribute respect or honour and contempt or derogation accordingly: status groups, for example peers of the realm or vagrants, form as social networks of those who share similar social prestige or life-style. Parties form out of the organized pursuit of social objectives; they are political parties, pressure groups, associations, and unions of those who consciously share a planned movement for the acquisition of power. In short, classes belong to the economic, status groups to the social, and parties to the political structure of society.[2]

Status and party will concern us in my third and fourth chapters. Here and now my task is to see how far inequality can be explained by class. But again, there is a welter of confusing terms. One thing is broadly agreed. Britain held a special historical place as the first industrial nation, which made it in the nineteenth century the classic home of an urbanized industrial working class or proletariat. But there agreement ends, and there is sharp debate about its older and its more recent history of a shifting balance of power and advantage.

A proletariat implies a bourgeois or capitalist class, and here it is essential to appreciate the long pre-industrial history of a landed aristocracy and gentry into which that capitalist class was absorbed. With due allowance for its sustained willingness and capacity to assimilate new elements, it may be said that an essentially hereditary medieval estate was slowly transformed into a fully developed class, retaining its hereditary character in a period stretching from late medieval times almost to our own day. There was no overt political revolution of the bourgeoisie. Control of state power and cultural advantage was virtually unbroken in the long journey from agrarian feudalism to industrial capitalism. The muddle of adjectives to denote classes comes from this history so that the terms upper, leisured, middle or middling, and lower are verbal deposits from the earlier pre-industrial age. It was the nineteenth-century analysts of industrial society who identified classes as capitalist, bourgeois, proletarian, and working. So the peculiarity of the British case is the mixture of confusing terms, reflecting history rather than logic. One consequence is that, in trying to name the classes which have evolved out of industrialism, Britons frequently divide themselves not into an upper and a lower but, absurdly, into a middle and a working class.

The class structure

The classical source of class analysis is Karl Marx. In some of his writings, for example in the *Eighteenth Brumaire of Louis Bonaparte* (1852), Marx distinguishes several classes for the purpose of refined analysis. But his main legacy is a two-class model of classes divided by ownership and non-ownership of the means of production (capital). This essential split determines the unequal distribution of power and advantage. Relations between the two great classes are exploitative and antagonistic. Capitalists in competitive pursuit of profit organize work in their own interests, seek to extend their control over all social institutions, especially the state, and extract surplus value (i.e. the value of products minus wages) from the proletariat. Society polarizes into two great warring camps as classes become more subjectively aware of their antagonisms. Classes form and develop from classes in themselves to classes for themselves through the experience of struggle against each other. The predicted outcome is revolution and eventually a conflict-free society without classes and with a voluntary division of labour.

History itself has been the severest critic of the theory of history to which the two-class model is tied. However, a two-class model, detached from this particular theory of the fate of industrial society, can be used as a simple starting-point for class analysis. The open questions are then whether power and advantage, especially state power and cultural advantage, may have sources other than or in addition to the class relations of production. Again following Max Weber and subsequent writers, most contemporary sociologists, and indeed most Britons, take a more pluralist view of the general system of stratification and the distribution of power and advantage.

On this more general view the importance of property is not denied but the elaboration of the division of labour is emphasized. As Frank Parkin puts it, 'the long-run tendency in Western Societies has been for the share of national income accruing to property steadily to diminish relative to income from employment'. The essential point is that in industrial society the anatomy of class is displayed in the occupational structure.[3] Groups and individuals differ first according to the terms on which they can sell their skills and their labour on the market, and second according to the actual conditions of their work—its autonomy, or lack of it, its intrinsic satisfactions, and its attendant amenities.

True, the British retain the archaic customs of an honours system through which they translate occupational achievement into feudal rank. They pretend, in other words, that power and advantage derive not from activity in the labour or capital markets, but from birth and breeding. True, too, that part of all social inheritance is immutable: birth gives us a family of origin, sex, race, and nationality. Some medieval estates—an extreme form of status—were legally hereditary. Class, too, in its fully developed form, shares this hereditary quality: but its foundation is in the market, not the law. An individual may move between classes in his own lifetime. The rise and fall of classes themselves is a broader and usually longer historical process through changes in the economy and polity which may be intended or unintended, violent or peaceful. Whether we follow the original Marxist orthodoxy and hold that legal ownership of the means of production is the crucial distinction or whether, with later writers like Dahrendorf,[4] we prefer to concentrate on authority in the organization of work, classes emerge out of occupational structure, and power and advantage are unequally distributed between them.

It is this definition of class in terms of occupation which is widely used in European sociology and which I use in this book. To do so implies adherence to no rigid orthodoxy as to the number of classes in twentieth-century Britain, nor to any preconception of their historical role, past or future. We shall look closely at the relation between class and voting in Chapter 4 below. Class analysis, like the Second World, has gone out of fashion and some like Ivor Crewe, David Butler, Peter Saunders, or Ray Pahl argue that the class structure has become looser, class-consciousness more complex and less determinate of political allegiances while old pure working-class communities fragment, new middle-class post-materialists seek life-styles distinct from old middle-class ways. We shall see that changes in social stratification have been and are part of the changing British pattern. But as Gordon Marshall and his colleagues have argued in their systematic review of class in modern Britain, both the structure of class and the ideological differences associated with it are strongly persistent as the twentieth century ebbs away.[5] The number of classes that may be identified at any point of time is partly a matter of convenience directed towards the degree of refinement required for the analysis of occupational-based power and advantage. For our purposes in this book—the analysis of Britain within living memory—it will usually suffice to distinguish three classes—the middle, lower-middle, and work-ing classes.

The first stratum can be taken to mean what most people mean by the *middle class*: professional, managerial, and admin-istrative occupational groups and higher technicians, and their wives and children—the 'service class'. The second stratum is a heterogeneous *lower-middle class* of non-manual employees, small proprietors, self-employed artisans—the petite bour-geoisie or lower-middle class—but also lower-grade technicians and supervisors of manual workers who might be thought of as a 'blue-collar élite'. The third stratum is the *working class*—industrial manual workers, and agricultural workers whether skilled, semi-skilled, or unskilled. Nevertheless, the reader should be aware that more refined class schema may be used, and indeed would be necessary, to identify groups with more homogeneous market and work situations.[6]

At the beginning of the century the occupational division of labour in Britain was such that over three-quarters of the em-ployed and self-employed population were engaged in manual work. Of these, 28.7 per cent were skilled, 34.3 per cent semi-skilled, 9.6 per cent unskilled, and 1.8 per cent were self-employed artisans in 1911. Above these manual workers stood a white-collar and professional class, more confidently divided then than now into the upper-middle class and lower-middle class. And above these stood the tiny group of a few thousand—the group which Lord David Cecil, whom I quoted earlier, termed 'the governing class' of his grandfather's day. By mid-century the proportion of manual workers had fallen below two-thirds and since then it has fallen still further to roughly a third. So the first impression is of a gradual movement away from what might be called a proletarian society: and this trans-formation has been gathering pace in recent decades. Thus be-tween 1964 and 1987 the proportion of employed people in manual work fell from 51 per cent to 36 per cent.[7]

By 1971, as John Goldthorpe and Catriona Llewellyn have described it,[8] the occupational structure was more differentiated and more balanced. In the middle there were now three main blocks of comparable size, each accounting for one-fifth to one-quarter of the total. There were first the semi-skilled manual workers, second the skilled manual workers, and third the clerical and sales workers. Flanking these three groups were three other small groups, each between 7 and 15 per cent of the total—on the one side the unskilled workers, and on the other the professional and technical workers and the administrative, managerial, and supervisory staff.

These shifts of occupational structure in the first three-quarters of the twentieth century, from the shape of a pyramid to that of an electric light bulb, are characteristic of advanced industrial societies in general. They are shown for Britain in Table 2.1, which was constructed by Goldthorpe and Llewellyn. Behind them lies economic transformation: from small to large scale; from manufacturing to so-called tertiary-sector activity; from personal dealing to bureaucracy: from handling things to manipulating words and numbers; and from private to public organizations.

Some sociologists interpreted these trends as involving the development of a middle mass of technical and clerical employees with a consequent decline of class antagonisms, and with the spectre of polarized capitalist society in retreat. We shall see below that the end of the post-war period and the resurgence of economic liberalism with high unemployment and privatization raise again the problem of class polarization.

But in any case, before drawing such inferences about Britain, it is prudent to notice what is perhaps the outstanding feature of occupational change, namely the growth of women's employment outside the home. The number of men in the workforce has remained fairly static in recent decades and will not change much before the twenty-first century. Yet the number of women has grown by about one million since the mid-1980s and will continue to grow until, by 2001, women will make up 45 per cent of the civilian labour force.[9] Male and female involvement in the economy have run different courses over the period we are considering. As may be seen from Table 2.1, in 1911 both sexes

were divided between manual and non-manual jobs three-quarters to one-quarter. Subsequently, the female labour force has
both grown and shifted substantially into non-manual work, so
that by 1981 three-fifths of the employed women were non-
manual while over half of the men were still manual workers.
And even the shift to non-manual jobs among men has mostly
taken place since the Second World War. What is more important about it is that the increasing numbers of higher-level professional and managerial positions have largely gone to men, while
women have filled the even faster expanding array of lower
white-collar jobs.

This development of the pattern of male and female employment raises two important issues, one with respect to the Marxist
two-class model, the other concerning the relation of women to
the class structure. The two-class model has to be adapted to
take account of the expansion of professional and managerial
occupations. Marxists have argued that these middle classes
are in a contradictory class position. They exercise control
over the productive powers but most of them own no capital.
Ralf Dahrendorf and other liberal analysts have called them
the 'service class'—those who provide a bridge between the
rulers (capitalists) and the masses (workers) by acting as the
agents of public and private authorities. From a Marxist standpoint these groups are explained as functionaries serving the
owners of capital which has brought them into existence as a
consequence of concentrations into larger enterprises. Large
scale necessitates delegation of capitalist control to bureaucratic
managers and professional experts. The capitalist development
of production, on this view, determines the division of labour.

Women and the class structure

The second point—women and class—is still more important
and has occasioned lively debate.[10] Are women a class? My
answer is no; but explanation is needed. Married women's paid
employment has certainly increased from about a tenth at the
beginning of the century to roughly half now: but employment
outside the home is not only largely treated as additional to

retaining the major responsibilities for domestic work but is also characteristically intermittent, part-time, and secondary to male employment. Whether or not women have young children has a major influence on whether or not they take paid employment. In 1991 those with children under 5 worked full time in only 13 per cent of the cases compared with 55 per cent of those with no dependent children. Those in professional or managerial jobs were moreover much more likely to work full time (67 per cent) than those in working-class jobs (8 per cent for unskilled manual workers).[11] The typical case remains that the 'head' of a family determines the class of its members, including wives, by his labour market role. The restricted and conditional nature of women's participation in the labour market also largely deprives them of the essential capacity for class action, i.e. the power to disrupt the productive process in any serious or effective manner. Instead, as Parkin has argued, women like other groups with status or 'party' disadvantages, 'are forced to rely far more heavily upon collective mobilisation of a purely social and expressive kind in order to press their claims'.[12]

Most certainly the evidence is overwhelmingly that women suffer systematic inequalities of power and advantage as against men. But, while warranting full recognition, these inequalities are more adequately explained as inequalities of status, party (organization), and kinship than as class phenomena, even though their character is related to class. Accordingly their discussion is deferred to Chapters 3, 4, and 5. Nevertheless, it should be remarked at this point that sexual stratification is a fundamental feature of the social division of labour in all complex societies and that the increasing involvement of women in the occupational (i.e. labour market) division of labour in the twentieth century has had important consequences for class structure. Sexual inequality is a dimension of social stratification in its own right. But its impact on class inequality, as Westergaard and Resler have suggested, is to sharpen class division.[13] Socially assortative mating increases the spread of income and wealth *between* families 'headed' by individuals (usually males) of different occupational class. Significantly also there is a high correlation between husband's and wife's unemployment.

The wealth of the nation

So much for a preliminary view of stratification using a simple conception of class. Now let us look at collective prosperity. At the outset, the reader should be warned against taking official estimates of the national income or the gross national product— those modern talismans of national virility—as ultimate measures of the wealth of a nation. They are the gifts of bureaucracy rather than social science. These economists' sums tell us roughly what are the products of the *occupational* division of labour: but there is a larger *social* division of labour which includes the exchanges in families, and the services of the Samaritans, as well as the fiddles unrecorded by the Inland Revenue. There is, in short, another economy of vast dimension. It was, for example, only by the fiat of the Victorian economist Alfred Marshall that the paid labour of charwomen is counted as part of the national product, while the work of housewives is not.[14] If we were to reckon the whole output of the social division of labour it is most likely that our sterling numbers would be more than doubled. Nevertheless, if we assume that outputs from the two economies are in less than completely inverse relation, the official figures can be used to indicate trends. They tell us that since 1900 the United Kingdom has at least tripled and possibly quadrupled its gross national product in real terms.[15]

In any case, there is general agreement that British levels of living rose throughout the century until the late 1970s and even in the 1980s for those in secure employment. If the word 'living' is taken quite literally, it may be noted that, compared with a hundred years ago, the average Briton lives thirty years longer, mainly because of a reduction in infantile mortality. In the childhood of the oldest readers the death of a baby in the house was a grim commonplace: now, less than two in a hundred die in infancy. Real earnings, income, and expenditure have risen throughout the present century. Real disposable household in-

Table 2.1 Distribution of economically active population by occupational category, Great Britain 1911–1971, males (M) and females (F) shown separately (percentages by column)[1]

Standardized Census occupational category	1911 M	1911 F	1921 M	1921 F	1931 M	1931 F	1951 M	1951 F	1961 M	1961 F	1971 M	1971 F
Self-employed and higher-grade salaried professionals	1.5[a]	1.0[a]	1.6		1.7	1.0	2.8	1.0	4.5[b]	1.1[b]	6.1	1.4
Employers and proprietors	7.7	4.3	7.7	4.7	7.6	4.4	5.7	3.2	4.8[c]	3.0[c]	5.2	2.9
Administrators and managers	3.9	2.3	4.3	2.1	4.5	1.6	6.8	2.7	7.5[c]	2.6[c]	9.9	3.3
Lower-grade salaried professionals and technicians	1.4[a]	5.8[a]	1.8	6.3	1.8	6.0	3.0	7.9	4.0[b]	9.2[b]	5.5	10.8
Inspectors, supervisors, and foremen[d]	1.8	0.2	1.9	0.3	2.0	0.4	3.3	1.1	3.8	0.9	4.5	1.2
Clerical workers	5.1	3.3	5.1	9.8	5.1	10.3	6.0	20.3	6.5	25.5	6.1	28.0
Sales personnel and shop assistants[e]	5.0	6.4	4.1	7.5	5.9	8.2	4.0	9.6	3.9	10.0	3.9	9.4
Skilled manual workers (inc. self-employed artisans)	33.0	24.6	32.3	20.3	30.1	19.2	30.3	12.7	32.3	10.8	29.4	9.3

Semi-skilled manual workers[f]	29.1	47.0	24.5	40.0	23.4	41.4	24.3	33.6	22.8	30.9	21.2	27.3
Unskilled manual workers[f]	11.5	5.1	16.7	8.1	17.9	7.5	13.8	7.9	9.9	6.0	8.2	6.4

TOTAL ACTIVE POPULATION

(Thousands)	12,926	5,424	13,635	5,698	14,760	6,263	15,584	6,930	15,992	7,649	15,609	8,762

[1] This table was constructed by J. H. Goldthorpe and Catriona Llewellyn

[a] Divided according to 1921 ratios. (The 1911 Census did not distinguish between self-employed and salaried professionals.)

[b] Divided on the assumption of a linear trend in the ratios from 1951–1966 (sample census),

i.e. $\dfrac{\times 61}{\text{Total } 61} = \dfrac{\times 51}{\text{Total } 51} + 2/3 \dfrac{\times 66}{\text{Total } 66} = \dfrac{\times 51}{\text{Total } 51}$

(The 1961 Census did not distinguish between self-employed and salaried professionals.)

[c] Numbers in Groups 3 and 4 divided according to a ratio arrived at by plotting trend lines for these groups from 1951 to 1961, i.e. $P_{61} = P_{51} + 2/3(P_{66} - P_{51})$. (The 1961 Census did not distinguish between employers and managers.)

[d] Of manual workers.

[e] Includes supervisory personnel and also a small number of self-employed workers.

[f] Includes self-employed workers.

Sources: The basic source is the Occupational Tables of the Censuses of Population for England and Wales and Scotland. We have, however, drawn to a large extent on the reworking of Census data by earlier investigators although modifying their procedures somewhat, and correcting what appear to be several minor errors. In various respects, therefore, our figures differ from those of our predecessors where they might appear comparable, but not to any very significant degree.

For 1911 to 1951 we began with the work of Guy Routh, Occupation and Pay in Great Britain, 1906–60, Cambridge University Press, 1965, Table 1, pp. 4–5, taken together with the further information provided in Appendix A, pp. 155–7.

For 1961 we have drawn on the work of G. S. Bain, The Growth of White Collar Unionism, Oxford University Press, 1970, Table 2A. 1, p. 191; and of Bain, Robert Bacon, and John Pimlott, 'The Labour Force', in A. H. Halsey (ed.), Trends in British Society since 1900, Macmillan, 1972, Tables 4.1 and 4.5, pp. 113–14.

come fell between 1990 and 1991—the first time for a decade. But over the longer period of twenty years it rose by 70 per cent. While it is difficult if not impossible to translate these money figures into real purchasing power by discounting for inflation, we can safely say that they also represent at least a tripling of real income. Nor can there be any doubt that the ordinary manual worker and his wife are very much less the slaves of toil than they were in Edwardian England. Their market freedoms, whether as earners or spenders, have been transformed.

Hours of work have been steadily reduced (from 54 to 43 per week between 1900 and 1980). After the Second World War, paid holidays became common; four weeks became the norm in the 1980s and in the 1990s the entitlement was extended to 94 per cent of the workforce. Even so, the holiday distribution is closely related to class. Eight out of ten in the managerial classes took a holiday in 1991 compared with half of the unskilled workers. The official statistics for 1991 record 54 million holidays by residents of Great Britain. This is a far cry from the experience of many, if not most, ordinary children between the wars—the annual charabanc trip to Blackpool or Skegness.

Yet inequality persists after a long period of economic growth. From this point of view the picture of prosperity looks very different, especially since the end of the 1970s and the arrival of a government determined to press policies of economic liberalism. The assumption of growing affluence is not beyond question. The old poverties of lack of property, low pay, poor health, inadequate education, and bad housing still disfigure, and many would say disgrace, the powerful engine of production which we call industrial society. The official rate of registered unemployment doubled from the beginning of the Thatcher administration to over 13 per cent of all employees in 1983 (Figure 2.1). The number of unemployed peaked in July 1986 before falling to 1.5 million in early 1990 followed by an equally dramatic rise back to 2.8 million in August 1992. Thatcherite unemployment was heavily concentrated in the working class, and within that class among the young, the old, the sick, and the disabled. Over seven million Britons depended on the Supplementary Benefits

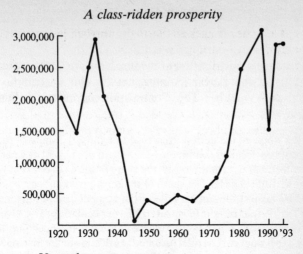

Figure 2.1   Unemployment 1921–1992

Commission. In other words, over seven million were living on the government's own estimate of the poverty line. And there were more below it who did not claim their due.[16]

How, then, are income and wealth shared among the population? Let us begin with two relatively simple statistics. In Britain in 1990 the richest 5 per cent still own 37 per cent of all marketable wealth. Income is less unequally distributed, but here again the richest 1 per cent take home about the same amount as the poorest 20 per cent. They each have, in other words, more than twenty times as much income. These are quite spectacular inequalities.

The distribution of market income

From the First World War to the 1970s there was slow and unsteady progress towards a more equal distribution of personal income. By the early 1970s the top 10 per cent of income receivers were taking about one-quarter of total income, and this one-quarter share was also the amount being taken by the bottom half of income receivers. Comparing manual and non-manual earnings a trend towards decreasing inequality can be traced at least as far back as the 1920s. In 1978 the ratio of non-manual to manual earnings was 1.25.

The trends in distribution of income from 1959 were carefully explored by the Royal Commission on the Distribution of Income and Wealth.[17] The Commission summarized them as follows:

Over the whole of the period from 1959 to 1974/5, the share of the top 1 per cent has declined continuously; the share of the next 2–5 per cent has declined but not continuously; the share of the 6–10 per cent group has shown little change. The share of the top 10 per cent as a whole in the before tax distribution has fallen from 29.4 per cent of total income in 1959 to 28.0 per cent in 1967 and to 26.6 per cent in 1974–5. Over the same period (1959 to 1974–5) the share of the top 1 per cent has fallen from 8.4 to 6.2 per cent of total income. The decline in the income share of the top 10 per cent as a whole is balanced by a corresponding increase in the overall share of the remaining 90 per cent, within which only one decile—61–70 per cent—did not increase. Approximately three-fifths of this increase accrued to the remaining 40 per cent of tax units in the top half of the distribution. Their share increased from 47.5 per cent to 49.2 per cent of total income between 1959 and 1974–5 while, over the same period, the share of bottom 50 per cent of tax units increased from 23.1 per cent to 24.2 per cent of total income.

These equalizing tendencies in the market fortunes of occupational classes came to a halt with the passing of the post-war period. Between 1976 and 1982 the distribution of market incomes became more unequal. The top one-fifth of households increased their share from 44 to 47 per cent, while the bottom one-fifth sank from a share of 0.8 per cent to one of 0.4 per cent.[18]

More recent and meticulously careful analysis has been conducted by Professor A. B. Atkinson. In his Keynes Lecture for 1991[19] he noted that the fall in income differences between 1949 and 1976 was a noticeable one, but most of the redistribution was from the top 10 per cent to the next 40 per cent, not to the bottom half. But after 1975/6, in the period to 1984/5, the top 10 per cent went back to having 5 times the average of the bottom half. And there was a further and sharper increase after 1985.

The share of the top 10 per cent rose from 24.4 per cent to 29.2 per cent.

Redistribution by the state

The impact of taxes and transfers is a complicated one and much debated. It operates, as R. M. Titmuss pointed out,[20] through three loosely related systems of state intervention—fiscal policy, the social services, and occupational welfare. Essentially these political interventions can only be understood as collective action to change the unacceptable outcome of market exchanges: and that means the outcome of class. Historically, the development of these elements of social policy starts from the liberal governments before the First War. Their complexity mirrors the increasing complexity of the division of labour. They give Britain now a social division of welfare which is not by any means simply a political antidote to class distribution of what is produced by collective labour. On the contrary, social policy itself has been powerfully shaped by class. For example, the fiscal system has been no simple extension of progressive taxation from its introduction in 1907. We have noticed that the richest one-fifth of households in 1982 took 47 per cent of the nation's income. After taxes and benefits that share was reduced to 39.4 per cent. The poorest one-fifth of households had taken 0.4 per cent of market income. Taxation and benefits raised that share to 6.9 per cent. These figures can scarcely be interpreted as evidence of a hugely redistributive 'welfare' state. Welfare, it would appear, is largely self-financed for the bulk of the population. The activity of the state makes for no dramatic reduction of market inequalities.

Most government money is raised from households. Some households will be taxed more than they benefit, and others will benefit more than they are taxed. Initially, households receive income from various sources: from their employment; from occupational pensions; from investments; and from other households—this is called original income. Cash benefits from the state (e.g. retirement pensions and income support) are added to original income to give gross income. Households lose money to

Table 2.2 Redistribution of income through taxes and benefits, 1989[1]

United Kingdom

£ per year and numbers

Average per household (£ per year[3])	Quintile groups of households ranked by equivalized disposable income[2]					All Households
	Bottom fifth	Next fifth	Middle fifth	Next fifth	Top fifth	
Earnings of main earner	770	3,160	8,050	11,730	19,780	8,700
Earnings of others in the household	80	520	2,060	4,330	6,640	2,730
Occupational pensions, annuities	200	610	810	840	1,290	750
Investment income	160	320	480	770	1,920	730
Other income	70	160	190	210	420	210
Total original income	1,280	4,760	11,580	17,880	30,050	13,110
+Benefits in cash						
Contributory	1,710	1,690	990	640	410	1,090
Non-contributory	1,640	1,320	770	470	250	890
Gross income	4,630	7,770	13,340	18,990	30,710	15,090
−Income tax[4] and NIC[5]	170	700	2,030	3,390	6,030	2,460
−Domestic rates[6] (gross)	500	520	580	620	710	590

Disposable income	3,960	6,550	10,730	14,980	23,970	12,040
Equivalized disposable income[2]	4,080	6,210	8,960	12,520	22,210	10,800
− Indirect taxes	1,120	1,570	2,460	3,050	3,890	2,420
Post-tax income	2,840	4,990	8,270	11,920	20,080	9,620
+ Benefits in kind						
Education	920	850	910	810	460	790
National Health Service	1,230	1,180	1,040	930	780	1,030
Housing subsidy	110	120	60	30	10	70
Travel subsidies	40	40	40	40	50	40
School meals and welfare milk	70	20	20	10	10	30
Final income	5,200	7,210	10,340	13,740	21,400	11,580
Number of households in sample	1,482	1,482	1,482	1,482	1,482	7,410

[1] See Social Trends, 23, Appendix, Part 5: Redistribution of income for definitions of the income measures. The 1987 and 1988 figures published in Social Trends 21 and 22 and these 1989 figures incorporate major changes to the methodology, and are not comparable with figures prior to 1987 published in earlier editions of Social Trends.
[2] Equivalized disposable income has been used for ranking the households into quintile groups. The average equivalized disposable income for each group is shown below disposable income, but all other incomes shown are unequivalized.
[3] Rounded to the nearest £10.
[4] After tax relief at source on mortgage interest and life assurance premiums.
[5] Employees' national insurance contributions.
[6] Community Charge in Scotland from April 1989 onwards.

Source: Central Statistical Office, from the Family Expenditure Survey Social Trends, 23, 1993. 75.

income-tax payments, NI contributions, and Council Tax to leave them with disposable income. Some of their spending goes to indirect taxes such as Value Added Tax (VAT) leaving them with post-tax income. Lastly, households benefit from government expenditure on services such as education and health. Adding in the value of these gives a household's final income.

The method for calculating the effects of taxes and benefits on household income was reviewed during 1989 and it was decided to move to an equivalized basis, and to rework the historic time series. Equivalization means adjusting household income to take account of household size and composition in order to recognize different needs. For example, to achieve the same standard of living, a household of five people would need a higher income than a single person and this is reflected in the equivalization. Distributions based on equivalized income put all households on an equal footing regardless of size or composition and therefore provide a better way of comparing incomes.

In 1989, original income ranged from an average of £1,280 per household for the bottom fifth to £30,050 for the top fifth (Table 2.2). After adding in cash benefits, taking off taxation and other contributions, and adding in benefits in kind, final income ranged from £5,200 to £21,400—narrowing the gap between the two groups. The effect of taxes and benefits on improving income is greatest for retired households and those non-retired households with no economically active people.

Inequality of wealth

Again, the third system of occupational welfare is more of a complement than a counterweight to class inequality. Occupational pensions are earnings-related. Sick pay and pension arrangements are better for non-manual than for manual workers. And there has been a considerable growth of tax-deductable fringe benefits since the war with the effect of increasing inequality between highly paid executives and the rest.

Up to this point we have documented continuing, if slowly decreasing, income differences: and we have shown that they are related to class. But the more challenging task is to explain them. For orthodox Marxists the distribution of capital is crucial: it fundamentally defines the class structure. Professor Westergaard and Miss Resler, who have produced a voluminously and soberly argued empirical account from the Marxist standpoint, conclude that it was the exceptional circumstances of war which produced lasting effects on the contrasts in income and wealth. They insist, however, that the two Wars

formed no part of a continuous trend toward equalization, and that they entailed only modest redistribution ... Disparities may indeed have widened since the 1950s. They certainly did not narrow significantly, from the early 1950s to the early 1970s under governments of either political shade.[21]

Moreover, these authors find the root cause of continuing inequality in the condition of property-less labour of most people: and this in turn they attribute primarily to the concentration of property ownership. 'It is for that reason above all', they argue, 'that capitalism can make no claim to a steadily more equal spread of wealth. Inequality is entrenched in its institutional structure.'[22]

Liberal theorists, for their part, do not deny the inequality of distribution of personal wealth. But they do not accept the importance that Marxists attach to it, and would contest the further Marxist theory that status and power in society are derived from it. Instead, they begin by arguing the significance of trends towards a more equal spread of both wealth and income. Argument about the exact measure of the distributions themselves is relatively unimportant. The various authorities would agree that the proportion of personal wealth held by the richest 1 per cent of the population before the First World War was about 70 per cent. By the mid-1930s it was reduced to 56 per cent, and by 1960 to 42 per cent. Subsequent official figures are on a slightly different basis. They show the percentage held by the top 1 per cent of people as moving down from 37 per cent in 1962 to 18 per cent in 1990. More detailed figures from 1960 are reproduced in Table 2.3 from the fifth report of the Royal

Commission on the Distribution of Income and Wealth. At first glance, then, these figures would appear to contradict Westergaard and Resler, and to show a strong and steady trend towards equality. But essentially Westergaard is right because the redistribution has very largely been a spread of wealth to the richest 5 per cent instead of 1 per cent, and much of it reflects arrangements for gifts *inter vivos*—gifts between the living as distinct from those bequeathed at death. In this way rich families have passed on their wealth and legally avoided tax.

The Royal Commission, chaired by Lord Diamond, was abolished by the Conservatives when they came into office in 1979, and the official statistics on inequalities of wealth distribution have become less detailed. They do, however, tell a somewhat different story. Table 2.4, derived from the government publication *Social Trends*, shows the trends since 1971. Its figures for marketable wealth among UK adults tally with those of the Diamond Commission in the early 1970s. But the authors of *Social Trends* go on to point out:

Apart from housing and land, few forms of marketable wealth have kept pace in value with inflation in recent years, and for many adults their non-marketable rights in pension schemes, whether occupational schemes or the state pension scheme, have represented an increasingly important component of personal wealth over and above holdings of marketable wealth. In 1982, the richest 5 per cent of the adult population owned 41 per cent of marketable wealth, but only 24 per cent of all wealth including all pension rights; thus inequality in the distribution of wealth is reduced by pension rights.

There were substantial reductions in the percentage of marketable wealth owned by the richest groups in the early 1970s, largely because of the fall in the prices of stocks and shares which form a significant part of the wealth of the wealthiest. The late 1970s and early 1980s brought very little change to the pattern of ownership of marketable wealth. The distribution of wealth including occupational pension rights broadly follows the same trend. For marketable wealth plus occupational and state pension rights there was also a movement toward less inequality in the early and mid-1970s, but since 1977 there has been little change.[23]

Table 2.3 Trends in the distribution of personal wealth 1960–1975

Percentage shares of estimated personal wealth of given quantile groups both of the population covered by the Inland Revenue estimates and of the total population aged 18 and over, with Gini coefficients; at specified dates between 1960 and 1975. The figures from 1960 to 1974 are for Great Britain, and those in the last two columns refer to the UK.

Quantile group	1960	1962	1964	1966	1968	1970	1972	1973	1974	1974	1975
Population covered by Inland Revenue estimates (Series A)											
Top 1 per cent	28.4	27.2	25.9	23.6	24.2	20.7	22.1	21.8	18.4	18.3	17.2
Top 5 per cent	50.9	48.8	48.5	43.7	45.2	40.9	41.8	38.8	36.7	36.7	35.0
Top 10 per cent	63.1	60.7	60.5	56.0	57.1	51.9	53.9	50.9	49.0	49.1	47.3
Top 20 per cent	76.2	73.9	74.1	70.8	71.2	66.4	68.5	66.6	64.9	65.0	63.3
Bottom 80 per cent	23.8	26.1	25.9	29.2	28.8	33.6	31.5	33.4	35.1	35.0	36.7
Gini coefficient	73	72	72	67	68	65	66	65	63	63	62
Total population aged 18 and over (Series B)[1]											
Top 1 per cent	38.2	36.0	34.4	31.8	32.7	29.0	29.9	27.6	25.3	25.2	23.2
Top 5 per cent	64.3	60.7	59.3	56.7	59.0	56.3	56.3	51.3	49.9	49.9	46.5
Top 10 per cent	76.7	74.0	73.5	71.8	73.8	70.1	71.9	67.2	66.0	66.1	62.4
Top 20 per cent	89.8	88.4	88.4	87.8	89.4	89.0	89.2	86.4	85.5	85.6	81.8
Bottom 80 per cent	10.2	11.6	11.6	12.2	10.6	11.0	10.8	13.6	14.5	14.4	18.2
Gini coefficient	89	87	87	86	87	86	86	84	83	83	81

[1] Assuming that persons not covered by the Inland Revenue estimates have no wealth.

Sources: Inland Revenue and the Royal Commission on the Distribution of Income and Wealth, Report, No. 5, Cmnd. 6999, 1977, Table 33.

Table 2.4   Distribution of wealth 1971–1990

Percentage shares of estimated UK personal wealth held by given quantile groups of the total population aged 18 or over.

Quantile group	1971	1976	1978	1979	1980	1981	1982	1986	1990
Marketable wealth									
Top 1 per cent	31	24	23	22	21	21	(18)	(18)	(18)
Top 5 per cent	52	45	43	40	38	40	(36)	(36)	(37)
Top 10 per cent	65	60	57	54	51	53	(50)	(50)	(51)
Top 25 per cent	86	84	83	77	76	79	(73)	(73)	(72)
Top 50 per cent	97	95	95	95	95	96	(92)	(90)	(93)
Marketable wealth plus occupational and state pension rights									
Top 1 per cent	21	14	13	13	12	12	11	10	11
Top 5 per cent	37	27	25	25	24	24	24	24	26
Top 10 per cent	49	37	36	35	33	33	34	35	37
Top 25[1] per cent	69–72	58–61	57–60	56–59	55–58	56–59	56	58	60
Top 50[1] per cent	85–89	80–85	79–83	79–83	78–82	78–82	79	82	84

[1] Estimates vary with assumptions. See *Social Trends*, 15, Appendix, Part 5: Personal wealth.

Source: Social Trends, 15, 1985, 90.

The technicalities leave room for further argument about the exact degree of concentration of private wealth and its long-run trends. But if, following R. H. Tawney, we distinguish between property for power, by which I mean property that carries with it control over the lives of other people, and property for use, possessions that free a man from other people's control, then we can reasonably say that, throughout the period we can collectively remember, three-quarters of the British have been virtually property-less in that area which covers the central part of life and occupations—how men and women earn a living and how they relate themselves most fully and creatively to their fellows. A minority has monopolized wealth, and an even tinier minority of that minority has monopolized property for power.

At the same time, of course, harking back to the fact of rising affluence, we should not ignore the social significance of the spread of property for use. Most of the under-40s take a wide range of amenities and consumer durables for granted. Only the over-40s remember those primitive instruments of washing day—the poss-stick and the dolly-tub.

To sum up a formidable ledger of evidence, we can say that distributions through the capital and labour markets were dramatically unequal at the opening of the century. Wealth, part of which is property for power, was always more unequally spread than income. And both distributions have remained unequal around a rising average level. Over and above such wealth for use as housing and personal possessions, property for power still has a most impressively unequal distribution. But the trend to a relatively more equal sharing of income has increasingly dominated the structure of inequality as a whole because the labour market distributes much more income than does the capital market. In 1976 income from employment accounted for well over two-thirds of all income though that proportion fell during the 1980s to 58 per cent in 1991. The self-employed account for one-tenth, and unearned income from rent, dividends, and interest payments a still smaller proportion. On the evidence so far, then, the problem is to decide whether to attach more importance to the remaining inequality, or to the expanded material freedom which has attended the rising norm. The judgement will turn on whether one is impressed by absolute or by relative riches, and how much significance we attach to polarizing trends.

Inequality and limited horizons

In either case, we have still not fully explained the inequality of a rich society. The question of how it has survived can again be put in class terms by quoting what J. B. Priestley had to say on his journey through England in 1933, when he came to Jarrow—a wholly working-class town.

> Wherever we went there were men hanging about, not scores of them but hundreds and thousands of them. The whole town looked as if it had entered a perpetual penniless bleak Sabbath. The men wore the masks of prisoners of war. A stranger from a distant civilization, observing the condition of the place and its people, would have arrived at once at the conclusion that Jarrow had deeply offended some celestial emperor of the island and was now being punished. He would never believe us if we told him that in theory this town was as good as any other and that its inhabitants were not criminals, but citizens with votes.[24]

Jarrow provides one example of the remarkable absence of resentment against class inequality. In an attempt to explain this feature of British society, W. G. Runciman has put forward the theory of relative deprivation.[25] On this theory, satisfaction or resentment is not a function of inequality as documented by economists, but of a man's assessment of his positive relative to other people with whom he compares himself. In Runciman's view the period from the end of the First World War up to 1962, against a background of trends towards the equalization of class, status, and power in Britain, working-class status resentment increased, and class resentment fluctuated, but at a remarkably low level. Working men compared their lot with other people in the working class and not with non-manual groups, who, incidentally, were just as likely to feel deprived despite their objective advantages. In the decades before 1962 there was seldom a close correlation between class inequality and resentment of it.

Both World Wars raised expectations and lifted the horizons of working-class people. But the egalitarian hopes thus engendered receded in both post-war periods. The economic depression of the 1930s inhibited comparisons between manual wages and white-collar salaries. After the Second World War there was widespread belief that a programme of class redistribution was taking place when in fact it was not. Runciman's 1962 survey showed that resentment was still low among working men and their wives because they compared themselves, in the traditional way, with those near to them in the factory and the neighbourhood. They did not compare themselves with barristers, or the residents of Mayfair. Relative deprivation was in fact more likely to be felt by middle-class than by working-class people.

Repeating the survey thirteen years later in 1975, W. W. Daniel found that the same patterns of restricted social horizons of comparison were still present.[26] Several years of serious inflation and still more years of high publicity to pay claims and incomes policy had not significantly altered them. Most importantly, the more recent survey showed that people cared not so much about how other people were getting on as about how they saw their own financial position this year compared with last year. It seems that government policy for 'gentling the masses' is more likely to be successful if it looks to economic growth for all, rather than to redistribution between unequally placed groups.

From this point of view the period from 1979 under both Thatcher and Major premiership has been grimly paradoxical. Government strategy was diverted avowedly towards economic growth for all but by means which have produced mass unemployment and a reversal of the slow long-run movement towards less inequality. Many occupational groups have continued to prosper alongside the three or four million unemployed.

Conclusion

For the twentieth century as a whole, though with an at least temporary and significant reversal in the 1980s and 1990s, we have explained the continuing inequality of a rich society mainly in terms of the slow growth of prosperity and the limited social horizons of the relatively poor. This explanation, however, still leaves open the question of whether we can properly call the inequalities we have found class inequalities. If we follow post-Marxist and liberal theorists and define class in terms of occupational structure rather than capital ownership and if, further, we treat the family rather than the individual as the unit of the class system, we shall have to recognize that many inequalities are of status rather than of class—those between men and women, or between older and younger people, or between ethnic groups. For example, if we take the average earnings of all white males to be 100, the comparable figure for black men is 88. Nor is this inequality of earnings between ethnic groups to be explained in class terms. Within classes the differentials are still to be found except among the lower-paid groups of semi-skilled and unskilled workers and personal service workers.

We must also refer to the postulated emergence of an 'underclass' in Britain. Most sociologists reject the idea, not because they ignore its antecedents in what Marx and Engels termed pejoratively the lumpenproletariat but because it is of American origin—a code word for inner-city Blacks. A sociologically as distinct from ideologically usable definition is of a group cut off from both work (the productive system) and family (the reproductive system). William Julius Wilson[27] has used such a definition to describe a minority in Chicago where the de-industrialization of the stockyards and the rise of a drug culture have systematically reduced the marriageability of males over the past thirty years. The possibility of similar developments in Britain cannot be denied: but the reality has so far not been demonstrated.

We shall return to this question in the next chapter. Meanwhile, we may conclude that class remains fundamental to stratification in Britain but it does not tell us the whole story.

3 THE RECONSTITUTION OF STATUS

Class is a necessary but not a sufficient explanation of the continuity of inequality in British society. Status must be added in a country where the tiniest detail of manner or style was once a symbol sufficient to place a person immediately in a national and unitary hierarchy of prestige. Such was the Victorian order on which the sun set for Lord David Cecil with the death of his prime-ministerial grandfather in 1903. It is now widely agreed from several different ideological standpoints that British twentieth-century history is the history of the decay of the values and status system of the Victorian period. My aim in this chapter is to trace the historical stages of the relation between status and class. The intended result is to dispose of both the Marxist theory that status is simply a by-product of class and the liberal assumption that status is an independent aspect of society. In reality they are mutually interacting forces: and, so understood, they throw light on the persistence of inequality, the social sources of belief in 'the decline of Britain', the emergence of a new division of social labour (Chapter 5), and the prospect of new patterns of intensified class conflict in response to the new Conservatism of the post-1979 period (Chapter 8).

These are, to be sure, large promises; but they stem from the combination of powerful theories. And they lead finally to an understanding of the emerging status of citizenship—a status quite different from the old status order. In the twentieth century citizenship has been pitted against the forces of class and, in the 1980s, faced a reactive challenge from the resurgence of economic liberalism, albeit presented by Mr Major in the 1990s as a promise of classless society.

Status and class theory

To understand these present and future issues we must return to the past and to the theory of class and status. My description of present disarray already implies that I will argue an important role for status, and later party, in understanding inequality—its continuities and its changes, and its relations to liberty and fraternity. There are two main arguments for the significance I accord to status. One is that some socially recognized distinctions which are highly salient to issues of equality are nevertheless not a basis for class formation. Thus, once it is accepted that the family, and not the individual, is the unit of class systems, it follows that neither age-groups nor sexes can constitute classes. Yet equally clearly there are social conflicts which turn on the claims to equality of women and young people. Both groups have status disadvantages; but their *class* interests in the allocation of resources are predominantly dependent on their families, first of origin, and later of affinity.

The second main argument is that a new form of status has been advanced in the twentieth century to claim a second distribution or redistribution of goods and services through the state and based on criteria of need as distinct from purchasing power. This has been explicitly aimed against the class distributions of capital ownership, labour market earnings, and work conditions, and against the traditional status inequalities of generation, sex, and race. We shall see, in other words, that a reconstitution of status has accompanied the dissolution of the old order.

But neither of these arguments is intended to deny the stubborn capacity of class to survive, nor, still less, to argue inequality out of our way. Class systems and their inequalities are intrinsically prone to persist. They resist change in two ways. Those who do well out of them do not usually volunteer to surrender their advantages, and they also use their powers to pass on superior opportunities to their own children. And the more this happens, the more are classes formed. A fully developed class system is both a structure of market inequality and also a hereditary system of recruitment, in practice if not in theory.

All this is obvious. What is not so clear is how class and status can either support or oppose each other. Here the first thing to notice is that class power can be translated into status power and vice versa. The encroachment of the one upon the other is a central thread in British social history. Medieval Britain was an estate society: power and advantage were primarily distributed to people on the basis of their rights and duties in relation to landholding, in a hierarchy extending upwards from the peasants, through the gentry and aristocracy, to the monarch. A class system was cradled in this pre-industrial order through the establishment of liberties and privileges for particular craft and merchant guilds. The origins of individualistic freedom, so basic to British ideological tradition, are to be found in this order of status inequality.

Class supersedes status

The outstanding feature of social development in Victorian Britain was the usurpation of status by class. Liberal nineteenth-century capitalism distributed the goods and services of an industrialized earth through the social mechanisms of the market. Distributions were therefore the outcome of interests. They arose from a division of labour which treated labour as a commodity and removed responsibility from the rich and powerful for the lives of the poor and dependent. The enlightened spokesmen of English liberal capitalism, Adam Smith, Ricardo, Bentham, and James Mill and John Stuart Mill, elaborated impressive theories of personal freedom and material plenty, which, for a brief period, formed a consensus of sound opinion among all classes. But the actual outcomes of the market were impossible to justify. The dogma of *laissez-faire* was no defence against the evidence of the horrors of women's work underground, the exploitation of child labour in the mills, and the squalor of the new industrial cities. To the men and women caught up in, exhausted, and demoralized by this system, the 'free market' seemed to be a canting phrase for organized plunder. Class polarization and class antagonism emerged from the very conditions of free and equal access that established the market system in the first place. The legitimacy of such a class-based social order could hardly be expected to escape challenge from revolutionary or reformist movements. In fact both types of movement appeared. Both based themselves on a principle of legitimation opposed to individualism. So socialism emerged into British politics. And a principal reason for the dominance of reformism and revolution was the role of status in supporting the legitimacy of a modified class system.

The integration of class and status

In the mid-Victorian period 'the upper class' meant gentlemen and gentlewomen, and was still basically a hereditary caste of titled persons and their families. However, this landed aristocracy and gentry had always absorbed new men, and in the last century the new rich of trade and industry were gradually drawn into it until in the end they overwhelmed it. A new upper class was welded together. By 1900 the House of Commons, previously an assembly of gentlemen, contained 250 bankers, merchants, tradesmen, stockbrokers, company directors, and the like, alongside and overlapping with 70 Lords, Baronets, and Honourables.[1]

The rise to high status of many British families in the nineteenth and early twentieth centuries, initially through class mobility, is both a myth and a reality. The stereotype is the factory owner accumulating capital in a Northern or Welsh industrial town in the first generation; the firm expands in the second generation; and in the third is a large public corporation, vertically integrated and with metropolitan headquarters. The status translation of family members runs from the original artisan—provincial, respectable, chapel-attending; the sons are educated in local grammar schools and perhaps Armstrong College in Newcastle, or Josiah Mason in Birmingham, and the grandsons in a major public school and an Oxford college. The family journey also runs from chapel to church, from Liberal to

Conservative voting, from business to the major professions and management, and from the Commons to the Lords. The Heralds' Office attends to the details.

This caricature indicates that, though classless societies have existed, and more are conceivable without classes, status depends in the long run on access to material resources, and such access in this case was primarily afforded through the capital and labour markets.

Edwardian Britain had a secure alliance of class with status. The bourgeoisie had adopted modified versions of the tastes and style of life of the aristocracy and the gentry. The old barriers between Church and Dissent had been widely breached, and trade had married title as Sybil had wedded Egremont in Disraeli's novel. This formidable combination dominated the manners and consciousness not only of its cadets in what Orwell called the 'lower-upper-middle class' of home and imperial administration, and not only of the slowly growing but still inferior ranks of the professions and the salariat, but also of its remote dependants beyond the great divide—the men, and particularly the women, of the manual working class.

I say remote, and the sense in which the word remote describes the relations of the upper to the lower classes is plain enough. But for some if already a declining number of working-class families, relations were intimate through generations of domestic service. Thus, while it was true of the status order that 'an Englishman had only to open his mouth to make another Englishman despise him', the language of U and non-U was not a simple binary division barring the middle from the upper classes, but also a language linking the 'governing class' to their 'lower-class' servants along a different dimension of symbolic subordination. This direct association was already declining, but its function of binding unequals together was still of some importance then. Along with the vocabulary and the routines of domestic management, larger conceptions of hierarchy and place were deferentially absorbed. An integrated inequality was the central principle of social life in Britain before the First World War. A status hierarchy lent legitimacy to class inequality.

Status control over time and social distance is one of the themes running through Robert Roberts's account of the working-class district of Salford in which he grew up in the first quarter of this century.[2] 'By 1900', he tells us, 'those cherished principles about class, order, work, thrift, and self-help, epitomized by Samuel Smiles and long taught and practised by the Victorian bourgeoisie, had moulded the minds of even the humblest.'[3]

The boys of Roberts's community avidly read the *Magnet* and the *Gem*—comic papers exalting the life and manners of public schoolboys. While they went daily to a seedy elementary school, they vicariously adopted Greyfriars as their Alma Mater. 'The "mouldering pile", one came to believe, had real existence: of that boys assured one another.' They placed it vaguely in the Southern counties—somewhere between Winchester and Harrow. It came as a 'curious shock' to Roberts, who revered 'the Old School', when it dawned upon him that he himself was a typical example of the 'low cads' so despised by all at Greyfriars. 'Over the years', he claims, 'these simple tales conditioned the thought of a whole generation of boys. The public school ethos, distorted into myth and sold among us weekly in penny numbers, for good or ill, set ideals and standards.' In Roberts's opinion, 'Frank Richards [the author of these fictions] during the first quarter of the twentieth century had more influence on the mind and outlook of young working-class England than any other single person, not excluding Baden Powell.'[4] Nor did these ideologies disappear with the new generation after the war. In the 1930s and 1940s too, working-class boys identified no less enthusiastically with the public school heroes of 'Red Circle', the mythical public school of the *Hotspur*, and with the imperial ethic in its purest form—'The Wolf of Kabul'. The adult, and more subtle, version of Harry Wharton, I might add, is Jeeves, created by P. G. Wodehouse, and widely enjoyed by a mass readership. Jeeves is essentially the servant, clearly more able than his feckless master, who none the less devotes a lifetime of service to the preservation of traditional privilege.

The Salford proletariat was arranged in an elaborate status hierarchy, rooted, of course, in the different market and work situations of workers with different levels of skill, but extending to cover all men, women, and children in a closed urban village of crowded streets, sharing a common culture of bare subsistence and survival. The arbiters of status in the community were women, centred on 'a powerful inner ring of grandmothers'. The poverty-stricken analogue of landed possessions was not even so much what one owned by way of domestic equipment, but what one pawned. To hock clean clothes gave higher status than dirty hearth rugs, or the pots off the table. When neighbours quarrelled the symbols of status were hurled back and forth

to prove to the world that the other party and its kindred were 'low class' or no class at all. One waved, for instance, a 'clean' rent book (that great status symbol of the times) in the air, knowing the indicted had fallen in arrears. Now manners and morals were arraigned before a massed public tribunal . . . Purse lipped and censorious, the matriarchs surveyed the scene, soaking it all in, shocked by the vulgarity of it all, unless, of course, their own family was engaged. Then later, heads together, and from evidence submitted, they made grim readjustments on the social ladder.[5]

Nor were the growth and grip of these virtues left to chance or the comic book. Similar legitimations were incorporated into the public agencies of child-rearing throughout the nation. With a confidence now unimaginable, the Elementary School Code of 1904 delineated in exact terms the morality to be inculcated by schoolteachers. They were to 'implant' in the children 'habits of industry, self control, and courageous perseverance in the face of difficulties'. The Catechism of the Anglican Prayer Book, repeated millions of times by the ancestors of these urban proletarians, was not wholly forgotten in the new unnatural world of the factory town.

My duty towards my Neighbour, is to love him as myself, and to do to all men, as I would they should do unto me: To love, honour, and succour my father and mother: To honour and obey the King, and all that are put in authority under him: To submit myself to all my governors, teachers, spiritual pastors and masters: To order myself lowly and reverently to all my betters: To hurt no body by word nor deed: To be true and just in all my dealing: To bear no malice nor hatred in my heart: To keep my hands from picking and stealing, and my tongue from evil-speaking, lying, and slandering: To keep my body in temperance, soberness, and chastity: Not to covet nor desire other men's goods; but to learn and labour truly to get mine own living, and to do my duty in that state of life, unto which it shall please God to call me.

The decline of the Victorian status system

The reinforcement of class inequality by status continues to this day, but it has lost much of its Victorian and Edwardian efficacy. One cause is to be found in the transformation of the class structure itself. Although, as we have seen, inequalities persist between classes, the internal composition and hence the status assumptions and outlook of the classes have drastically changed. At one end, the old upper class of the landed aristocracy has virtually disappeared, to be replaced by a more varied collection of employers, celebrities from the media and the arts, politicians, administrators, and professional people, between whom social connections have loosened, to whom recruitment from white-collar and manual origins has greatly increased, and among whom there is less agreement and confidence as to the symbols of social superiority.

Status distinctions within the working classes have often been ignored or simplified. I have used Robert Roberts's description of Salford to illustrate the internal status structure of the urban working class in the earlier decades of the twentieth century. But in so doing, I have avoided his title, *The Classic Slum*, and this is deliberate. While it is true that Engels (in his *Condition of the English Working Class in 1844*) had used this phrase to describe the Salford through which he passed daily in the early nineteenth century, it is dangerously misleading to suggest that there was an identity between working-class communities and slums in the early part of the twentieth century. The slum existed in the Edwardian industrial town, but was typically a sharply segregated and distinctive quarter within a working-class district, within which domestic violence, child neglect, drunkenness, and the low brothel were concentrated. These quarters were in no way representative of working-class life, and the working class is wrongly and romantically depicted if it is thought of as having been rescued from the slum. The underclass with which Britain is threatened in the 1990s is similarly to be differentiated from manual workers in more or less regular employment. Working-class districts, including those where incomes were very low, and housing and amenities poorly provided, were also areas of domestic peace and neighbourly trust of a standard which we do not know today. People never thought of locking their houses if they went out during the day, and theft would have been cause for amazement. The traditional problems of the slum have since been more widely spread through the town and cities, with the result that old working-class areas have lost their capacity to police the activities of strangers with the almost total efficiency of the period before the First World War. These districts and neighbourhoods have also lost the capacity, even if not the cultural aim, of 'keeping up standards', such as they were, of 'workman', 'workmate', 'neighbour', 'mother', 'housewife', etc. These standards were neither noble nor 'cultured', and indeed may be argued to have been pathetically misguided expressions of status conformity. Nevertheless, what Roberts calls 'the cherished principles' were not the values of the 'classic slum'.

Journalism and quasi social science continue to find the myth that identifies 'the working class' with the slum fatally attractive. But historical accuracy gives us a quite different picture. The point may be illustrated by recalling how Beatrice Webb made her 'romantic' discovery that there was a wage-earning family among her kith and kin whom she visited in Bacup, whence she wrote to her father in 1883:

You would have laughed, father, to see me sitting amongst four or five mill-hands ... I was surprised at their fair-mindedness, and at the kindliness of their view of men and things ... This class of respectable working man ... The old man and his daughter with whom we are staying, are a veritable study of Puritan life on its more kindly side ...

I can't help thinking that it would be well if politicians would live among the various classes they legislate for, and find out what are their wishes and ideas ... Of course, it would be absurd to generalize from such a narrow basis: but ... Mere philanthropists are apt to overlook the existence of an independent working class, and when they talk sentimentally of the 'people' they really mean the 'ne'er-do-wells'.[6]

This less dramatic description of the working class was no less (and probably more) typical of the first half of the twentieth century than of the 1880s when Mrs Webb was writing. Richard Hoggart's description in *The Uses of Literacy*[7] of Hunslet in the 1920s and the 1930s is a similarly accurate account of working-class life in this period, and his more recent autobiography confirms the picture.

Over the past two generations, since the Second World War, and of perhaps greater import, there has developed a more homogeneous and indeed more hereditary working class in Britain. This is not, by any means, the expanded and impoverished or 'immiserated' proletariat of classical Marxist prediction. Quite the opposite. It is contracted, better off, and more collectively powerful. But it is largely recruited from second- and third-generation people of working-class antecedents. This development is not yet widely appreciated even by sociologists, but emerged clearly from the studies of the English and Welsh population in the 1970s and 1980s which have been carried out at Oxford,[8] and from a parallel enquiry in Scotland. An older study led by David Glass at the London School of Economics, looking back from 1949, depicted relatively caste-like conditions at the top of British society.[9] In the post-war period, however, it is the working class which has to be thought of as closed and stable in its membership, and the middle classes as relatively open to a wider range of new recruits from different class origins. Two out of every three middle-class men today were not born into a middle-class family.

In consequence, the status claims of those with class advantages have become less clear and less confidently uttered. Appeals to blood or family connections are now seldom heard; and in any case are discordant with the meritocratic values which offer them ideological challenge in a modern industrial society. Ascription is not in practice, however, debarred from presenting itself as achievement in a competitive labour market. The older upper and upper-middle classes recruited on both criteria, but the resulting fusion of a class weakened its status pretensions: and meritocracy by definition continually invites further recruitment from below.

The development of a more homogeneous working class, with reduced differentials and therefore less sharp status distinctions between skilled, semi-skilled, and unskilled workers, had complementary effects. The skilled man's rate of wages was twice that of the labourer in 1867. By 1914 the skilled rate was about 50 per cent more than the unskilled, and by 1952 the difference had narrowed to 16 per cent.[10] The material basis for status differences within the working class was, thus, eroded. It was not until the 1980s with the return of mass unemployment that these trends towards narrower economic differentials were reversed.

In part, of course, the unheavenly host of ennobled or honoured leaders of the British proletariat served to maintain a modified form of the older status hierarchy. There was, it is true, debate within the socially conscious elements of the Labour movement as to whether Ramsay MacDonald should wear ceremonial dress (in fact he loved it), or Walter Citrine accept a knighthood. When, earlier, Ben Tillett was criticized for dining too often at the Ritz, he had to defend himself with the rejoinder that 'only the best is good enough for the working class'. But few advocated direct rejection of upper- and middle-class styles of life. It was a Rugby, Balliol, Church of England, middle-class socialist, R. H. Tawney, who refused a peerage in a letter to MacDonald saying that 'no cat ties a tin can to its own tail'. Nevertheless, in the process, the symbols lost some of their lustre.

The Victorian status hierarchy of respectability continues to decline with the falling away of religious belief and is peculiarly vulnerable to revelations of marital and sexual irregularity in the Royal Family. The tabloid press seizes its opportunities with enthusiasm. No doubt Edward VII was at least equally eccentric but the flow of information about Queen Elizabeth's children has been much amplified by technology and the receptive prurience of a wider modern public. Nor is it essentially different with the House of Lords. A case can be made for its continuation. But, as the late Baroness Wootton of Abinger recognized in her autobiography (*In a World I Never Made*), it was 'totally indefensible in a democracy'. As Labour Party leader, Tony Blair has confirmed the intention to reform the House of Lords, first by stripping hereditary peers of voting rights. The price or reward of dismantling the Victorian order seems to be a republican classless inequality.

In any case, the slowly growing affluence and mobility of the working class supplied the material base for new and less dependent status positions. Between the Wars these came in fantasy form from Hollywood through the screens of the local picture palaces. After the Second World War international 'pop stars' were carried into every house and flat by what we now call the media. A history of football heroes would sharply illustrate the point: it would run from Eddie Hapgood of Arsenal and England in the 1930s, with short back and sides, deferential to the manager, Mr Chapman, proud to play for his country, paid the wages of a skilled manual worker, and leaving Wembley or Highbury to return home by bus and train. By the 1970s the archetypal hero had become George Best of Manchester United, idolized by teenagers, forever flouting the authority of referees and trainers, frequenting boutiques and nightclubs, practising widely publicized sexual promiscuity, driving a Jaguar, and catching planes to Los Angeles.

By the 1990s, status through sport was so thoroughly international that Paul Gascoigne could shuttle easily between Newcastle and Milan.

Geographical mobility, quickened by the two Wars, broke the grip of the working-class matriarchs. The patterns of social mobility over the past generation have had still more far-reaching effects. Men and women, moving and marrying between different occupational levels, both over the generations and also within their own working lives or careers, have become an increasingly common feature of British social life in the past half century.

The patterns are complicated. They have occurred over both long and short occupational distances; they have often involved geographical migration; they are different for men and women. Pathways through education have broadened. The net result has been an upward movement through the generations. Mobility in the course of working life has not, as some Marxists have argued, developed a counterbalancing narrowness.[11]

All this might appear, incidentally, to overturn the picture of persistent inequality that I previously drew. But this is not so. It is perfectly possible that a high degree of inequality of relative chances of mobility for people of different social origins should exist alongside high and rising absolute rates of movement between classes. Where there is an inverse correlation between class and fertility, as well as an expansion of professional and managerial jobs, this coincidence of unequal relative chances and high absolute chances of upward mobility can easily result.

I shall return to a more detailed consideration of class mobility in Chapter 6. The point here is that people carry images of social worth from their older to their newer class positions, and this weakens any pre-existing accord on a hierarchy of lifestyles. This is what has happened in Britain. It has added to the problems of social control, whether by employers, managers, policemen, tax gatherers, parents, or teachers. It goes, in other words, beyond class to the social order as a totality. The stabilizing force of the status order we inherited from the nineteenth century has been comprehensively dismantled. Moreover, and what is perhaps more important, attitudes of resentment to the remaining status distinctions have moved in the opposite direction; they have been strengthened. This is argued cogently by Runciman in his study of attitudes to social inequality in twentieth-century England. As he puts it, 'the magnitude and frequency of relative deprivation of status in the manual stratum has, on the whole, risen as inequality of status has declined'.[12]

If, as sociologists now agree, such a supportive status system had been dissolving in Britain, then class must also have been losing its legitimacy; and its persistent inequalities are less and less protected from challenge. This is in fact what has been happening, especially since the Second World War (which, incidentally, was itself a period of accelerated decay of traditional status assumptions).[13] In the last two decades most Britons have had the sense that the social contract is being renegotiated; that all the methods which distribute and redistribute burdens and benefits—the collective bargain, the statute, the judge's ruling, the executive decision, the routine of administration in central and local government, the customary expectations of work places and bus queues, and even the give-and-take of family life. In short, the arrangements for the social division of duty, wealth, and welfare are in debate, their principles and procedures in question.

The rise of citizenship

Social status, then, has a peculiar history. Yet we have still to explore its most significant feature, namely the rise of citizenship as a special form of status. At this point we reach a crucial step in the discussion of class and status. What I am essentially arguing is that the Marxist emphasis on class interest trivializes status by relegating it to a subsidiary role as a more or less complicated apparatus of control over subordinate classes. At the same time, I am also arguing that the liberal emphasis on status, which comes in one form or another of a pluralistic theory of stratification, constitutes the reciprocal error—it trivializes class by denying its role in undermining the freedoms promised by a liberal society.[14] In the Butskell period from 1945 to 1979, the Marxist error was increasingly obvious. In the 1980s the liberal error was revealed. But both theories lead to false doctrines of historical progress, and neither deals adequately with the problem of social order.

There is, however, an open channel between this Scylla and Charybdis of sociological mis-explanation. It was charted by T. H. Marshall as long ago as the 1940s.[15] Marshall avoids both traps, and accurately pictures the history of conflict in Britain over the distribution of work and reward, by postulating a developing battle between the two great dramatis personae of our social history—*class* operating through the labour and capital markets, and *status* operating through the political and legal systems to define the rights and duties of citizens.

The double thrust of Marshall's theory goes to the heart of social change in twentieth-century Britain, and places contemporary struggles in the wider context of the slow and contested development of citizenship through civil rights during the period from the middle of the seventeenth century and the revolution of 1688 to the First Reform Act of 1832—including Habeas Corpus in 1679, the abolition of Press censorship, and Catholic emancipation. Quoting G. M. Trevelyan,[16] Marshall points out that by the early nineteenth century 'civil rights had come to man's estate and bore (except for the right to strike) in most essentials, the appearance they have today'. The Hanoverian epoch had established the rule of law, 'and that law, with all its grave faults, was at least a law of freedom'.[17]

Subsequently, in the nineteenth century, citizenship began slowly to acquire the dimension of political enfranchisement. Class and traditional status began a long retreat from direct control over organized politics. This conquest of politics by the principle of citizenship remained incomplete down to our own period: the enfranchisement of women was not completed until the 1918 and 1928 reforms, and the dual voting for businessmen and university graduates was not ended finally until 1948. Indeed, it can be argued that political rights were not entirely freed from their attachment as privileges to a restricted economic class to become attributes of citizenship until full manhood suffrage was adopted in 1918. In the early years of the century the registered electorate was only 60 per cent of all British men, and those left out were mostly working class.

The development of the *social*, as distinct from the civil and political, rights of citizenship belongs pre-eminently to the twentieth century. The 1834 Poor Law had been the last monument to the sharp separation of social rights from the status of citizenship. The break-up of the Poor Law is the central element in the even now unfinished story of the struggle of this new status against class in our lifetime. Its first milestone is to be found in the legislation of the Liberal landslide government of 1906. No wonder that Robert Roberts, from the vantage point of a corner shop in a working-class street, tells us how the new old-age pensioners—new, that is, since 1909—when spending their allowances of 7s. 6d. per week for a married couple, 'would bless the name of Lloyd George as if he were a saint from heaven'.

Citizenship won further victories in the field of social rights as the century advanced, especially after the Second World War with the establishment of Beveridge's social security programme based on insurance, and the National Health Service based on direct taxation. By 1977 the 'social wage' distributed by the Welfare State had become a sizeable sum: it was nearly £1,500 a year for each member of the working population of the United Kingdom.[18] But the story remains unfinished because the two principles of distribution—class and citizenship—remain in contention. Indeed the struggle has intensified since 1979 in battles over the level of public expenditure, welfare rights, and the National Health Service. A class society uses the market as its distributive instrument. It had evolved historically under powerful impulses toward economic freedom, as Marx, as well as the liberal theorists, well appreciated. Citizenship, on the other hand, is a special form of status which looks to the state and seeks a different type of distribution which turns on the political process and on the secondary form of industrial citizenship which has developed in its wake. Citizenship is also different from class in that it is intrinsically levelling. But it is not simply an assertion of equality against freedom. As Marshall was at pains to point out, it permits sanctioned inequality, for example in advanced education, or specialized medical need.

Citizenship, we should note in this context, has been defined nationally. This point is fundamental. It has been fateful for Britain in this century that the nation state was seen as the political unit appropriate to its purpose. The emerging political organization of the working classes aimed, from the start, to conquer national politics. In so doing, it necessarily took on the immense challenge of forming a national community: for citizenship status depends for its support on fraternity. Looking at the

Labour party in this way—as a movement aspiring to transform a hierarchical social order into a national community—its handicaps become plain.

The Labour movement at the beginning of the century was based on the solidarity of local class communities. Labour markets and kinship networks were bounded by walking distances. For the vast majority of ordinary people national concerns were remote from daily life. Only war made Britons out of people whose social horizons were normally enclosed by the street, the village, or the neighbourhood. The bid for men's minds, which was made by appeals for a broader national or even international class solidarity before the First World War, was in any case weak. In peace, class solidarity was dissipated in day-to-day preoccupations with survival in the close social networks of the industrial town and the agricultural village. In war, it retreated before the siege-solidarity of response to external threat. Both phenomena, of course, parochialism and nationalism, may be interpreted as expressions of social control by the governing class. But this, too, further emphasizes the barrier to national community which stood in the way of the Labour movement. A political organization committed to universal and democratic freedom had also to face the dilemma of either persuading the powerful minority to join a new national community by giving up its privileges, or forcing them to do so by reducing the economic freedoms they had previously won for themselves in the establishing of free capitalism. Moreover, the very process of economic growth, on which state welfare depended for its development, also involved changes in the occupational structure which steadily diminished the size of the working class and enlarged the lower-middle- and middle-class groups of white-collar, technical, and professional people.

Class and status have, then, been in complex contention in our time, and that contention has largely determined the application of the social principles of liberty, equality, and fraternity.

The theory of citizenship

The theory of citizenship which I accept can be challenged. It can be misinterpreted as a benign, even complacent assumption that history is the evolution or progress of civilization towards a welfare society. It can be so-called Whig history—a self-congratulatory account of the gradual ascent of liberal values. T. H. Marshall can be misread in this way, particularly with respect to what he termed the secondary system of industrial citizenship.

Marshall treated industrial citizenship or economic rights more briefly than either political or social rights. His history in this respect is all the more likely to be misinterpreted as Whig— that is the gradual unfolding of liberal principles through enlightened institutions of bargaining and conciliation, parallel or assimilated to the steady evolution of the institutions of parliamentary democracy. On this view, as Alan Fox describes it, 'the growth of strong trade unions and systematic collective bargaining [was] an evolutionary triumph of liberal principles and civilized restraints, with workers coming gradually to "learn" what was required of them in this best of all liberal worlds'. Fox's alternative view is that 'groups of workers fumbled their way towards [collective bargaining] as the most promising way of reducing the uncertainties of their immediate work experience; employers reacted in the light of their particular interests and exigencies'.[19] Marshall would agree, but remains less easily read as one concerned to stress the contingencies as well as the continuities of history.

Anthony Giddens, however, takes this criticism further and remarks on an 'odd similarity here between [Marshall's] interpretation of the development of contemporary capitalism and that of some Marxist authors who in other respects have very different views from those of Marshall'.[20] These authors interpret citizenship rights (what Marx himself had dismissed as 'bourgeois freedoms') as a form of concessionary social control by the ruling class. In a wider context Frank Parkin takes a similar view when he emphasizes 'how readily an "equality of opportunity" version of socialism can be accommodated to the institutions and values of modern capitalism' and that 'the allocation of benefits to the less privileged serves to damp down radical or revolutionary movements'.[21]

Giddens's point is that such accounts, Marshall's or Marxist, put too little emphasis on *struggle*. He is empirically justified in insisting that all three elements of Marshall's citizenship rights had to be fought for over a long period by those classes and organizations which were excluded from power and advantage by the development of capitalism. And the recent resurgence of market liberalism in Europe and America demonstrates that none of the three elements is either secure or irreversible.

Yet Giddens's criticism cannot be fully sustained when, as he himself notices, Marshall describes class and citizenship as principles or social forces which have been 'at war in the twentieth century'[22] and this conflict of principles 'springs from the very roots of our social order'.[23] Unlike Durkheim and unlike some of his own interpreters, Marshall saw conflict (though he would not have used the Marxist term 'struggle') as a permanent and indeed desirable feature of a dynamic society.

'The affluent societies of the mid-20th century', he believed, 'contain within themselves elements producing a discord that has not yet been resolved and which . . . could remain unresolved for a long time without disrupting the social order.'[24] In his very last essay he concludes with respect to 'democratic-welfare-capitalism':

The system survives in . . . a precarious and somewhat battered condition . . . It is obvious that an acute incompatibility of values prevalent in different sectors may cause intolerable friction or possibly the destruction of one value system by another. But it would be absurd to assume that the coexistence of different value systems in different contexts must necessarily be on balance 'disfunctional', since this kind of ethical relativity has been a feature of very nearly every society since civilisation began. The question is whether potential conflict can be managed . . . Each case must be judged on its merits.[25]

In the same essay Marshall returns to a personal affirmation of both his liberalism and his belief in the chronic conflict embedded in what Richard Crossman had called 'civilised capitalism':

I am one of those who believes that it is hardly possible to maintain democratic freedoms in a society which does not contain a large area of economic freedom and that the incentives provided by and expressed in competitive markets make a contribution to efficiency, and to progress in the production and distribution of wealth which cannot, in a large and complex society, be derived from any other source. But I also believe that the capitalist market economy can be, and generally has been a cause of much social injustice. The vital question whether this is an inevitable outcome of its ethos or a malady which could be treated . . . without destroying all that is of value in the system, has yet to be answered.[26]

Marshall was, on balance, optimistic about the future of the Welfare State. Though insisting on open possibilities rather than any inevitable trend, he believed in the probability of a favourable balance of collective welfare against private acquisitiveness.[27]

Of course it is no less rational to put a more pessimistic value on these probabilities. Recent experience, particularly in Britain and the USA, strongly suggests a stable possibility *in a parliamentary democracy* of majority support for 'the spirit of acquisitiveness' and its associated market inequalities buttressed by social and political control of dispossessed and deprived minorities minimally maintained by state charity. Even so Marshall's non-historicist view of history, his weaving together of ideological with institutional factors in a theory of change, and his scepticism about structural solutions to the problem of inequality still stand as firm contributions to our understanding of the genesis and contemporary state of capitalist society.

Moreover, Giddens's picture of the importance of struggle— 'the outcome of the active endeavours of concrete groups of people'[28]—can itself easily be overdrawn. The clash between the interests of capital and labour in the development of the industrial relations system in Britain, though real enough, is no simple story. For example, as Alan Fox reminds us: 'Even within the socialist element [of the working-class movement] there was a strong tradition which gave only qualified support to the international Marxist appeal—a strand of indigenous as against exotic socialism, characterized by such names as Morris, Blatchford, Tawney, and later Orwell and Edward Thompson, which remained strongly libertarian and shared the old radical love of country.'[29] And the political ruling class was never a mechanically reliable 'executive committee' of the capitalist class. It maintained a commitment to constitutionalism, law, and a not-too-heavy hand on the lower orders, partly no doubt, as Fox points out, because it was not wholly dependent on the domestic economy, but in such a way as to make the struggle for civil, political, and social rights into a process far more complicated than one of crude class conflict. In short, the system of industrial citizenship, and still more the development of political and welfare rights, was neither a predictable process of liberal enlightenment nor a new set of controls invented out of the cunning of a Fabian ruling class.

None the less Giddens is able, I think successfully, to find a weakness in Marshall's account of the sequence of the establishment of civil, political, and social rights as they developed from the status hierarchy of feudalism in the capitalist era. Marshall gives the impression that civil rights were fully and finally established before the long march of political enfranchisement and the subsequent expansion of social rights in the nineteenth and twentieth centuries. Giddens argues that civil rights, or we might say legal citizenship, established in the courts, always remained at issue. Especially in what Marshall treated as their extension into industrial citizenship, these civil rights were at least as much a battle-ground of class conflict as the basis for class abatement or amelioration. Present struggles serve Giddens's view that the separation of the economy from the polity as arenas of conflict between class interests and citizenship principles, which was so characteristic a feature of the history of capitalist society, throws doubt on the classification of economic citizenship as an extension of civil rights. Such struggles have also to be seen as a challenge to the separation of the 'economic' from the 'political' by labour movements. Working-class entry into parliament was a necessary step towards reforming anti-working-class law. In Marshall's own terms, political rights have been used to gain extended civil rights just as much as civil rights were used as a basis for demanding the extension of the political franchise. The

'political' strike is notoriously contentiously defined. More generally in the analysis of contemporary capitalism we are well
advised to think of the three citizenships as in mutual or inter-
active fragility, always threatened by class conflict, just as we
must think of the civil rights of individuals under state socialism
as always diminished by monopolized party political power.
Thus the Marshallian analysis, rid of its residual evolutionism,
can be turned powerfully against both the tendency of liberal
theory towards envisaging a 'post-industrial' society in which
citizenship has replaced capitalist class conflict and against the
shortcomings of Marxist theories of the state in both capitalist
and socialist societies.[30]

In any case, as Dahrendorf has shown,[31] the modern social
conflict has to be seen in the context of provisions and entitlements. The problem of defining and delivering a full employment economy is now much more difficult than it was in
Beveridge's day, given the changes in sexual division of labour
and the sophistications of industrial bargaining, even if the commitment of government to full employment were unequivocal.
Modern provisions are immense but their availability socially
and geographically is fraught with uncertainty. The nation state
has neither perfect control over its constituencies nor perfect
potency with respect to international exchanges. Moreover, on
the side of entitlements the nation state no longer exercises
complete legal control. Westminster continually faces both
Brussels and its own provinces. Maastricht, 'the social chapter',
and monetary union have all given dramatic illustration of the
modern lines of cleavage, and of the challenge to harmonize
economic provisions with civil entitlements. The social chapter
remains unsigned by Britain while Wages Councils are abolished, safety regulations relaxed, and unemployment benefit
reduced in Orwellian language to a 'job-seekers' allowance'.
Britain in 1994 remained on the edge rather than at the heart of
Europe.

Citizenship and ethnicity

Perhaps the most difficult test of the strength of the citizenship
principle has been its application to the immigrant population of

ethnic groups with origins in the so-called 'New Common-wealth'—mainly from Africa, the West Indies, India, Bangladesh, and Pakistan. These are the Black and Brown Brit-ish, small ethnic minorities in a dominantly white society. The most recent estimate of their numbers (1989–91), including those born in Britain, was 2,682,000 forming 5 per cent of the total population of England, 1 per cent of Wales, and 1 per cent of Scotland.[32] Their contribution to births in 1991 made up a total period fertility rate of 2.5 per cent compared with 1.8 per cent for Britain as a whole.[33]

The coloured ethnic groups in Britain therefore constitute a small, but significant, minority. They suffer both class and status disadvantages and discriminations. Their citizenship is assured in law, but fragile in practice. Their history in Britain is a short one, dating from 1948 when the former German pleasure cruiser, the *Empire Windrush*, brought 492 West Indians to work in Britain. Policy towards them was timidly pragmatic. There was a restricted preoccupation with the facts of immigration. Thus, in the 1950s, the 'stranger hypothesis' in sociological theory[34] was the academic equivalent of a policy of assimilation. Academic theory and official policy were mirrors of each other. The problem was seen as that of a small number of newcomers who would be either willing and able to learn a learnable British culture, or would accommodate temporarily and return whence they came. The process of assimilation assumed capacities on both sides—on the part of the host 'to be kind to the foreigner, the poor chap can't help it', and on the part of the immigrant to understand the reluctance of his host to expose himself hastily or to commit himself unduly by identification with a stranger whose behaviour, by definition, was imperfectly controlled by the tacit understandings of a complex, historically evolved, and slowly learned code of morals and manners. The conceived scale of the problem is well illustrated by the story of Leary Constantine's arrival between the Wars to settle in a mining town as a pro-fessional in Lancashire league cricket. On the Sunday morning after his arrival he went for a walk and, true to his nature, joined in with a group of boys kicking a football in a side street. The first boy's greeting was, 'Hasta been downt' pit, then?'

But both theorists and policy-makers were forced in the 1960s to recognize that the assimilationist policy was no longer possible in the face of the rapidly increased rate of immigration, especially from India and Pakistan, at the end of the 1950s. Hence restrictions on entry were brought in by the 1962 Commonwealth Immigration Act. The paradoxical consequences were a temporary reversal of the intentions of the Act, which brought a sharply increased flow of Indian and Pakistani families to settle permanently in place of the groups of male temporary workers intending to return.

These developments undermined the assumption of the older assimilative policy that the coloured population was a homogeneous collection of individuals. This was never a fact. Distinctions have to be drawn not only between different nationalities and ethnic groups, but also within these between castes, classes, and occupations, and between individuals, families, and types of community group. E. J. B. Rose showed at the end of the 1960s that the pattern of group formations among the British coloureds was changing rapidly and in different directions among West Indians, Pakistanis, and Cypriots, as well as between the first and second generation of immigrants.[35] In particular, an unassimilated group of depressed status within the working class was being formed. More generally, the developing size and heterogeneity of the coloured population demanded not assimilation but integration where the process had to be seen as a highly differentiated one of absorption, incorporation, and accommodation to the multiple relationships of locality, occupation, politics, religion, and indeed the whole network of society.

Similarly, effective race relations policies had to take account of the facts of change in the host society. The terms of assimilation have been transformed. British society is no longer as assimilative as it was when the earlier wave of Jewish immigrants arrived at the end of the nineteenth century. There has been an 'Americanization' of British society with decreasingly certain use of informal sanctions through tacit understandings, and with growing impersonality, mobility, and aspirations towards privatized affluence. Moreover, the quiet and polite xeno-phobia of the average Briton has been overlaid with explicit racism ranging from the ugly militancy of the National Front or the British National Party (with their links to French, German, and Belgian neo-Fascist parties) to the intellectualized prejudice of Enoch Powell.

What was needed, it was generally agreed, was an attack on three fronts—against urban poverty, racial discrimination, and language disabilities. Such an approach would require extra money directed specifically at improving the situation of coloured minorities, particularly in the areas of housing, educa-tion, and employment. It also demanded a clear government policy on race relations rather than mere declarations of princi-ple. Meantime, ugly confrontations with the police, as in Bristol, or with the National Front, as in Wolverhampton, continued to rend the social fabric of Britain in the 1980s. For, although successive governments had declared their support for policies of positive discrimination, they gave no lead themselves in treat-ing Black and Brown people as equivalent to whites.

There were serious riots in Brixton and Toxteth in 1981. A crisis of relations between citizen and the law was recognized in the inquiry subsequently led by Lord Scarman. The crisis re-ceded in subsequent years in the sense that no further riots took place until 1985. But the underlying conditions of citizenship denial scarcely changed.

A typical example is the Granby triangle in the ethnic mixing-bowl of Liverpool, which has concentrated a fantastic variety of human faces, crowded together in economic decline, bad hous-ing, poor amenities, low morale, and high crime. At its worst, Toxteth is the jostling proximity of the rawest community at the lowest common denominator of individuals thrown together with no common social inheritance. The best dream of what it could be is the hope of multi-cultural harmony in a civic stability of Merseyside cosmopolitans.

Put in public and constitutional terms, the question is whether Toxteth belongs to Britain, whether the Blacks are British citi-zens—or whether these territories are to be seen as under the alien occupation of foreigners (more politely described as 'immigrants' or 'New Commonwealth'). If they are citizens, then they have equal rights and duties with the white majority. They have a claim to equality, not only before the law, but also before the teacher, the employer, the doctor, and the social worker. If they are not citizens, the white majority should explicitly renounce the promises which brought them, or in most cases their ancestors, to these islands, and the state should be obliged to negotiate real citizenship for them elsewhere. I have no doubt myself that the first is the more honourable and, indeed, the only practical answer. We are talking here about 40,000 people, and the majority of this Liverpool minority is strictly Black British: they were born here, brought up here, and know no other home.

Whether by the ancient and cruel accidents of slave-trading, the propaganda of colonialism, the labour demand of the once buoyant British economy, or the plain fact of birth in the United Kingdom, the 5 per cent minority have just as much right to a place on the island as any descendant of a Saxon or Norman invader.

But citizenship status policy has been quite otherwise. Its outline is most clear with respect to immigration control. The 1960s saw legislation aimed at excluding Black immigrants. The 1971 Act took away the right of Black Commonwealth immigrants to settle. The Labour government of 1974–9 maintained immigration controls and race relations policies. Margaret Thatcher and the Conservative party in the run-up to the 1979 election emphasized the threat of 'swamping' to ordinary British culture by already established Black and Brown communities. Immigration was a code for Black. Immigration control was tightened by the Thatcher administration, and clothed in the language of British citizenship by the British Nationality Act of 1981. The argument for racial discrimination at the immigration office was given official expression at an OECD conference in 1986.[36]

In recent decades, the basis of policy in the United Kingdom has been the need to control primary immigration—that is, new heads of households who are most likely to enter the job market. The United Kingdom is one of the most densely populated countries in Europe. In terms of housing, education, social services and, of course, jobs, the country could not support all those who would like to come here. Firm immigration control is therefore essential, in order to provide the conditions necessary for development and maintaining good community relations.[37]

The focus on immigration control is now built in to British race relations. It flared as sentiment to rival the Powell 'Tiber foaming with much blood' speech when Mr (now Lord) Tebbit proposed his 'cricket test' in 1990. He questioned the loyalty of those Asians and Caribbeans who did not cheer for England in test matches. There is again here the fear of swamping the natives by newcomers determined to bring their own culture and nationality to the island. Resistance to immigration from Hong Kong had similar social sources, though here a 50,000 quota was allowed. The exclusion policy was even applied in 1992 to Bosnian refugees from the collapsed Yugoslavia. As to the policy of any future Labour government, an assurance was given by Gerald Kaufman (Hansard, 83, 1985, cols. 909–10) that while firm control on immigration would continue, such control would be applied equally to all immigrants regardless of race. Elsewhere in Europe explicit anti-foreigner politics is rife. Britain so far, despite such isolated examples as the success of a British National party candidate for Tower Hamlets Council in 1993, has avoided the emergence of racism as a major political force.[38] Small parties find national success difficult in the British electoral system and the Conservative party manages to accommodate some who might otherwise join extremist parties.

Finally, it should be mentioned that there is recent evidence these ethnic minorities have found educational and training opportunities in Britain in encouragingly increasing numbers in recent years, and we return to the point in Chapter 8.

All in all, the changing circumstances point to the need to develop a complex policy of integration. Social inequality, conceived as differences in power and advantage, is the basic condition of the Black British. There is overwhelming evidence that the coloured population suffers discrimination on grounds of colour in employment, housing, leisure activities, and over the whole range of social relationships. Differences in power and advantage, whether based on colour or any other socially evaluated attribute, tend to be generalized and to be transmitted between generations. The social outlook for the ethnic minorities is accordingly bleak. Whether admitted directly to citizenship through the immigration office, or indirectly through an upbringing in Britain and through the school system, they typically have all the disadvantages of the lower levels of the native working class, as well as those of colour prejudice.

The effectiveness of the deliberate pursuit of equality through governmental action in the twentieth century has been severely limited in respect of the relative chances of the working class. In so far as the integration of Africans and Asians is thought of as a recapitulation of the gradual admission of the working class to full citizenship, the task calls for much more politically forceful action than is embodied in the Race Relations Act of 1968 or 1976, or the mild gestures towards 'positive discrimination' which have been incorporated into the government's Urban Programme. Without such action, the position of the second and third generations of coloured people is likely to worsen.

Obvious and persistent inequality, quite apart from its moral effectiveness, is a threatening source of conflict. In the context of class relations, John Goldthorpe has analysed the paradox of the coexistence of gross inequality with a high degree of political consensus. [39] He divides the current explanations into two main types, 'social psychological' and 'culturalist'. I have discussed W. G. Runciman's contribution to the first type. What determines behaviour is not actual but *felt* deprivation. Limited imagination has served to integrate an unequal society. Goldthorpe's second type of analysis complements Runciman's. The British political culture is characterized by a balance 'that holds, even across lines of class and party, between participant, activist attitudes on the one hand, and acquiescent, passive attitudes on the other, between emotional commitment to political principle and cool pragmatism; between consensus on matters of procedure and conflict over particular issues'.[40] Socialization into the culture makes for apolitical and unfanatical citizens. In the past it has offered little basis for politically extremist egalitarian movements. Thus, as Runciman put it, 'there has been woven a social fabric in which traditional privilege blends with egalitarian socialism and class-consciousness with a veneration of existing institutions'.

Will race relations in Britain tear this fabric apart? Continuing conflict leaves open such a possibility. Race relations legislation is explicitly egalitarian. But the question remains of what responses are likely from those who are legally declared equal in an unequal society of conflicting interest groups, what economic and social costs will have to be paid for the absence of moral consensus, and what external controls will be required by those who prefer to maintain the status quo. The answers are far from comforting.

Conclusion

In this chapter we have traced the complex interplay of class with status. The decline of the Victorian status order which so powerfully legitimated a class society was a feature of British social stratification at least until the end of the post-war period. The reconstruction of status on the basis of the principle of citizenship also emerged as a fundamental conflict in British society. The war of citizenship against class won some battles for social equality against class inequality in a polity of parliamentary democracy and a mixed economy. But the war continues, and the position of the ethnic minorities shows grimly that an equal commonwealth of citizens remains an unattained objective of social reform.

4 THE FORTUNES OF PARTY

Class and status, it has emerged, are social structures which both constrain the lives of men and women and offer them opportunities. We have described the continuities and changes in this enveloping framework of life-chances. Yet still the picture of social inequality is incomplete. A full view of the stratification system, following Max Weber's analysis, must include those movements through which individuals band together to seek collectively for power and advantage. A dynamic theory of stratification is a three-sided analysis of class, status, and party. The next task therefore is to examine how people have used deliberate organization in pursuit of their ends. By studying organized movements we can begin to answer the question of 'structure' and 'agency', that is, how far have or could people alter the framework of constraint and opportunity by deliberate social action? How far can power and advantage, which we have seen in Britain as a structure of class and status inequality, be changed by political and industrial interest groups? In short, what, in Max Weber's terminology, is the power of party?

An answer for Britain at the end of the twentieth century involves five elements: first the rise of working-class organization geared to the market and the state, second the containment of these movements by a resourceful and adaptive Conservative party, third the incorporation of Labour leaders, fourth what sociologists call the institutional segregation of industrial conflict, and fifth a resurgent economic liberalism which captured the Conservative party at the end of the 1970s. This movement, which survived strongly into the 1990s, together with disintegrative conflict in the 1980s within the Labour party,[1] finally raises the question of whether the whole balance of British politics has been transformed with momentous implications for the future shape of British society. In the 1990s the issue could well be phrased as the relation between society and state.

At the beginning of the twentieth century the trade unions and the Labour party were the practical means of those whose weak market position could only be transcended by mobilizing their superior numbers both industrially and politically. Consideration of these popular movements of class, status, and party will lead to the conclusion that they had eventually to face the problem of 'alienation of the organizational apparatus from the membership'.[2] This fate befalls all large organizations. They tend to become remote from the interests they are created to serve, the more so the more successfully they recruit members. In other words we are talking about a society in which *Gesellschaft* increasingly replaces *Gemeinschaft*, the secondary substitutes for the primary tie. There are fewer siblings (and lately less marriage), fewer known neighbours, and correspondingly more associations or 'parties' including organizations for marriage and cohabitation, reconciliations for spouse and neighbours, community centres and churches as substitutes for neighbours, car boot sales as substitutes for formal markets.

The age of organization

There is no more commonplace description of the twentieth century than 'age of organization'. If we pursue that phrase we find as its corollaries the age of alienation and the age of anomy (or normlessness). I shall not cover the whole sweep of advancing organization, nor shall I more than refer to what Professor Finer termed the *Anonymous Empire* of pressure groups which lobby Westminster and Whitehall, and fill the gap between government and electorate between elections. There are many such interest groups. Some obscure and some ephemeral, some of long standing and widely known, they cover the whole gamut of social, economic, and political life. Confining examples to the first letter of the alphabet there is the Automobile Association, Aims of Industry, Amnesty, Alcoholics Anonymous, Action on

Smoking and Health, and Associations of almost anyone anywhere ascertainable. My main concern, however, is with the central phenomenon of party in twentieth-century Britain—the rise, and in the 1990s the possible demise, of an organized working class.

The more general background of the age of organization can be summarized as one in which more people are more involved in social relations beyond kinship at every stage of their lives. One indicator of the general trend is the number of enquiries received by the advice network of Citizens' Advice Bureaux (CAB). In 1971 there were 512 branches, by 1991 there were 2,111. The number of clients multiplied by five in twenty years. Another indicator is the likelihood of being employed in a local firm. People now typically work for an organization which is unlikely to be confined to their town or even their country. It is more and more likely to be a multinational company. Concurrently there has been increasing concentration into a smaller number of larger firms. The invention of the limited company in the nineteenth century had paved the legal way for this development,[3] and sounded the knell of classical political economy as a valid theory applicable to the real world. Though at the beginning of the twentieth century the hundred largest companies still produced only 15 per cent of manufacturing output, today the hundred juggernauts of industry account for half the output. On the other hand economic liberalism encouraged people to start their own businesses in the 1980s with the result that, by 1992, 3 million people were self-employed. Of these six out of ten work in the services sector and as many as one in four of Pakistanis and Bangladeshis are so placed. The once all-dominant manufacturing industry of the classical British industrial revolution has shrunk until by 1992 it accounted for only a fifth of the workforce while services expanded to nearly three-quarters. As many critics insist, industrial capitalism was displaced by casino capitalism and in the process, part-time, female, and less secure employment came to dominate the productive process. Overall, the number of workers declined (from over 22 million in 1971 to $21\frac{3}{4}$ million in 1992). It is also noteworthy that men in the UK worked longer hours than in European countries generally (44.0 hours per week against 40.4 in 1990) but women worked shorter hours (30.5 hours per week against 33.1). Correspondingly only 6 per cent of men compared with 45 per cent of women were in part-time employment in 1992.

In short, the organizations of production have expanded their range, reduced their numbers, and enlarged their scale. Married women have moved into paid employment, and what the Registrar-General is pleased to call 'the economically active population' has therefore expanded, despite the fall-off in economic activity rates among older men and the parallel increase in the number of old and retired people. Leisure experiences, too, as well as work and education, are supplied by large-scale organizations, or take place in premises or with apparatus controlled by them. Even to watch television in the home is in fact to participate as a consumer in the final result of an enormous organizational effort. Similarly, in the case of children's play, the humble *Dandy* is replaced by the video game, and juvenile prestige has come to depend less on skill with four old pram wheels and a few bits of wood and more on the ability to buy the most sophisticated and fashionable products of technology.

The largest organization is, of course, the state itself. The state supplies cash, personnel, buildings, and other resources for a vast network of financial, personal, educational, and social services. The Welfare State remains a huge employing agency. For example, in the National Health Service the staff remains at over a million in 1991 as in 1981 though the proportion of administrators has risen.

The growth of trade unions

At the beginning of the century economic organizations were dominated by a private owning and controlling class, and political organizations by the Conservative and Liberal wings of the middle and upper classes. The Labour party did not exist, and the trade union movement, though it had deep roots, especially among skilled workers, in the earlier stages of industrialism, was struggling to extend its organizational sway among semi-skilled

and unskilled workers. There were 2 million union members at
the beginning of this century, out of a total potential membership of nearly 16 million. In other words, only one-eighth of all
possible recruits had in fact been recruited. Put more technically,
the density of membership was 13 per cent in 1900. This figure
rose rapidly to reach 45 per cent by 1920. Since that date unionization has had fluctuating fortunes, but did not attain a higher
density than it had in 1920 until the 1970s. By 1979, it had
reached 55.4 per cent.

At this point, which we now see as the end of the post-war
period and the re-emergence of economic liberalism, it now
appears that traditional unionism reached its zenith (Figure 4.1).
Economic recession and political opposition combined to reverse the tide of union strength. Union density was down to 48
per cent by 1982, a level more like that of the 1960s. During the
first half of the 1980s union membership declined from the high
point of 13.3 million in the UK in 1979 (compared with less than
10 million in 1961). In the first three Thatcher years membership
fell by 13 per cent, the highest losses occurring among unions
recruiting in manufacturing industry, where unemployment rose
most rapidly. Figures for unions affiliated to the TUC show
membership falling by 17 per cent between the end of 1979 and
the end of 1983. By 1991 total membership was down to 9.6
million and density had fallen to 37.7 per cent.

Figure 4.1   Density of union membership 1901–1991

Were it not for the relative buoyancy of unionism among women, professionals, and public-sector employees, the picture of a traditional male working-class union movement in retreat before Thatcherism would be still more dramatic, especially perhaps with the miners' strike of 1984, which ended in 1985 with the miners returning to work without any satisfaction of their demands for greater protection from pit closures. Both public sympathy and political vulnerability were confirmed in the parliamentary battles and final defeat of the coal-mining interest in 1992 and 1993.

Unionization of women has always lagged behind that of men: so, too, has that of white-collar employees compared with manual workers. But after the Second World War, unionization of white-collar workers increased very quickly. Thus while union membership among manual workers increased by only 0.9 per cent between 1948 and 1970, the increase among white-collar workers was 79.8 per cent. The densities in 1979 were 63 per cent for manual workers and 44 per cent for white-collar workers.[4] Unionism remains an organized force or 'party', but its march has been reversed and its male working-class character is drastically modified.

The class struggle in economics and politics

The end of the nineteenth century had brought the period of peaceful bourgeois domination to its late autumn of economic progress, imperial expansion, and national security. Political conflict divided contestants by religion more than class. But class politics were soon to sweep away the old divisions. The class struggles previously fought in an autonomous economic sphere were to enter into the political sphere, forcing governments to move from a passive 'keeping of the ring' into economic intervention and management. These movements towards a kind of 'Britain incorporated' were essentially the consequences of developments in class structure, but the form they took, and particularly the part played in them by an organized working class, was conditioned by those developments in the status of citizen-

ship which T. H. Marshall has analysed[5]—the civil right to
free association, out of which the trade unions were built,
and political enfranchisement, which gave the Labour party
its opportunity.

Class conflict and political consensus

These interconnected industrial and political movements were,
to be sure, class and collectivist organizations. But, much more
so than their counterparts in the continental countries, their
character was outstandingly individualistic and social democratic in their commitment to the idea that opposition and dissent were not merely tolerable but essential to a progressive
society. Part of the explanation lies in the strong historical link
between the period of religious cleavage and that of class cleavage in British politics. In its secular effect, organized religion is
usually and properly seen as primarily an apparatus of social
control. The 'heart of a heartless world' as Marx acknowledged,
but also, then a striking phrase if now a cliché, 'the opiate of the
people'.[6] In industrial Britain, the nonconformist chapels were
the bearers not only of religiosity but also of a radicalism which
schooled more than one generation of activists. Even the
Church of England nurtured its socialists—men like R. H.
Tawney, or Archbishop Temple, whose conception of the social
order began with the morality of the New Testament, and who
saw capitalism not simply as unchristian, but antichristian in that
it converted economic means into overriding ends and thus in-
troduced the worship of false gods. I remember as a child in the
1930s intoning the Magnificat at evensong in a Northampton-
shire church—'He hath put down the mighty from their seat and
hath exalted the humble and meek.' And I vaguely assumed that
the archaic language of my elders had led them to essential truth
but with wrong tenses, just as they appeared also to be confused
as to the geographical location of Jerusalem.[7]

At all events, the religiously moulded inheritance of native
radicalism of the early years of this century was responsible and
respectable. It was a radicalism that accepted many traditional
and middle-class values, not a radicalism of class warfare. It was

therefore less terrifying to the dominant classes, making their
resistance to the spread of political suffrage weaker and encouraging the political wing of the ruling class to stay as far as
possible out of the battle between capital and labour in the work
place—a policy in any case enjoined by nineteenth-century liberal theories of economics and politics. It gave working-class
leaders to the twentieth century who, though tenaciously defens-
ive of union interests in dealing with owners and managers, were
anti-Marxist, non-revolutionary, pragmatic, and piecemeal in
their reformist intentions.

At least until the 1960s there was a marked asymmetry in
the class relations of economics and politics in Britain—the
one characterized by low and the other by high relations of
trust. This asymmetry was formed out of a long history. Relations in the work place in industrial Britain reflected liberal
doctrines of the market, defining labour as a commodity.
The 'laws of market economics' provided an external 'scientific'
substitute for ethical principles in the division of the fruits
and declared that private charity rather than the employer was
responsible for the mitigation of hardship, with the state as
the ultimate but minimal provider when neither charity nor self-
help prevented destitution. In the work place itself, the working
class accepted the definitions imposed upon it by its economic
masters. Collective bargaining resulted between employers
enforcing a commodity conception of labour and a largely
alienated work-force conditioned by the system into a zero-sum
game conception of management/worker relations. As Alan Fox
puts it: 'So far as work relations were concerned, the classes
existed alongside each other, self-contained and independent;
mutually alienated; the one seeking to protect itself against the
superior power of the other by means of a process of low-trust
bargaining.'[8]

Fox chooses his words carefully. He uses the phrase 'existed
alongside', rather than 'confronted', because working-class independence ran only along certain dimensions of class relations. It
was not an independence grounded in any generalized conception of class war in the Marxist sense.

Indeed it could be argued that the working-class independence that expressed itself through Trade Unionism, collective bargaining, and the sub-culture which celebrated solidarity and collectivism, was only conceded legal status and . . . social acceptance by the more powerful groups in society because working-class independence showed clear signs of limiting itself to relatively marginal challenges of a bread-and-butter kind at the work place.[9]

Political relations were able to rest more directly on social bonds outside the work place that were strongly antithetical to doctrines of class struggle. That is why it can be reasonably argued that the norms of political attitudes were ones of high trust by contrast with the established and enduring low-trust industrial relations.

Paradoxically, the General Strike of 1926, which may reasonably be described as a moment of tense confrontation between the two main classes, also provided unmistakable evidence of a consensual political culture. The stories of good humour and fair play between strikers and soldiers have since taken their place in national mythology. I am not thinking of those, but rather of the exchanges in the House of Commons and in Downing Street before and after the event between the Conservative Prime Minister, Stanley Baldwin, and the Labour members. The year before the strike, two Tories (one a Conservative trade unionist) put down a Private Members' Bill to end the political contribution to the Labour party from trade union dues. The Bill would probably have succeeded, but Baldwin opposed it. After discoursing on the growing power of the organized employers and organized workers, and on the tradition of letting Englishmen develop their own associations in their own way, he went on as follows:

We find ourselves, after these two years in power, in possession of the greatest majority our party ever had . . . because, rightly, or wrongly, we succeeded in creating the impression that we stood for stable Government and for peace in the country between all classes of the community . . . I want my party today to make a gesture to the country . . . and to say to them: We have our majority; we believe in the justice of this Bill . . . but we are going to withdraw our hand; we are not going to push our political advantage home. Although I know that there are those who work for different ends from most of us in this House, yet there are many in all ranks and in all parties who will re-echo my prayer: 'Give Peace in our time, O Lord.'[10]

Fourteen years later David Kirkwood, described by G. M. Young as 'once the firebrand of Clydeside', wrote a letter to Baldwin remarking on the change in attitudes between 1914 and 1938. In it he said 'it seemed to me . . . that in your speech you made flesh the feelings of us all, that the antagonism, the bitterness, the class rivalry, were unworthy, and that understanding and amity were possible'.[11]

We are listening here to two characteristic voices of British politics even after the organized working class had become the major opposition party. Disraeli's one-nation Toryism and social-democratic Labour were those two voices. The hard heads of right and left poured scorn on them then, and still do today. It is easy to dismiss them as rhetorical sentimentalists. It is wiser perhaps to recognize that the creation of universal suffrage, and all the apparatus of industrial bargaining and conciliation, also entailed the creation of vested interests in them for both classes.

The deferential British worker?

Alternatively, these British political peculiarities have been explained by the thesis of a deferential working class. On this there is a large literature.[12] The point of departure of the thesis is that, extension of the suffrage notwithstanding, a country with a hugely preponderant proletarian electorate has returned more Conservative than Labour governments. Even if we start from 1918, so as to ignore the early period of Labour party formation and the still restricted male franchise, the party of the working class has held office for only twenty of the subsequent seventy-six years to 1994.

This comparative electoral failure cannot be explained away by denying the proposition that Labour has been the working-class party. The Communist party has never attracted more than a fraction of 1 per cent of votes,[13] and the decline of the Liberals after their split in 1916 took more Liberal voters into the Conservative than into the Labour camp. Between the Wars the class base of the Labour party took a long time to establish. Consolidation came only with the Second World War when there was a profound national shift of political outlook which led to the Labour landslide of 1945. The share of the vote at general elections taken by Labour is shown in Figure 4.2. Even so, the capture of the working class as a potentially overwhelming political force was never complete. Labour electoral support levelled off after the Second World War to leave the two main parties in fine balance until Labour's decline in the 1960s to 1980s.

Between the Wars, the Labour party increasingly attracted the loyalties of working men and their wives, partly at the expense of the Liberals and the Conservatives, but most of all among those families with no history of party allegiance. Nevertheless, a large residue of cross-voting, that is, voting for the party of the other class, remained, and it is at this point that interest in the Tory-voting worker becomes salient. As Butler and Stokes put it, there was

one grand historical paradox: the first major nation of the world to become industrialized, a nation in which 70 per cent of the people regard themselves as working-class, has regularly returned Conservative Governments to power. Between 1886 and 1964 the Conservative

Figure 4.2   Labour's share of the vote 1900–1992

Party was defeated by decisive majorities only twice—in 1906 and 1945.
Such a record could only have been achieved through heavy 'defection'
to the Conservatives among the industrial working class . . . the working-class elector was likelier than the middle-class elector to support the
party of the opposite class.[14]

This is true, at least on a generous definition of the working
class—and incidentally crucial for the survival of the Conservative party in the period we are discussing. In 1970, the Conservatives took 45 per cent of their votes from manual workers.
Nevertheless, it is also true, and no less important, that in that
same year the manual-worker vote was split between Labour
and Conservative 64 per cent to 36 per cent. At first glance, these
figures appear to contradict one another—the one showing Conservative success in attracting nearly half of its votes from
manual workers, and the other showing that nearly two-thirds of
manual workers voted for their natural party. They are, in fact,
the same figures put in two different ways as answers to two
different questions. If we ask where parties *got* their votes, we
find that the Tories got 45 per cent of them from the working
class. But if we ask where the classes *sent* their votes, we find that
only 36 per cent of the working class sent them to the Tories. The
difference is due simply to the fact that the working class was
still, at that time, larger than the middle class.

The slow growth and limited success of the Labour party as
the political organization of the working class was therefore to
be explained partly by its relatively late start, partly by the
inevitably slow process of building up loyalty as parents passed
on their party commitment to their children, and partly from the
brilliant ingenuity of the Conservative party in rebutting the
twentieth-century assumption that political parties should be
seen solely in terms of class interest. It is the success of the
Conservatives in combating this one-dimensional view of politics, and the corresponding failure of Labour to maximize its
appeal to class that accounts for British electoral history, not the
deferential working-class Tory voter. Such voters are, of course,
to be found: and those manual workers who vote Conservative
are more likely to be strong supporters of the monarchy than are

their workmates who vote Labour. But before the inference is accepted that the working-class Tory vote is deferential, we must also notice that more than half of the working-class *Labour* voters are royalists, and that monarchist sentiment is more common among the Labour-voting working class than among the Labour-voting middle class.

We are dealing here, to be sure, with only one indicator of what writers have in mind in defining deferential voting: but weighing all the evidence we are forced back to Walter Bagehot's judgement that the English *as a nation* are deferential. We have no need to ascribe these attributes exclusively to the Tory working class.

Why did Labour lose?

The incomplete but steady consolidation of class loyalties to a two-party division of society continued for half a century. But this description fits only half of the graph of Labour's share of the vote (Figure 4.2). The complete graph is an inverted U-curve followed by a recovery of Labour fortunes after 1983. Labour dropped its share of the vote in the 1979 election, and Mrs Thatcher's Conservatives turned a defeat into a disaster for Labour in 1983 when a further dramatic decline of Labour support reduced its share of the vote to 27.6 per cent, with 42.4 per cent going to the Conservatives and 25.3 per cent to the new SDP/

Table 4.1   Party Voting 1983–1992

	1983	1987	1992
Conservative	42.4	42.3	41.8
Labour	27.6	30.8	35.2
Social Liberal Democrats	13.7	12.8	17.0
Social Democrat Party	11.6	9.7	—
Plaid Cymru	0.4	0.4	0.4
Scottish National	1.1	1.3	1.9
Northern Ireland Party	2.5	2.2	2.1
Green Party	0.2	0.3	0.6
Others	0.5	0.2	1.1

Liberal Alliance. The comparable figure in the general elections of 1987 and 1992 were 22.5 and 17.0 per cent of all votes. The question therefore may still be put as to whether the old political mould is broken or, in terms of our concerns in this book, whether the class base of British politics has come to an end involving the collapse of the political organization of the working class.

The short answer is no. The analysis of the 1983 and 1987 elections by Dr Anthony Heath and his associates[15] rebuts the theory that politics has become detached from the traditional stratification of British society. Admittedly class loyalties have been attenuated: middle-class Conservative voters plus working-class Labour voters fell as a proportion of all voters from 64 per cent in the 1964 election to 51.7 per cent in 1983 and 51.6 per cent in 1987. But within this framework of attenuating class loyalty the differences between occupational classes in their alignment with the parties have remained stable. The odds of middle-class electors voting Tory compared with the odds of a manual worker voting Labour (i.e. the odds ratio) have changed little. The odds ratio was 4.8 in 1945, 6.1 in 1959, 4.5 in 1970, 3.7 in 1979, and 3.9 in 1983. There has been, in short, trendless fluctuation and certainly not a de-alignment of politics from class.

The really significant change therefore has been not so much the political propensity of the classes as a change in the class structure itself. As Dr Heath puts it 'in focussing on class dealignment, political scientists have concentrated on a minor rearrangement of the furniture while failing to notice a major change in the structure of the house'.[16] In the 1960s, 1970s, and 1980s, Britain has been moving strongly from a blue-collar to a white-collar society. I drew attention to this transformation in Chapter 2. On Heath's class schema, whereas in 1964 the working class was nearly three times the size of what he terms the dominant class (our middle-class professional and managerial groups, and Dahrendorf's or Goldthorpe's 'service class') and constituted nearly half the electorate, in 1983 these two classes were of almost equal size. The dominant class had grown from

18 per cent of the electorate in 1964 to 29 per cent in 1983 while the working-class proportion had dropped from 47 to 31 per cent. Heath also distinguishes three intermediate classes—routine non-manual (22 per cent in 1983), petty bourgeois (8 per cent), and foremen and technicians (10 per cent).

Incidentally, the advantage of this five-class model over the Marxist two-class model, which I criticized in earlier chapters, becomes crucial in this question of interpreting the emerging relation of class to politics. The two-class model (paradoxically in the light of its historical and ideological origins) yields an impression of a much looser relation between class position and party preference than is warranted in reality. Using the five-class schema, Heath is able to show much more precisely the middle-class character of the Conservative and the Alliance parties (the former most solidly based in the petty bourgeoisie), and the working-class base of the Labour party. The organization of British politics along class lines is actually obscured by the historically outmoded two-class model. Heath and his associates have further improved their analysis in 1991 by using both a refined class scheme and a better method of distinguishing absolute from relative class voting. The five-class scheme—a scheme based on both employment status and occupation—is:

Salariat (managers, professionals, and administrators)
Routine non-manual workers (clerks and secretaries)
Petty bourgeoisie (employers and self-employed)
Foremen and Technicians
Working Class (rank and file manual workers in industry and agriculture)

Using this scheme Heath shows the relative strength of parties. The Labour party is strongest in the working class followed by the Foremen and Technicians. The Conservatives are strongest in the petty bourgeoisie and next in the Salariat. The Liberal and Social Democratic parties are strongest in the Salariat. Labour decline is reflected in their loss of votes in every class (except the petty bourgeoisie) in 1983 and 1987 compared with previous elections from 1964. The Liberals rose reciprocally. Using log linear modelling Heath is able to take into account both the changing size of the classes and the changing overall share of votes going to the three main parties. The analysis finds little support for the thesis of 'class secularization'. Trendless fluctuation remains the relation of class to politics. Politics, not change in social class structure, explains the history of party fortunes from 1983 to 1992.

To be sure, the declining electoral fortunes of the Labour party are not wholly attributable to changes in (a more elaborately conceived) class structure. There have been short- and long-run changes in the organization of the parties, their ideological outlook, and the subjective values of the nation as a whole. For example, while left-wing militancy has captured some constituency parties and trade unions, popular views on nationalization and privatization have moved significantly to the right in all classes, and hostility to the bureaucratic apparatus of the state has grown in post-war experience. The Falklands episode of 1982 demonstrated a deeply entrenched nationalism (which supported Mrs Thatcher) and possibly reflected a resentment of lost imperial glory which is felt in different ways among widely different class and status groups. And the defection of prominent middle-class Labour leaders and supporters to the SDP was a serious blow to the electoral effectiveness of the Labour party. Nevertheless the class basis of politics remains central to the understanding of the parties. The Conservative party as well as the Labour party has become a less successful class party in the sense of retaining as high a proportion of the voters of its natural class supporters. The Conservative heartland has, however, waxed while the Labour heartland of industrial manual workers has waned.

Prosperity

In any case, political action is responsive to the quality as well as the quantities of class relations. From this point of view the periods before and after 1979 may now be seen as involving opposite tendencies. Discussing the earlier period in Chapter 2, I was at pains to juxtapose two contradictory features of British economic development—the persistence of inequality, and the growth of affluence. Affluence unquestionably made the stronger impact on popular political perceptions. Post-war prosperity, continuing into the 1970s, gradually established expectations of annual increments of income and welfare, with the political parties increasingly seen less as class organizations than as competing instrumentalities—a competition, incidentally, in which Macmillan was at least as adept as Gaitskell in the eyes of ordinary voters. And intellectual fashion supported popular opinion. There was, in the 1950s, a confirmed confidence in Keynesian economic management. Full employment seemed to be assured by it, and bitter memories of the slump years could be dismissed as irrelevant relics of a banished society.

Indeed in the pink glow of 'Butskellism', and the politics of the centre ground, inequality was difficult to discern. The traditional call to uneasy conscience from the survey traditions of Booth and Rowntree seemed to have ended with the last short book published by Rowntree in 1951.[17] This told us that the percentage of the working class who were in poverty, which had been nearly one-third in 1936, was now reduced in 1950 to less than 3 per cent. And the triumph was attributable to Keynesian full employment. Poverty was no longer a class phenomenon. Indeed it was widely regarded as no phenomenon at all, and had to be rediscovered in the 1960s. Not until well into the 1980s did beggars become a commonplace on the streets of Britain's towns.

Ironically, in those years Labour party intellectuals, even at a time when the class alignment of voting had gone as far as it ever did, became more than half convinced that the social base of their party support was being eroded by embourgeoisment—the assimilation of the working class into the life and manners of the middle class. The famous study of Luton workers by a group of Cambridge dons[18] dealt severely with this doctrine and called instead for a new and determined political leadership of the Labour party. The Cambridge dons got no response from the Labour leaders, but meanwhile the 1964 election left no one prepared to argue further the crude form of the embourgeoisment thesis with them. In retrospect, what was most telling in Goldthorpe and Lockwood's study was the identification of *privatization* among the relatively prosperous new working class, and of *instrumentalism* in the work place among employees of all classes. Affluent workers were becoming more privatized in that they sought the good life more at home with their wives and families than at work or in the traditional male organizations of the pub and club. And all employees were becoming instrumental in that they increasingly regarded unions, politics, and work not as ends in themselves but as means to private ends. The Royal College of Nursing increased its membership by 38 per cent between 1979 and 1982. The unionization of white-collar employees is the story of a principle treasured by the working class—collectivism—disseminated to other classes, but at the same time made instrumental. In the process the trade unions began to lose their class character, if not their class rhetoric. Even the Association of First Division Civil Servants affiliated to the TUC.

Incorporation of working-class leaders

Where embourgeoisment *had* taken place was not in the rank and file, but among the political leaders of the organized working class. The social composition of the Labour benches and cabinets had undergone a striking transformation. Between the Wars 72 per cent of Labour MPs came from rank-and-file employment, and 15 per cent were university graduates. By 1945 only half came from the working class, by 1970 only one-quarter, and by 1992 scarcely more than one-fifth. By this time the proportion of graduates had risen to more than half (56 per cent in 1992). Among cabinet ministers the trend was even more striking. In MacDonald's 1924 cabinet, 30 per cent were graduates. In 1969, under Wilson, the graduates made up 83 per cent. In the 1992 Parliament there were 59 Labour members of working-class occupation and 4 Conservative—making 10 per cent of the two parties combined. This working-class element among the Labour parliamentarians is not trivial, is higher than in Europe generally, and is therefore at least partly attributable to local

Labour party selection procedures. Nevertheless the party MPs differ more in the type of middle-class professions from which they are recruited than in class origin. A quarter of all Conservative MPs are from the private sector (mainly lawyers and accountants) while 40 per cent of Labour MPs are from the public sector professions (mainly education).

In short, there has been class incorporation of the Labour leadership. But we should also notice that MPs are no more socially representative in the sense of reflecting the nation by age, sex, and ethnicity. More than two-thirds of those elected in 1992 were aged between 40 and 60. Only 9 per cent were women and only a handful came from the ethnic minorities. But in both respects the Labour party has been more hospitable. Of the 60 women returned (the largest number ever), 37 were Labour and 20 Conservative.

These changes in the social antecedents of Labour leaders do not, of course, demonstrate subversion of working-class interest. It is what people do, not where they come from, on which that question has to be settled. What the statistics do indicate, however, is a gradual change in the image presented to the electorate. In the case of Labour politicians, that image never was and never became exclusively proletarian, whether revolutionary or gradualist. In a more literal sense, the television image further emphasizes the common social personalities of Labour and Conservative party leaders. They both have their extremist wings—a 'looney' Left and a hard racist Right—each playing off the other, amplified by the media. The SDP and the Liberal party complicate the stage with further claims to recognition as the moderate political solution. Television is *par excellence* the centre ground over which the parties squabble, and they do so decorously, reinforcing an indistinguishable impression of alternative teams of natural governors.

In parallel with these developments, participation in local Labour parties has become pathetically weak. Since 1952 the individual membership of the Labour party has fallen continuously. It had risen to a peak of over one million in 1950. But by 1976 it had declined, even on official returns, to two-thirds of that figure, and on other estimates was as low as a quarter of a million.[19] On the basis of individual party membership per hundred party voters, Labour is now numerically among the smallest socialist parties in Western Europe.[20] In short, the increasing incorporation of the Labour party at the national centre of power has been accompanied by a spectacular decline of participation by members in local organizations.[21] While it is too early yet (1995) to gauge the impact of Labour Party reform we can note that in the 1994 elections for the leadership, while 4.3 million were entitled to vote only 952,109 actually did so. They constituted 69.1 per cent of the 172,356 constituency party members and 19.5 per cent of the union members.

On the other hand, the rise of locally based direct-action groups is also a marked feature of modern Britain. They are, at least in part, a response to the alienation of leaders from members in organizations of massive scale. In the workplace, these forces contributed to the increasing power of shop stewards. In consequence, the capacity of the TUC to maintain agreements with Labour or Conservative Chancellors was undermined. Control over the membership by the union leaders, who represented them in the corporatist negotiations with government, was just as uncertain as is that of the CBI over its 12,000 member companies and 200 trade and employer associations. Wages and even local plant management were more and more determined on the local shop-floor, and not by conversations in Westminster. This is one powerful reason why observers like Alan Fox refused to accept fashionable warnings of the imminent coming of a British corporate state. The continuance of low-trust relations in the direct dealings of shop stewards and plant managers was the principal manifestation of the class struggle. What Fox describes as 'arms-length contractual bargaining' is deeply ingrained: on the one hand, it is a defence against corporatism; on the other hand, it holds little prospect for industrial democracy because such a development requires managers and employees to pursue efficiency together in something other than a zero-sum game.

Thatcherism and opposition

Thatcherism did not fundamentally change the pattern of organizations or 'party', though it gave renewed emphasis to their class character. The 1978 'winter of discontent' excited wide-spread popular antipathy towards the power of the unions, exposed the weakness of the Labour party in relation to them, and provided electoral support for Mrs Thatcher's new Conservatives as well as for the subsequent anti-union legislation. The rolling back of the organizational frontier of the state has also failed to show dramatic results. But the effort again reinforced class antagonisms. The policies of monetary control to combat inflation and 'non-interference' to promote market efficiency led to declining national standards of living, mass unemployment, impoverished public services and civic amenities, and increasing inequality. While dole queues lengthened and bankruptcies were commonplace, it was announced in 1993 that Peter Wood, Direct Line Insurance banker, had been paid a bonus of £18 million. Thus does the market distribute its rewards, as von Hayek has calmly explained.

Such news together with the experience of an extended and, in the end, bitterly futile miners' strike had begun by 1985 to affect popular opinion. The polls of March 1985 gave Labour a six-point lead over the Conservatives (38 per cent against 32 per cent), with the Alliance in third place and commanding one-quarter of the intended vote. Nevertheless organization in Westminster and Whitehall, as distinct from opinion, still heavily favoured the new Conservatism, and opposition, at least up to 1987, came as effectively, or ineffectively, from traditional Tories (the 'Wets') and from the Church of England bishops as from Her Majesty's Opposition in the House of Commons. We shall return to these issues in Chapter 8.

Conclusion

Meanwhile, to sum up nearly a century of organizational development: we have witnessed the massive development of working-class political and industrial combination, and a parallel response by the dominant classes through the Conservative party and the employers' associations. In this sense, we have seen the rise of party; and between them they have created a vast proliferation of the organs of state. We have also seen the rise of a host of sectional interest groups about which I have said little. One aspect, however, deserves special emphasis. Margaret Thatcher and economic liberals came into office clad in ideological opposition to the proliferation of state power and the incorporation of the estates of the modern realm. Experience has, however, driven organization in the opposite direction to that favoured by ideology. Quangos by 1994 were more numerous, more funded, and more powerful than ever. 'Placemen' were again as prominent in British administration as they were in the Napoleonic wars. The new Conservatives discovered a vast patronage for their party members and their business supporters. It is true that 'non-departmental public bodies' (NDPHs) fell in number from 2,167 to 1,412 between 1972 and 1993. But this trend has been swamped by the huge centralization of the public sector and the wholesale attack on local authorities. In particular the reforms of health, education, and policing being pursued by John Major's government are set to quadruple the number of unelected agencies and to give them control over nearly a quarter of governmental spending by 1996. The notion is to press 'market disciplines' on formerly public-service bureaucracies, and the number of quango appointments at the disposal of ministers is estimated at 40,000. The Citizen's Charter Minister at that time, William Waldegrave, saw it all as a strengthening of democratic accountability through giving power to consumers over public services. The critics see it all as a growing democratic deficit. The citizen is overruled by the consumer: but a national community is primarily a body of citizens.[22] That finally is the central conflict between the political Left and Right. As a whole, these developments amount to an organizational revolution. But it has been no revolution in the Marxist sense. Certainly the working class became consciously organized, industrially and politically, in the first two decades of the century, and certainly some of its members envisaged social ends inspired by the Russian Revolution. After the First World War, many poor families who had voted Tory when first admitted to the franchise, were drawn not to Liberal but to Labour allegiance. Older men might grumble that before the War there was, as one put it, 'very little o' that clap-trap about profit an't' bosses an' Socialism an' there being no God . . . Now everyon's at it.'[23] Fellow-travelling was fashionable in small intellectual circles,[24] and the Webbs thought of Russia as a new civilization.[25] But no serious Leninist vanguard movement ever emerged. Class struggle was muted and fragmented.

The main consequence of the rise of the working-class party was national incorporation of its leaders—a development as unanticipated by its pioneers as it was intended by the liberal-minded elements of the upper and middle classes. Over the following half century, a new Establishment was welded together and supported by the vested interests not only of the traditionally powerful, but also of the new men of power who now also stood to lose by any departure into radical adventures from the established framework of industrial bargaining and parliamentary procedure. And these convergent interests always had popular support. Class was never the sole dimension of life as subjectively experienced by ordinary people. It had its place in politics and the Labour party came to occupy that place: but it was limited by rising affluence and mobility, and by localism as well as nationalism—both entrenched sentiments which enabled Conservatives to hang on to a vital segment of votes across the class divide. 'My country Right or Left' was not only Orwell's instinct in the early days of the Second World War: it was also a national disposition.

Yet organizational decay was eventually the price that had to be paid for incorporation. The Labour leaders who set out to conquer national politics could not have anticipated either their metropolitan success, or their later provincial failure. Local Labour parties now are even more deserted than the chapels to which they owed so much of their early education. The mass membership is alienated and inert.

After the Second World War there was a gradual consolidation of trade union strength under conditions of full employment. The market continued to be the regulator of both political and industrial relations until the mid-sixties. Since then, economic stagnation and inflation have together created a new situation which we can describe as the spread of politics into the economy. Even the revival of liberal doctrines by a Conservative government pursuing monetarist policies in the 1980s has to be seen in the same terms. Unions have extended their organization far beyond the industrial proletariat. The state has become less parliamentary and more the centre of attempts to incorporate and pacify competing economic interests—all of whom are recalcitrant corporatists. And localized conflict is rife. Some old struggles have shifted back to the work place and the locality where they began, and where horizons are narrowest and objectives most limited and sectional.

Since 1979, the shop-steward movement has been weakened by economic recession and unemployment, and the national union leadership has been excluded from political decision-making. Thatcherism has supported these movements with explicit ideology and through monetary and fiscal policies which have sharpened conflict between classes, created new inequalities between regions, and divided the employed against the unemployed. The balance of power between organized capital and organized labour has re-emerged, though little is said about it in newspapers or on radio and television, after a long period of compromise and consensus between class interests.

5 BETWEEN THE GENERATIONS

Whether or not a society changes its structure, the ineluctable fact of mortality dictates that it must change its members. So in this and the next chapter we are concerned with social reproduction, with people rather than institutions, incumbents rather than roles, agent rather than structures. How do individuals come to be fitted into institutions? How does a society reproduce itself? To answer these questions, I shall deal in this chapter with kinship and in Chapter 6 with mobility and education.

Again, however, the discussion is based on the analysis in earlier chapters of the changing structure of class, status, and party. We may begin with a maxim from the liberal school of sociology.

'What the few have today the many will demand tomorrow.' That is Professor Daniel Bell's summary of the social history of industrial society.[1] Michael (now Lord) Young and Peter Willmott have called it the principle of stratified diffusion and turned it into a metaphor. They picture successive ranks of families in Britain drawn up in a column of social class, but a column on the march. 'The last rank keeps its distance from the first and the distance between them does not lessen. But as the column advances, the last rank does eventually reach and pass the point which the first rank passed some time before.'[2]

With this metaphor in mind, let us look back for a moment to the beginning of the century. Here is G. M. Young remembering the coronation year of 1902,[3] when he was an Oxford undergraduate:

We looked forward to living, with some improvements, the sort of life our fathers had lived. By *we* I do not mean the wealthy classes but the sort of people who filled the public schools and the two ancient universities, not rich, but comfortably off, who took games, books, and hospitality for granted: sons of lawyers, civil servants, MPs: young men who might succeed to their father's share in some old family business, or seek an outlet for their energies in India, or the Sudan, with Cromer for their ideal, and Milner for their example. It was an attractive life, I think we might say the most attractive that European civilization had ever fashioned for itself, and the prospect of living that life and transmitting it to our sons and daughters was an incentive, I should judge, more powerful than any quest for wealth or power. In a word, and it was a word often spoken in those days, England was a very good country for gentlemen. And it all rested on two things—an income tax so moderate that it was hardly felt: and an unlimited supply of cheap and efficient domestic service. Pull those pillars down, and that social hierarchy topples. That also we could not foresee.

That was the England of G. M. Young's youth. But at the same time, some two hundred miles further north in the same country, Robert Roberts was growing up in industrial working-class England, and tells of how his elders told him

of a man with a large family struggling to keep his sick father with them. At last the old man insisted he should be taken to the workhouse. They set off, the wife picking up his few belongings, and the father on his son's back. *En route* they stopped to rest a while on a stone seat. 'It was here', said the old man, 'I rested, too, carrying my father to the workhouse.' The son rose, took the burden on his back again and turned with his wife for home. 'We'll manage somehow', he said.[4]

Here, then, are the vanguard and rearguard of the extended column of class in Edwardian Britain. There was much for future generations to demand.

Significance of the family

My theme in this chapter is the relation between the generations: and my focus is on the primordial link between them— the family. There is no widely agreed explanation for the rather sudden transformation of the Western European or British type of family. Yet the history of individualism is a useful approach to such a theory. As Alan Macfarlane has shown,[5] modern attitudes are essentially individualistic and the relatively low fertility, non-peasant, small, mobile, late-marrying, spouse-chosen, two-generation resident type of nuclear family was established at least in medieval times and probably earlier. What has become dominant since the 1960s is an amalgam of feminist resolve, technical ease of birth control, shifts in occupation opportunity, and compulsory schooling with its accompanying equalization of educational chances, albeit hampered by resistant social prejudice and a government unwilling to provide the funding required to develop public services as support to the emancipation of mothers and wives. The slow pace of change has so far, in the 1990s, left both public discussion and public policy in relative chaos. The nuclear family of parents and dependent children is the basic ascriptive unit of society. But it is much more. It is the reproductive social cell of class, of status, and of culture. If, therefore, we examine its history, we should see from another angle the continuities and changes of social structure in Britain in the period covered by our collective memory. We can map the journey of the advancing column. That we shall find significant differences in the substance and meaning of family life between now and three generations ago is already implicit in my account of the transformations of class, status, and party. The question now is how the pressures of these macroscopic social forces have modified the shape and process of the microcosm of their reproduction.

But before setting out to follow the trail of biological, social, and cultural reproduction, let us recognize the strange character of intellectual discussion of a subject so thoroughly known, so commonplace, so deeply and comprehensively learnt by everyone. The very word 'familiar' is used to denote what everybody knows. Can there then possibly be anything to add? I think so: and this is because we can have recourse to macroscopic information and to history—both necessary additions to the idiosyncratic experience on which personal knowledge is based.

I should also remark on the passion that lies between personal knowledge and scholarship on the family—a vast literature of ideology. The family is both eulogized and vilified down the ages. Its immense power over the shaping of minds is constantly rediscovered. Confucius of the Analects tells us that: 'Those who in private life behave well towards their parents and elder brothers, in public life seldom show disposition to resist the authority of their superiors. And as for such men starting a revolution, no instance of it has ever occurred.'[6] Resentment of that power was vehemently expressed by Sir Edmund Leach in his Reith Lectures: 'Far from being the basis of the good society, the family with its narrow privacy and tawdry secrets, is the source of all discontents.'[7] There is no lack either of celebration of its beneficence. Here is Eleanor Rathbone in 1924:

Yet when we are considering society from any other point of view than the economic, we can all see well enough that, of all its institutions, the family is after all the institution that matters most. It is at once indispensable as a means to all the rest and, in a sense, an end in itself . . . the strongest emotions, the most enduring motives, the most universally accessible sources of happiness are concerned with this business of the family.[8]

But the place of the family in reproduction and upbringing of the next generation has moved rapidly on, not only since Eleanor Rathbone and the 1920s, but also since Edmund Leach and the 1960s. We live now, in the 1990s, in a new age of challenge to the nuclear family as the locus of childbirth and child care. Between 1971 and 1991 the number of marriages fell by a fifth, while divorces doubled and a quarter of those involved a person who had been divorced before. Births outside marriage became a third of all births by the early 1990s. Cohabitation is the main factor here: three-quarters of births outside marriage in 1991 were registered by both parents and a half gave the same address for both parents. The old culture of shot-gun marriage before childbirth is virtually gone: only 4 per cent of pregnancies in 1991 were followed by marriage before the birth.

Needless to say the emotional upheaval of divorce and separation usually gives rise to high conflict and often to expensive litigation. The Child Support Agency, which was inaugurated in

1993 to enforce the government's resolve to collect maintenance from absent fathers, is at the centre of heated controversy.

Demographic transition in Europe

So if we retreat awhile to the calmer and more arid regions of demography, it is to gain the light of factual perspective rather than to escape the heat of fierce engagement. Demographers have evolved the quaint custom of comparing fertility rates with the even quainter customs of the Hutterites—a flourishing community of agrarian fundamentalists in North Dakota. Demographers have chosen these people because they have the highest known levels of what is termed 'natural fertility', that is that fertility which is not affected by fertility-reducing social practices which are themselves dependent on the number of children already born. They have no deliberate birth control within marriage. On average, their families have over ten children. Against the Hutterite yardstick, Britain and Europe have low reproductivity. Even in the 1870s, before the onset of widespread fertility control, Britain recorded little more than one-third of the Hutterite rate. By 1931 fertility had plunged still further, by more than half of the 1871 level in England and Wales, and slightly less than half in Scotland.[9]

But we must not rely on the Hutterite yardstick (which in any case has shown signs of instability since mid-century). A more general measure is the *total fertility rate* (TFR), i.e. the number of live-born children a woman would have if she survived to the end of her child-bearing period and had children at the rate specific to her age-group and period. In other words, TFR measures what completed family size would be if current patterns of fertility continued from a particular point of time. In the 1870s the TFR for all women was 4.8, and for married women only was about 6. By 1931–5 the TFR was at its lowest point in history (until the 1980s) at 1.78 for England and Wales. In 1991 it was 1.8.

This remarkable demographic transition is not peculiar to Britain. British reproductive history is not specially remarkable by comparison with other European countries, except that it might have been expected that the first industrial country would have been the first to experience it, whereas in fact the transition came nearly a century later than in France. It is also worth noting that, within Great Britain, there has been more similarity of experience between regions, apart from Scotland, compared with the variability within countries like Germany, Belgium, or Spain. Over the centuries British fertility and mortality have both been relatively moderate by comparison with countries on the European continent.

Consequences of demographic change

The demographic transition in Europe had three stages. In the pre-industrial stage a slowly growing population was maintained by a balance of high death-rates and high birth-rates. In the second stage of early industrialism extending well into the nineteenth century, fertility habits remained from the first stage, while a growing array of life-preserving practices reduced mortality. Then in Stage III, fertility declined at a rate which overtook the still-falling mortality rate until a new population equilibrium was reached by a balance of low birth-rates and low death-rates.

This simplified description, leaving out migrations and variations, though it roughly fits the facts and places our period in Stage III, is useful more for the questions it raises than for those it answers. Above all, it invites attention to changes in the place of the family in society, both causal and consequential. It has become clear from modern demographic research that the population history of England up to 1800 was pretty much as Malthus described it. Population growth was held back largely through the 'preventive check' of delayed marriage which was in turn a response to movements in prices and wages.[10] Rates of growth fluctuated more through fertility than mortality. Accordingly it would be difficult to overemphasize the importance of the West European pattern of relatively late and avoidable marriage which was particularly strongly developed in England. This pattern, which still to some extent persists, created a uniquely low-pressure demographic regime in Western Europe.[11] There is, however, at least one modification to the simple description which must be added in order to bring experience since the Second World War into view. There was a fertility upturn after the War, followed by a downturn in the 1950s, and a longer birth-rate bulge in the 1960s. Stage III does, nevertheless, seem to be real. Births fell to 870,000 in 1971, 704,000 in 1981, and rose slightly to 766,000 in 1991.

Fertility in the twentieth century has shown unprecedented volatility. Fluctuations have occurred not only because of the traditional variations in rates of marriage but also because of the advent of virtually complete contraception within marriage. The volatility in question is primarily due to changes in the timing and spacing of births rather than to changes in intended sizes of family. Yet they have had dramatic effects on the size of successive birth cohorts—the variation in the birth-rate has been as much as 20 or 30 per cent in less than a decade. The difficulties of planning the number of school places, for example, have been consequentially increased in Western Europe.[12] Demographically Britain belongs closely to this group of countries which in the second half of the twentieth century have converged in their levels of fertility, marriage, divorce, mortality, and even in their demographic fluctuations.

The consequences of the Victorian population explosion are an important part of the social heritage of twentieth-century Britain. They include the growth of industrial cities at home,[13] and the global sweep of what might aptly be termed 'white peril'

Figure 5.1   United Kingdom population 1901–2001

abroad, colonizing continents. Together foreign domination and domestic urbanization created an unprecedented empire within which the reminiscences of G. M. Young in Oxford and of the working man in Manchester combine to illustrate the comment that, if it was an empire on which the sun never set, there were parts of its heartland on which the sun never rose.

The birth-rate, when our period opens, was still very high by today's European, if not by Hutterite, standards. In 1900 one-quarter of the married women were in childbirth every year. Yet thirty years later that proportion was down by one-half to one in eight. The earlier history of Stage III of the industrial demographic cycle need not concern us, though it continues to attract careful scholarship to its still unsolved problems.[14] One thing, however, is clear. For whatever reasons, the head of our metaphorical column had long since taken a decisive turn towards the ideal of the small family. And among the whys and hows of this movement towards what Young and Willmott describe as the symmetrical family, there was a fall in infant mortality after 1905 (Figure 5.2), especially among professional and middle-class families, which set conditions for subsequent generations that have enabled us to think of the twentieth century as 'the century of the child'.

Figure 5.2   Infant mortality 1846–1994

It may be, as Sir John Habakkuk has suggested, that it took time before people became fully aware of the implications of lower levels of child mortality, that the middle classes did so first, and responded by planning and reducing their fertility within marriage. Working-class men and women followed more slowly. When child mortality had been high, it was both more difficult for married couples to predict the size of their surviving family, and less urgent for them to do so. But it must be acknowledged that the problem of explaining fertility decline in the modern period is an extremely complex one. It is certainly no single consequence of reduced mortality. A full explanation has to take into account the vast transformation of relations between men, women, and children which has accompanied the development of industrial society. These changes include those in the economics of reproduction—for example the declining market for child labour, the Factory Acts, and the gradual introduction of compulsory and extended schooling—and the rise of professions and administrative careers recruited by public examination. All these forces weighed in the balance of the decision to have children among couples of different class and status positions. Moreover, the quality of gender relations was itself changed with the increasingly secular definition of means and ends and the decline of religious observance.

Falling fertility during the first three decades of the century may be thought of, then, first as an adaptation to these changes of circumstances and attitudes including a continuing fall of child mortality: people wanted, and were increasingly able, to control procreation according to their notion of a desirable style of life. But second, following the principle of stratified diffusion, we must notice that the course of reproduction in the twentieth century eventually, and at least temporarily, arrested the inverse relation of social class and fertility which had been inherited by Edwardian Britain as a feature of the demographic transition we have discussed. At that time, social distribution of the reproductive burden operated on the exact, if lunatic, principle of largest load on weakest back. In the following thirty years, the working class moved towards the earlier middle-class fertility norms.

Those at the rear (or at any rate, towards the rear) of the historically marching column of social ranks aspired to catch up with those ahead of them; and this they were able to do at roughly a ten-year distance. Class differences in fertility began slowly to be reduced: so that, in this sense, the stratified diffusion metaphor has to be modified—the tail was closing up on the head of the queue, the queue was beginning to re-form into an advancing line abreast.

Could this very different principle of progress be fully realized? Perhaps not, for there was yet another change of direction among the social leaders in the 1940s and 1950s. They changed course towards larger families, while manual workers and their wives continued along the old path. Thus we find Habakkuk in 1968 asking 'May it not be that the middle classes who in the 1870s led the country into the fashion of small families, are now leading us back to big families?'[15] He doubted whether the steps would be retraced very far, and the evidence of later years has justified his doubt, and there has been an important consequence. The fertility of those who have married since 1965, when projected to estimate completed family size, comes to 2.06 children for the average wife which is just below the so-called 'replacement' figure of 2.1, and just above the completed family size of the lowest point of fertility reached by those who married around 1930. The demographic transition to an equilibrium of low fertility and low mortality may at last be complete.

Nevertheless, there remain two unresolved questions for demographers. One is whether there is any naturally stable level of fertility appropriate to an industrial society like Britain where children now have negative economic value. Since 1971 all Western European countries have dropped and stayed below replacement fertility. Their total fertility rates are 1.7 or 1.8, not the replacement level of 2.1. The renegotiation of sexual relations which is so central a feature of contemporary society has the possibility of long-run population decline as one of its outcomes. In Italy and Spain the approach of total population decline is now rapid.

The other question is that of the future relation of class or family income to fertility. In the 1960s and 1970s there was the prospect of the elimination or even the reversal of the inverse relation between class and fertility which began in the middle of the nineteenth century. There was, in other words, a possible future in which births are distributed between families in roughly the same way as income. One view insists that the natural relation between income and fertility is a positive one and that the U-shaped pattern of class and fertility which was shown to exist in the 1971 Census was caused by incompetent family planning among the poorer and less well educated—a feature of reproduction which might be expected to diminish. Trends in fertility by class or income tend to support this view. Some evidence from Britain since 1971 is given in Table 5.1.

In 1970 only 22 per cent of births within marriage occurred in Social Class I or II. By 1982 this middle-class proportion had risen to 32 per cent and remained at that level in 1988. Total fertility fell in the 1970s and 1980s. Among women in manual

Table 5.1 Social class difference in number of legitimate births, Britain 1971–1986 (figures expressed as a percentage of all legitimate births in each year omitting 'other')

Year	I & II	IIIN	IIIM	IV & V	All
1971	22	11	43	23	100
1976	28	11	40	22	100
1981	31	11	37	21	100
1986	32	11	36	20	100
1986[a]	15	7	43	36	100

Note: The 1981 and 1986 figures are based on different occupation definitions and thus are not strictly comparable with the earlier figures. Percentages may not sum to 100 because of rounding.

[a] Jointly registered illegitimate births in 1986.

Sources: OPCS *Birth Statistics 1977*, Series FM1 No. 4; OPCS *Birth Statistics 1988*, Series FM1 No. 15.

worker families the fall was one-third for 1970–85, among routine non-manual workers it fell by the national average, but women with husbands in Social Classes I and II did not share in the decline at all. The class balance of future generations had in the process shifted. By 1988 the ratio of middle-class to working-class births had moved to 1:1.2.[16]

Between 1973 and 1983, the overall number of legitimate births in England and Wales declined from 618,000 to 530,000, while births to the professional and managerial classes (Classes I and II) actually increased. The relative fertility of middle-class married women over 30 was especially high, and more markedly in the early 1980s.

But the evidence must, of course, be interpreted against a background of marked retreat from marriage, a rise in pre-marital cohabitation, and a growing contribution of the total births outside marriage. Figures for births outside marriage where the social class of the father is known are included in Table 5.1. There is a disproportionate contribution of paternity from the manual classes, especially Social Class V.[17]

The consequences for family income and fertility are in effect the reversal of history. Poverty is apparently more concentrated on children in the 1990s than in earlier, more hopeful, decades. In 1990/1 nearly a third of all children in the UK (3.9 million) were living in poverty in the sense of having incomes below half the average after housing costs (compared with a quarter of the population as a whole). In 1979 there were 1.4 million children (10 per cent) in the same position and other evidence shows that 2.7 million (over $\frac{1}{5}$ of all children) were living on income support in 1992.[18] In this respect at least the century of the child seems to have become the century of child neglect.

Gender relationships

The place of women in society has been transformed. In his essay on *The Origin of the Family, Private Property, and the State*, Engels confuses class with status analysis, but arrests our attention by declaring that 'the first class antagonism which appears in history coincides with the antagonism between men and women in monogamous marriage, and the first class oppression with that of the female sex by the male'.[19] No one can read the history of marriage in our own time without being struck both by the material inequalities suffered by earlier generations of wives, and also by their reduction in more recent decades.

The burden of childbirth is central to the story. At the mid-point of the century, R. M. Titmuss summed it up by pointing out that, at the beginning of this century, a British woman aged 20 could expect to live 46 years longer. But approximately one-third of this life expectancy was to be devoted to child-bearing and maternal care of infants. In 1950 a woman aged 20 could expect a further 55 years of life. Of this longer expectation only about 7 per cent of the years to be lived would be concerned with child-bearing and maternal care.[20] By 1990 life expectancy had risen still further to 78 and fertility had fallen to 1.8 (TFR).

But no less important than the virtual slavery of Edwardian working-class women on the wheel of child-bearing was the relation of women to the economy and the state. In the earlier decades the great majority of families depended entirely for their material support on male employment. The establishment of a new position for the mother, independent of her link to the economy through her husband, was therefore a prominent theme of feminist reform. Eleanor Rathbone is again an outstanding voice. Child-rearing, she argued, should be seen as a public service as well as a private pleasure, and the costs spread accordingly. The only practicable agent was the state, and Miss Rathbone was, in effect, arguing for an extension of the social rights of citizenship for women. The main working-class demand in her day was for a 'living wage' for men. This she attacked as a continuation of ancient male tyranny. Even if achieved, the 'living wage' was intrinsically unrelated to family size. Women should not be regarded as dependants of the male in the labour market.

A wife and children and the wherewithall to keep them, are conceded to the wage earner as though they were part of the 'comforts and decencies promotive of better habits' for which he may reasonably ask

... But if he prefers to use the margin thus allowed him for breeding pigeons or racing dogs, or for some other form of personal gratification, instead of for keeping a family, that is assumed to be his affair, not the State's or his employer's.[21]

In the event, the state response was less than fulsome and the political descendants of Eleanor Rathbone, like Margaret Wynn,[22] or Frank Field,[23] still vigorously point out that both social security and taxation policies continue to treat families less favourably than bachelors, spinsters, and childless couples. As late as July 1993 Professor Jonathan Bradshaw wrote:

between 1979 and 1991 average living standards increased by over 30 per cent. However, inequalities widened dramatically, families with children drifted down the income distribution and many more families found themselves dependent on income support and relatively worse off. This need not have happened. It was the result of this government's tax, benefit and employment policies. If we aim to begin to improve the living standards of children and avoid separating the very large number of them on income support from normal patterns of life in Britain, then the child scale rates of income support must be increased now.[24]

The state has contributed indirectly towards the liberation of women, especially through the expansion of health services and education. But the loneliness of mothers with young children is still well attested and the absence of communal provision for such women remains an unsatisfied need. Meanwhile, more direct emancipating influences have come from developed methods of birth control and, most important, the gradual movement of women, including married women, into employment. In the first two decades of this century less than 10 per cent of married women in Britain went out to work: in 1951 the percentage was 21.74: by 1966 it had risen to 38.08. These upward trends continued to 1980 and then halted or partly retreated from a high point of 60 per cent in 1982. The slow spread of affluence has also played its part in combination with the invention of power appliances to relieve some of the drudgery of housework. Suburbanization and geographical mobility have provided escape for some from the matrilocal matriarchies of the traditional urban working-class communities—a point which reminds us that partial women's liberation has discriminated so far in favour of younger as against older women. So we could go on through a catalogue of economic and technical changes, and their consequences, which have made possible the trend towards *The Symmetrical Family* of Young and Willmott. By 1991 only 26 per cent of all women aged 16–59 were economically inactive: and this was true for only 52 per cent of those with children of 0–4 years.[25]

The correlative history, which is rather less noticed, is that of husbands and fathers. This too is a social transformation deserving its own detailed history. It would begin with young men of the Victorian upper-middle classes moving into marriage with prejudices mitigated at least to the point of co-operating in planned parenthood. Stratified diffusion would again emerge. Later, working men returning from the First World War had to accommodate, in many cases, to wives who had acquired a more independent outlook from having worked in the munitions factories, and from having run their homes unaided. Literacy and the wireless pushed back horizons between the Wars. Unlike previous wars, the Second World War did not tip the demographic balance so sharply in favour of men: the number of men and women remained roughly in balance, the reserve army of women disappeared.

Still more important, seventy years ago, working men typically lived in local occupationally homogeneous communities, of which mining and dock work were the classic examples.[26] Such communities evolved essentially male public organizations—the pub, the betting-shop, the football club; organizations which loosened marriage bonds and took resources away from women and children. But the newer patterns of inter-war industry around London and Birmingham, in the Home Counties and the Midlands, took their toll of the older male domination—reducing class solidarity perhaps and inviting more romantic love certainly. Particularly after the Second World War, hours of work were reduced, holidays lengthened, home ownership became more common, children were less ever-present, and men were drawn into a more intimate and longer spousehood than their predecessors had ever known. We noted in Chapter 4 that privatization was a key description of the affluent worker in Luton by the 1960s. It involved a closer, more co-operative, domesticity for millions of men. Perhaps the growth of the pornographic industry and the verbal obscenities which are hurled across football stands are each in their way further correlates of the pressure on men to adopt the new familial civilities.

Quite apart from the well-documented inequalities of pay, status, and promotion opportunities for women in the labour market, the sexual division of labour in households seems to be stubbornly traditional. A national survey by the Harris Research Centre in 1984 reported that half the adult population agreed that 'the man of the house should be the main breadwinner and the woman should be mainly responsible for looking after the home and the children, even if she works'.[27] Moreover, when asked about the sharing of household chores, men thought of themselves, and women thought of their husbands, as doing considerably less than the average man, especially with respect to cooking, looking after the children, and the menial tasks of household cleaning and washing. Thus British couples have an inflated notion of the norms of sharing and/or low expectations in their own households of what domestic labour should be contributed by men. The symmetrical family, whether as an ideal or as an idea, is yet to be realized.

There are still inequalities of access and pay despite much exploitation and publicity. But a gap remains in both the formal and the domestic economy between attitudes and realities. Summing up the latest British Attitudes Survey, Kathie Kiernan writes:

Behaviour still seems to be lagging behind attitudes and ideals ... particularly since the late 1980s, there has been a flattening of the trend towards equality between the sexes both in the workplace and the home ... It is very unlikely that the division of labour and specialisation between the sexes that persists will disappear quickly. But it is equally unlikely that the long-term trend towards equality will actually be reversed.[28]

Nor is it the only possible end to the journey. Looking back we can say that the social column has advanced and that the working class is much less conspicuously relegated to its rearguard. Yet the new freedom is by no means costless. Divorce and separation have largely replaced death as disruptors of the early and middle years of marriage. We cannot, of course, weigh the cost or gauge the misery caused by marital breakdown now or at any point in the past. We can estimate roughly that four out of ten of contemporary marriages will founder before reaching their twenty-fifth anniversary. We can also agree with Young and Willmott that their symmetrical family, since it asks more of its partners, exposes them also to greater strain and higher risk of failure. Moreover, as Juliet Cheetham has put it:

the possibility of controlling fertility, although usually accepted as an unqualified blessing, brings its own problems. It challenges women to contemplate social roles other than full-time motherhood. Acceptance of this challenge threatens prevailing assumptions about family life and about equality. Efforts to maintain the status quo frustrate women's aspirations and achievements. Discontent and conflict may be necessary preliminaries to human advancement but they are not comfortable to live with.[29]

One indicator of family instability is the record of one-parent families. The number of such families has grown from around 600,000 to over a million since the early 1970s and the children number over one and a half million, i.e. about one in eight children now live in such families. Such reproductive circumstances are typically (though not exclusively) concentrated in the lower echelons of class and income with higher rates of unemployment and poorer housing conditions. All in all the evidence is of mounting multiple instability of marriage and increasingly tenuous support for mothers and children outside wedlock. To be sure, it is a situation of great complexity and heated dispute. There are pessimistic traditionalists who believe that the family is collapsing with consequent chaos, crime, and crisis of civilization. There are also optimistic modernists who see a new dawn for opportunity, and equality for women, the end of the stigma of illegitimate birth, and the demise of male tyranny.

Justice for Children and the Collectivist ethic

Could it be that the gains for adults are at the expense of the interests of children? That is the central question with which we are here concerned. From a democratic socialist point of view it could end in disaster. Modern society has strange superstitions. Perhaps the central one is the belief that if ego maximizes his or her choices we are all better off.[30] Put more portentously it is the fallacy that individual freedom is collective good. The family is the age-old disproof of this contemporary nonsense. The traditional family is the tested arrangement for safeguarding the welfare of children. Only a post-Christian country could believe otherwise. The individualist doctrine is an hallucination with two main sources. First is the spectacular advance of human power over nature, which has relieved so many of us so much from the life of toil that our grandparents had to take for granted. They invented the work place, the career, the substitutes for human muscle and sweat, and we, with our microchips and washing machines, have both inherited and refined these escapes from the 'curse of Adam'. We call it the economy or the productive system and we employ economic statisticians and Treasury politicians to celebrate its continual growth. We use a language of productivity, employment, capital, and education which encourages us to imagine that the family has nothing to do with national prosperity.

Then, second, there is the developing assumption, so rampant in the 1980s, that the adult ego is self-sufficient. Children thereby become commodities—quality objects to be sure—but none the less things just like cars or videos or holidays which adults can choose to have in preference to other consumables. And if they do, that is their choice and their responsibility. Contraceptive control of our bodies enhances the illusion. So who needs a family or a community or, for that matter, a government other than to prevent ruin of the market for these good things by thieves and frauds? Surely technology has conquered nature and we can safely allow individuals to choose a consuming style, limited only by their willingness to work for money. Everybody is then free to buy the good life of their own definition. Marriage becomes a mere contract. The quality of life is measurable by calculation through methodological individualism rather than contained in organic conceptions of man and nature.

Our ancestors were poorer but wiser. They understood the notion of political economy. They knew what the modern fantasy forgets, that we are all dependent on one another. Atomized individuals calculate only for themselves and only for their own lives. Yet their very existence depends on calculation across generations. Few women and fewer men would rationally choose to have children in a world of exclusively short-term egotistical calculation. The costs and forgone satisfactions are too high. Hence rich countries with modern methods of birth control have declining or incipiently declining populations. The individualized as distinct from socialized country eventually and literally destroys itself.

Nor is this the whole of the modern mirage. In reality the family is part of, not separate from, the economy. Parents are the main producers of tomorrow's wealth and we all consume what they produce. That is why we need a just political economy to ensure that the beneficiaries pay their due. Behind the fiscal and monetary façade, old-age pensions are dependent on the future work of today's children. Yet paradoxically our political economy far from paying parents, actually punishes them for their folly in producing the producers of the future.

How can all this be turned round? The first step is to get the facts right. We appreciate that 'facts' always appear in the context of assumptions about what is good or bad for human beings. We deal today with heated value discord in these matters. We share with our colleague Norman Dennis the value position of the ethical socialist.[31] Central to that position is the doctrine of personal responsibility under virtually all social circumstances. People act under favourable and unfavourable conditions but remain responsible moral agents. History heavily conditions them; their own actions eventually become history and therefore determine the future balance of favour and disfavour in the ceaseless effort to become good people in a good society. The whole question of the quality of life remains for ever open. There are no ineluctable laws of history; only a continual reloading of the dice by millions of individual decisions. It follows that reproductive decisions are crucial to human destiny. Whatever the character of society or state, polity or economy, religion or culture, parents cannot escape responsibility for the quality of their children as citizens.

In the light of this political morality we see incontrovertible evidence of a weakening of the norms of the traditional family since the 1960s. It is not that we see a golden age of traditionalism. Material deprivation, and inequality between the classes and the sexes, were integral to British society in the first half of the century. There was no Utopia. There was cruelty, a double standard of sexual morality, incest and child abuse, savage treatment of unmarried mothers, desertions and separations. Nevertheless the traditional family system was a coherent strategy for the ordering of relations in such a way as to equip children for their own eventual adult responsibilities.

The much needed reform of the system required comprehensive strengthening of supporting health, education, and security services if quality children were to be produced, women were to have freedom to combine motherhood with career, and men were to be encouraged to take a fuller part in the domestic rearing of their offspring. The parental generation can be proud of its efforts to build up these elements of a modern Welfare State. But the evidence of more recent change is that the supporting services have deteriorated, the increment of economic growth has been transferred disproportionately to the individual pocket horizontally and to the rich vertically through the running down of family allowances, the raising of regressive National Insurance contributions, the abandoning of joint taxation for spouses, the failure to fund adequate community care and so on. In the 1980s the economic individual was exalted and the social community desecrated. Mrs Thatcher may well be

seen by dispassionate future historians as a major political architect of the demolition of the traditional family.

She was, to be sure, vigorously aided by other social and
personal forces. Divorce, separation, birth outside marriage, and
one-parent families as well as cohabitation and extramarital
sexual intercourse have increased rapidly. Many applaud these
freedoms. But what should be universally acknowledged is that
the children of parents who do not follow the traditional norm
(i.e. taking on personal, active, and long-term responsibility for
the social upbringing of the children they generate) are thereby
disadvantaged by their parents in many major aspects of their
chances of living a successful life. Such children tend to die
earlier, to have more illness, to do less well at school, to exist at
a lower level of nutrition, comfort, and conviviality, to suffer
more unemployment, be more prone to deviance and crime, and
finally to repeat the cycle of unstable parenting from which they
themselves have suffered.[32]

The evidence is formidable as well as tallying with common
sense. But we must be clear what the thesis does not say. The
comparison is of averages. It is not maintained that traditionally
reared children will all be healthy, intelligent, and good; nor that
children from parentally deprived homes will all turn out to be
sickly, stupid, and criminal. Like all social science, the relevant
studies deal with multiple causes of multiple effects and give us
estimates of statistical association for particular groups at particular moments in history. Nevertheless it must be insisted that
no contrary evidence is available to contradict the average differences postulated by the stated thesis. Accordingly the conclusion must be drawn that committed and stable parenting must
be a priority of social policy. If that view is accepted, it is no
comfort either to the Right or the Left. Committed parenting
cannot be the outcome of the market policies of economic liberals nor of what Norman Dennis has dubbed the 'egotistic socialism' of irresponsible fathers. The challenge to social policy is to
avoid both of these evils.

The essential background, of course, is the decline of infant
mortality and the spread of the small family. Yet this move to

smaller families, though important in itself, has to be seen in the wider context of a more general trend towards higher standards of upbringing. Infant mortality in 1991 fell to 7.4 per thousand, one-third less than in 1981 (Figure 5.2) and continuing a trend from 1900. Of those children born in the decade around the First World War only one-fifth grew up in owner-occupied houses, though in families with, on average, 3.4 children. Those born in the decade after the Second World War belonged to families with on average 2.1 children, and well over one-third of them were owner-occupiers.[33] Most children in the early years of the century grew up in the streets of industrial cities. After the Second World War there was a planned move to the suburbs in council estates and private dwellings. A working-class area is not now, so much as it once was, a kind of dormitory annexe to the workplace. The working-class family has become less closely geared to the factory hooter. This, combined with shorter hours of work, could have increased the amount of attention men give to their children. On the other hand, there is evidence of the opposite trend with rising divorce and separation. Moreover the gradual growth of women's employment outside the home may have had an opposite effect on mother–child relations.

Children now are more likely to come from middle-class families. The working class has fallen and the middle classes have risen as suppliers of children. Before the First World War more than two-thirds were of working-class origin. Even within the working class, the chances of being born into the home of a skilled rather than an unskilled worker, and into a smaller rather than a larger family, with rather higher income and rather better housing, gradually improved for those born later in the century. The norm shifted, in other words, from the description given by Richard Hoggart[34] of his childhood in Hunslet in the 1920s to the modest but still polarized prosperity enjoyed by Britain since the 1950s.

Changing relations between generations

What, then finally, are we to say about relations between the generations? From one point of view, the changes I have traced in the twentieth century seem to have created a children's paradise. No age has ever been more child-centred, or gone so far towards making death socially invisible. Yet family break-up, unemployment, parental anxiety, exacerbated by marital uncertainty, is endemic. Fathers, and more especially mothers, inhabit a world which takes away their control over, and simultaneously insists on their responsibility for, the fate of their children. Most parents have lived through a dramatic shift in the standards expected of them. It is not enough, as it once was, to look after bodily health and physical security. Parents must also answer for the mental and moral character of their sons and daughters, despite rising crime and drugs, despite influences from the street, the so-called peer group, the mass media and youth culture which children cannot escape, and with which parents cannot contend. They are increasingly made to feel amateurs in a difficult professional world. The old 'Us and Them' of the working-class mother is now a more generalized division between the inner life of families of all classes, and the external public forces. Such circumstances, together with the appreciation of schooling as a matter largely beyond family control, which determines the future jobs and incomes of their children, may add up to intense frustration. Relations between the generations in all classes are prone to anxiety and conflict, and the family is hard-pressed.

This is strange when we consider how much the twentieth century has deserved its description as the 'century of the child'. So much of modern politics has been about children. Not only increasing educational expenditure but also infant and maternity services, population policies, family allowances, adoption and fostering, treatment of young offenders, and so on. Even the principal objective all over the world of economic growth is essentially justified as 'for the children'. The old are relatively political outcasts. The future is all. 'Trailing clouds of glory do they come.' We have lived through a revolution, demographic, economic, and social, as a result of which the child has become the quality product of industrial society. The recalcitrant Andy Capp who says, 'What have my grandchildren done for me that I should care for them?' is at best a pre-freudian anachronism.

We should start by recognizing the frustration of the modern parent—whether a West Indian mother in Brixton who is baffled by the apparent failure of the school to teach her boy either good letters or good manners, or the anxious suburban father calculating the costs and benefits of buying a place for his boy in the private sector now that the comprehensive school is the only alternative.

Despite the increasing central *dirigisme* of the Department of Education and Science since 1979 it can be argued that Her Majesty's Inspectors have lost confidence as to what schools ought to be doing and therefore the authority to guide those they inspect. They deserve sympathy, for the loss of confidence is not only theirs. We *all* live in confusion as to what is the good life. Rereading Richard Hoggart's account of working-class life before the 1950s,[35] I am struck by the integration of ordinary families in those days with the moral traditions of the old class and Christian society which he so accurately and lovingly described. That moral structure has ebbed away fast under the assault of the classless inequalities and the secular materialism of the post-war world and, in the process, the familial controls over upbringing have steadily attenuated.

A traditional culture weakened by multiple forces of change falters in its transmission to the next generation and the lonely crowd of adolescent age-mates look to each other for guidance. They too, like their parents, are essentially powerless, even those who enjoy relative material prosperity. Their powerlessness is reflected in their collective amnesia, their unknowingness of the history of their conditions, and even more in their uncertainty as to their future. No wonder that fashionability, hedonism, and a desperate individualism serve as substitutes for a securely held morality. Hoggart's working-class family is romantically remote in the 1990s.

Of course, they were never church or chapel attenders in substantial proportions but, as Hoggart put it:

They believe, first, in the purposiveness of life. Life has a meaning, must have a meaning. One does not bother much about defining it, or pursue abstract questions as to its nature or the implications which follow from such a conclusion: 'We're 'ere for a purpose', they say, or 'There must be some purpose or we wouldn't be 'ere.' And that there is a purpose presupposes that there must be a God. They hold to what G. K. Chesterton called 'the dumb certainties of existence', and Reinhold Niebuhr, 'primary religion'. Equally simply, they hold to what George Orwell called 'those things (like free-will and the existence of the individual) which we know to be so, though all the arguments are against them'.[35]

Since Hoggart wrote not only the further decline of church and chapel, but also the changes in the typical position of married women—their reduced fertility and their sharply increased rate of paid employment—have been of greater moment in changing the character of the learning process among children than all the expansion and reorganization of schools which has gone on since the Education Acts of 1944 and 1988, including the development of schooling, the provision of secondary education for all, and the raising of the school-leaving age.

Institutional child-rearing

In short, a weakening of the bond between parent and child, and exacerbation of conflict between them, are a fundamental and paradoxical part of the so-called century of the child. From one point of view this may be seen in the growing power of public authorities to override the traditional rights of parents over children, albeit justified in the name of ever-rising standards of child care. Standards belong to experts. From another point of view, weakening bonds and sharpened conflicts are seen in child-avoidance by adults. This was, of course, always the way of the rich down the ages through such bodies as house-slaves, tutors, and (in this context aptly named) public schools. Characteristically, it now takes the form, in middle-class districts, of an endless round of parties and play activities which in effect share out the stint of child-minding on an informal rota system, releasing the other mothers. In the working class, the childminding industry has become an essential adjunct of recognized women's employment, punitively contained by a public administration in the vain hope that it will somehow go away. From another point of view, the parent and the teacher tacitly conspire to retreat from the harsh realities of their own lack of confidence to leave the children corralled before the television set. Later, adolescents are given up to their peer-group activities in segregated territories which they increasingly monopolize, such as the disco, the football terrace, the student union, and the pop music festival. These age-segregated phenomena are surely among those which the Martian anthropologist would pick out as significant features of a modern urban upbringing.

Class reproduction through the family

Meanwhile, the impact of class on upbringing may have been changing with respect to the nature of transmitted capital. In a pure class society it is, or was, material capital which differentiated the classes, and education basically served to put a stamp of class culture on fates already decided by class origin. The social reproduction of generations was primarily a transmission of material capital and therefore of its attendant inequality of income and opportunity.

But as the economy slowly developed its technology, and gradually complicated its division of labour, the fate of a family's children began to turn more on the successful transmission of cultural rather than material capital. Both still exist, of course, and are partially interchangeable—for example, conspicuously in a private or marketed system of schools. But cultural capital is of increasing importance. It is affirmed and publicly recognized in degrees, certificates, and credentials. And it is acquired first and foremost through familial transmission—for example, through knowledge of how to use the public properties of libraries and museums, through elaborated language codes which are indispensable to success at school, through appropriate levels of academic aspiration reinforced in the home, through information about learning or job opportunities.

The result is (just as much in post-Communist Russia or Capitalist America as in Britain) that the social reproduction of generations is a reproduction of a hierarchy of cultural capital.

This permits considerable mobility for a minority upwards and downwards in the hierarchy, but its main feature remains the continuity of familial status between generations and the raising of stakes through the evolution of a bottom class of structured unemployment.

Conclusion: a renegotiated division of labour

Social scientists, working in apparently unrelated fields, seem to be converging on to a more adequate conception of social change, showing that the traditional division of labour in classical industrial society is being radically renegotiated—the division of labour, that is, between the sexes, between the classes, between childhood, adulthood, and old age, between the family and the economy, and between the economy and the state.

The old conception of industrial society posited an essential triangle; the family, the economy, and the state. The conception of the life cycle was congruent. Families raised children; men worked; women ran households. The economy produced, the state redistributed, and the family consumed. The state collected taxes from the exchanges between the family and the economy and used the proceeds to redistribute resources for the education of the child, the relief of men temporarily out of work, the maintenance of women without men to connect them to the economy, the sustenance of the old, and the protection of the health and safety of the population as a whole. In the new conception, however, all of these relationships are revised. The family produces as well as consumes. Women are incorporated into the formal economy and men into the household and the informal economy. It is recognized that people live as well as work in factories and work as well as live in houses. Adults learn as well as children. Leisure becomes do-it-yourself work. It is also recognized that part of the growing informal economy lies outside the apparatus of tax collection and is therefore independent of the redistributive activity of the state. This leads us not only to revise conventional economic calculations of national income, but also to reappraise the politics of welfare (and taxpayers' revolts are not the only manifestation of that reappraisal). So childhood, education, work, and leisure are all words acquiring new meanings.

In the short run the division of labour, despite rising unemployment, divorce, and DIY, changes slowly from its traditional forms. But technological change, in interaction with the increasingly vigorous claims of disadvantaged class, ethnic groups, women, and regions, holds out the ultimate possibility of radical social transformation.

6 MOBILITY AND EDUCATION

Vilfredo Pareto pointed out that 'history is the graveyard of aristocracies'.[1] Marx recognized that 'the more a ruling class is able to assimilate the foremost minds of a ruled class the more stable and dangerous becomes its rule'.[2] Though rupturing primary bonds of kinship and neighbourhood, in a different sense mobility stabilizes social structures by moving individuals within and between generations. So to draw a complete picture of social and cultural reproduction we must take account not only of the family but of all the institutions which pass on skills, knowledge, and belief through channels other than those of genetic transmission. The development of education as an active agent of cultural evolution and social selection is one of the more obvious features of change in British society in the twentieth century.

I want, in this chapter, to ask about educational change and social reproduction by putting one version of a central question about any society: is it an open one? And I choose this approach because 'the open society' has been the traditional aim of liberal policy, with education in the forefront as one of its principal means.

The question can, of course, have many meanings. For the liberal it may turn on whether there is access to knowledge and freedom to use it. The interest of the egalitarian is different. He is typically concerned to question unequal distributions of skill and knowledge and to assume that, unless there is proof to the contrary, inequality of outcome in the social distribution of knowledge is a measure of *de facto* inequality of access. The ensuing debate has provided the stuff of educational politics in

Britain, as in other countries in this century. Behind it lies the more general question of what distributions between the members of each new generation are possible and desirable.

Is Britain, as a capitalist society in the late twentieth century, moving towards greater openness? Do boys or girls whose lives will be lived mainly in the twenty-first century, have more or less equal chances of becoming rich or professional or unskilled or unemployed compared with their fathers or mothers or each other? Are we to believe, with Marxist labour process theorists,[3] that the work-force is becoming more and more proletarianized as work itself is necessarily degraded or deskilled under capitalism? Or are we to prefer the more optimistic liberal theory of upward march to greater opportunities for everyone in a post-industrial society[4] and a service economy offering more and more professional and technical careers?

These contrasting theories of the 1970s can now be appraised in the light of empirical evidence from studies of social mobility. The idea of mobility implies movement from somewhere to somewhere else and the 'somewhere' in question may in principle be any social or geographical position. In the sociological literature it usually means some kind of class, status, prestige, or socio-economic position.

The chances of poverty

Has post-war reform equalized opportunity? What happens to those who are born into different circumstances of power and advantage? We can begin with a historically important and particular version of the question, 'Who falls into and who escapes poverty?' Professor Atkinson and his colleagues have offered compelling evidence.[5] In 1950 a tired but triumphant Attlee government had launched the Welfare State. Its supporters were comforted after their 1951 defeat by good news from social researchers in York.[6] Poverty had been virtually abolished under the impact of full employment and Beveridge's social security. Earlier Rowntree and Booth had exposed both late Victorian and inter-war Britain as a society in which one-third of its people had incomes too small to support a decent subsistence. Such mass misery was now to recede into unhappy historical memory. We were entering an age of secure abundance. Though biblical sociology warned us that the poor would remain with us till the crack of doom, we were now assured that they henceforth would be largely banished to afflict backward countries, leaving only a tiny proportion of our unfortunate or feckless compatriots to be looked after by social workers and the functionaries of the (then) National Assistance Board.

What, then, happened to these first children of the Welfare State? Did they stay poor if born poor, or move up in the world to be replaced by the children of the better off: and, whatever the case, what explains their financial fortunes? Atkinson and his colleagues provide an answer as well as a lucid lesson on how social science can formulate the complex varieties of such apparently simple questions. The authors adopted a heroic research design. They decided to find, to describe, and even to explain the fate of the children of the families surveyed by Rowntree and Lavers in York in 1950. This earlier study of a sample of the working class was chosen because it included both income data and the names and addresses of the sample members. Other extant studies did not satisfy both criteria and official records proscribe access. It would, of course, have been possible to begin a longitudinal study. Such studies lend themselves to the testing of hypotheses about life cycles if one has the patience to wait a generation for results: and the sample can be both national and directed towards particular social groups—the very poor, the unemployed, or, for that matter, the very rich. Alternatively a sample of the nation can be taken from which it is possible to reconstruct history by asking retrospective questions and arranging the answers into successive birth cohorts. But this always involves unreliable data—not least in the case of incomes—and hazardous inferences. To follow the Rowntree children was to avoid impatience and some inaccuracies. But this method too has hazards enough and Atkinson not only does not hide them but points to others and their implications which might easily have escaped the notice of an incautious reader. So much so that the book is just as valuable as a guide to method as it is a substantive answer to the question of how and how far poverty is inherited.

Of these children of the 1950s, two-thirds were still in York in 1975–8, and a further one-fifth in Yorkshire and Humberside. Were they better off than their parents? To arrive at a precise answer we must follow Atkinson's lead and be sophisticated about the words, such as income and earnings, which ordinary people use and about words like life cycle or measurement error or perfect mobility which sociologists use. Here is an answer from the numbers set out in Table 6.1.

'Low-income' is defined as below 140 per cent of the National Assistance scale in 1950, or below 140 per cent of the Supplementary Benefits scale in 1975–8. 'Intermediate-income' is defined as 140–199 per cent of the NA/SB scale. 'Comfortably-off' is defined as 200 per cent or more above the NA/SB scale. These three categories divide the 1,430 descendants into approximate thirds. The top row shows what happened to the 465 who were born into low-income families: 224 stayed in the low-income group, 155 moved up to the intermediate range of income and 86 became comfortably off. The raw numbers in each row show the passage from income origins to income destinations of all the Rowntree children. Putting the same story into percentages ('transition proportions'), we see that 48.2 per cent of those who

Table 6.1 The fate of the Rowntree children

Parents 1950	Children 1975–8 (percentages by row)			
	Low-income	Intermediate-income	Comfortably-off	All
Low-income	224 (48.2)	155 (33.3)	86 (18.5)	465
Intermediate-income	95 (25.8)	129 (35.1)	144 (39.1)	368
Comfortably-off	158 (26.5)	174 (29.1)	265 (44.4)	597
TOTAL	477 (33.4)	458 (32.0)	495 (34.6)	1,430

were born poor stayed poor, 33.3 per cent became ordinary and 18.5 per cent became comfortable. All this is 'outflow' analysis, i.e. how the children are spread along the rows from their origins to their destinations.

A second version of the question can be answered by turning the table sideways and looking at 'inflow', i.e. where the children who ended up in an income category were recruited from. The first column, for example, tells us that of the 477 who ended up in the low-income group, 224 had been born into low-income families and 158 had been born comfortably off. So, looking at it either way, there was both continuity and discontinuity between the generations.

Taking a third version of the question we can ask what were the chances of 'income mobility'. For example, for those who were born poor the chances of staying poor were 2.6 times better than of becoming comfortably off ($48.2 \div 18.5$).

A fourth approach is to compare the actual pattern with the pattern which would have obtained if there were no connection between income origin and income destination. This is the notion of a perfectly open or perfectly mobile society, i.e. one in which there is a random relation between the incomes of parents and their children. Under those hypothetical circumstances the transition proportions would be the same for all rows. The table shows that post-war Britain was not completely open in this sense. But neither was it a caste society. It was in an intermediary position, which can also be given a precise measure—an index of association between the incomes of parents and their children. Atkinson patiently shifts the angle of vision of the raw table of numbers (and the proportions calculated from them) from one statistical viewpoint to another, so as to enable the reader to see just how complex was the original question.

Among the many results to emerge is that Rowntree's famous life cycle of traditional working-class poverty, which typically pulled people above the poverty line only in the brief periods of adolescence and of middle age between the departure of children and the advent of old age, is still with us. Nevertheless the fate of individuals can only be described in terms of chances not continuities, probabilities not predestinations. The poor were not mechanically doomed to transmit their poverty. For the most reluctantly numerate student perhaps it will suffice to say that the Rowntree children were scattered from their parents more in income than they were in height.

Sir Keith Joseph suggested in speeches in 1972 that a cycle of deprivation rolls on down the generations and accounts for a significant burden on the social services. Joseph's hypothesis never captured much substance either in his relatively humane formulation or in the harsher Victorian original version of Social Darwinism. Some of the poor are descended from the poor but others escape and the causes of poverty are to be found much more in the circumstances of people than in their personal traits. And in any case the implications for politicians in general and current Conservative members in particular are that poverty can be increased or reduced by *their* actions.

Mobility between classes: the 1972 evidence

From this focus on a particular social division—the poverty line—we can now turn to the more general phenomenon of social fluidity on which there is a long history of British 'political arithmetic'. In 1949 Professor Glass and his colleagues at the London School of Economics pioneered a study of mobility in that tradition.[7] Twenty years later, my colleagues and I at Nuffield College, Oxford, judged that, after an intervening generation of social-democratic reform, it was time to look again.[8] And studies of the 1983, 1987, and 1992 general elections have yielded still more recent evidence.

Political arithmetic is by no means the only approach to the complicated question of social mobility. Another pursues an interest in the process of class formation. A third, which we glimpsed in Chapter 4, examines the correlates and consequences of mobility in electoral choice.[9] But whatever the approach we do well to appreciate the complexity of movements between social positions to which I pointed in Chapter 3. The intricacy of the structure of class, status, and party in Britain has already emerged in previous chapters. None of these dimensions, separately or together, yield a unitary hierarchy. Nor is the passage of individuals through the social structure a simple repetition of the experiences of one generation by the next. As we have seen, there have been fluctuations and trends in births and deaths, and in the occupational and other social positions to be filled. Moreover, mobility can be thought of as either group or individual, and either between or within generations.

With these various meanings and methodological cautions in mind we can begin to analyse the fluidity of the society experienced by recent generations in Britain. We can again use the simplification of three social strata of social classes, ignoring or evading the many sociologically created conceptual traps which are found in the study of social stratification, for example the vulgar Marxist theology of two classes at war in capitalist society, or the vulgar liberal conception of a continuous hierarchy of prestige or status which would make every individual a class.

The first of our three strata can be taken, as before, to mean the *middle class* or *service class*: professional, managerial, and administrative occupational groups and higher technicians and their wives and children. Taken by their *origin* (that is, classified by their fathers' occupation when they were 14 years old) these formed 13.3 per cent of men in England and Wales in 1972. The second stratum is a heterogeneous *lower-middle class* of non-manual employees, small proprietors, self-employed artisans, but also lower-grade technicians and supervisors of manual workers. They made up 30.8 per cent of the 1972 men by origin. The third stratum is the *working class*—industrial manual workers and agricultural workers whether skilled, semi-skilled, or unskilled. They made up the other 55.9 per cent by origin.

In this simple classification each individual has one of three classes as an origin, but also (judged by his own job ten years after entering the labour market) one of the same three as a destination.[10] Distributed by destination as distinct from where they had started as boys, they appear in the following array:

Social class destinations
(percentage)

Middle class	20.1
Lower-middle class	24.9
Working class	55.0

It is immediately apparent that the structure of origins is different from that of destinations for this generation of Britons. On balance there has been movement out of the working class and lower-middle class into the middle class. We will return to this question of trends. But for the time being let us stick to our snapshot survey and put the origins and destinations together to form a grid of intergenerational class mobility (Table 6.2).

We now see nine kinds of intergenerational experience, each one measured as a percentage of the total. The columns of the grid tell us about *inflow* between generations to the three *destination* classes. The rows show *outflow* from *origin* classes. The diagonal cells from top left to bottom right denote those who were found, ten years after starting their working lives, in the social class where they started. The cells below and to the left of the diagonal are occupied by those who would be correctly described as having had upward mobility if our three social classes were arranged in a strict hierarchy. The cells to the right

Table 6.2   Intergenerational class mobility: adult males, England and Wales 1972 (percentages)

Origins	Destinations (ten years after entry to work)		
	Middle class	Lower-middle	Working class
Middle class	7.0	3.7	2.6
Lower-middle	7.0	9.9	13.9
Working class	6.1	11.3	38.5
			100

and above the diagonal would be men who have been down-wardly mobile.

We should again remind ourselves at this point that this is a simplified picture. It conflates the experience of successive cohorts of births and entry into the labour market, it ignores the heterogeneity of the three social classes, it tells us nothing about the mobility of women, and it obscures intragenerational movement. Thus, for example, of those who had been born into the middle classes, and were also found in them as adults in 1972, half did *not* start their working lives in this social class, but began in a lower non-manual or manual job and later moved to a middle-class job.[11] In other words, our patterns and proportions of intergenerational stability of the middle class disguise intragenerational instability, what the researchers who gave us this evidence call 'counter-mobility'.

Nevertheless, returning to the simpler intergenerational picture, we can say that the typical Englishman or Welshman was born into and stayed in the working class. This is the largest group, more than three times as big as the next largest, which is those who started in lower-middle-class families and became manual workers. The three smallest groups are all mobile ones—from working class to middle class (6.1 per cent), from middle class to lower-middle class (3.7 per cent), and from middle class to working class (2.6 per cent).

Is this an open society? Certainly it is not a caste society. If we add all three diagonal cells, it turns out that the proportion who stay as adults in the social class in which they spent their child-hood is little more than half (55.4 per cent). A very substantial minority of Englishmen and Welshmen in the last generation have been socially mobile (44.6 per cent). If we look at the rows (outflow) it turns out that, while 7 per cent were born into the middle class and stayed there, 3.7 per cent went to the lower-middle class, and 2.6 per cent went to the working class, together accounting for the 13.3 per cent of middle-class origin. If we look at the columns (inflow) it further becomes clear that the idea, which is quite widespread among sociologists, that the élite have effective means of closing their ranks against the entry of other men's children is clearly a false one if by élite we mean what we have here defined as the middle class. The number of new-comers from other social classes is getting on for twice the number of those who are, so to speak, middle-class by birth. This is a similar picture to that presented by Geoff Payne for Scot-land.[12] The number of middle-class sons who moved into the lower-middle or the working class is not very far short of those who stayed where they were born.

Thus if we look at our three social classes in the 1970s expect-ing to find closed hereditary groups then the middle class disap-points us. Indeed it was the working class which approximated more to this notion. The typical factory worker was at least a second-generation proletarian, while the middle-class man who looked at his fellows found that nearly two out of every three of them had come from birth in another social class. The first industrial nation now combines a mature working class with an *arriviste* middle class.

So far we have examined outflow and inflow as they have occurred and in relation to each other. An alternative is to consider them in relation to an external criterion. Politically this may be conceived as the open society. Statistically, in the way which the London School of Economics 1949 study made stan-dard for subsequent mobility research, the same notion may be represented as that of 'perfect mobility', that is what the numbers or percentages would have been if destinations were randomly related to origins. The point is to compare actual movement with a defined hypothetical pattern of movement. Essentially the same method is to compare the *relative* chances of moving from given origins to given destinations. For example, the chances of becoming middle-class are highest for middle-class sons, more than half of whom retained their position, while fewer than one in nine working-class sons moved into the middle class. Notice too that the chances of moving out from the work-ing class were less than one in three, while the chances of moving out from a middle-class childhood were very nearly one to one. A fifth and summary way of answering the 'open society' ques-tion is to measure the strength of the bond between fathers and sons. In a fully open society the correlation between the social class of fathers and sons would be 0.0 and in a rigid caste society it would be 1.0. In fact, calculated on our 1972 data, the correlation between father's occupation and son's occupation in 1972 is about 0.36.[13]

Trends in mobility

Now, we may ask, what are the trends in mobility? In terms of our metaphor, this means turning a snapshot into a film. The method in one form or another is that of cohort analysis. But there are many dangers here. The birth cohorts of our sample are not strict random samples of birth cohorts in the history which they are made to represent, if only because while all sons have one and only one father, the converse is far from true. Moreover, it is difficult to know how far differences between birth cohorts are attributable to age or to the particular period of history in which a cohort reaches a given age. Given the background of change in the occupational structure which we have already discussed in Chapter 2, there is every reason to be cautious in interpreting trends from a survey of the kind on which we are relying here.

   Nevertheless, bearing in mind all these qualifications, I cannot do better than to paraphrase the findings from the Oxford mobility study.[14] These authors show that the view one can take of the question as to whether Britain has become a more open society will depend crucially on the method of measurement. They use three methods. First, following the method we have used in Table 6.2, they gauge 'absolute mobility rates' by tabulating the percentage movement from origins to destinations (which may be transit points in the case of first jobs or jobs ten years after entry to the labour market, and in any case cannot be taken as a pure definition of 'occupational maturity') in defined classes or occupational groups. On this measure they conclude that there has been a trend towards greater openness in that the younger men in the sample had better chances than older men of similar origins, of being found in the higher-class positions, that is, in professional, higher-technical, administrative, or managerial jobs.

Then, second, these authors turn to a simple measure of 'relative mobility rates', using disparity ratios. Absolute rates are those which are more or less visible to the participants (social actors) themselves. Relative rates are sociologists' concepts and not necessarily part of the social consciousness of participants: they relate the chances of mobility of men in different classes to some statistically defined norm or model, such as that of random relation between fathers' and sons' class position to which I have referred as perfect mobility. Measurement of relative rates of mobility by disparity ratios is a method which allows for change in the structure of classes or occupations. It enables us to gauge changes in the chances of being found in given destinations among men of differing origins. The disparity ratios are ratios between outflow percentages. For example, in a society divided into two classes the proportion of sons of Class I who themselves held Class I jobs as a proportion of all Class I sons is expressed as a ratio of the proportion of Class II sons who gained Class I jobs from the total number of Class II sons. Put formally, the disparity ratios would be

$$\frac{f_{11}}{f_1} \Big/ \frac{f_{21}}{f_2} \quad \text{and} \quad \frac{f_{22}}{f_2} \Big/ \frac{f_{12}}{f_1}$$

On this measure, the authors conclude that stability rather than change is the outstanding feature of intergenerational class mobility in Britain in recent decades. Whereas absolute rates give an impression of trends towards greater openness in the sense of there being increasing rates of upward movement into the expanding higher levels of the class structure, the relative rates show that these expanding opportunities have been fairly evenly shared out between men of different class origins so as to produce no change in their relative chances of access. In the recent period, moreover, while the working class has been shrinking, the relative as well as the absolute chances of men of middle-class origin being found in manual work have also declined. In short, relative class chances have been stable or increasingly unequal.

Then, third, the authors use a more complex measure of relative rates by the use of odds ratios defined formally in a 2×2 mobility table as:

$$\frac{f_{11}}{f_{12}} \Big/ \frac{f_{21}}{f_{22}}$$

That is, measuring whether the relative chances of the son of a Class I father being himself found in Class I rather than Class II are changing over time at the same rate as the relative chances of the sons of a Class II father being found in Class I rather than Class II.[15] On this approach the conclusion is again reached that there have been no systematic or general shifts in relative mobility. The relative chances of men from two different classes of origin being found in one rather than another of two different class destinations have not changed.

In short, in a period in which the occupational division of labour in Britain was transformed to offer more middle-class opportunities, there was continuity in the underlying processes of intergenerational class mobility. Moreover, though there may have been some specific trends in relative chances of movement between particular classes, the evidence is that increased fluidity is to be found only when the class positions of sons and their fathers are compared at a relatively early stage in the working life of the son. When intergenerational mobility is measured using class origin and the point of 'occupational maturity' (beyond which there is little likelihood of further major shifts in class position), such trends as are to be found are in the direction of reduced social fluidity. In general, however, a model of 'constant social fluidity' best fits the data, and the finding has been established as a general one in advanced industrial societies.[16]

Mobility in late twentieth-century Britain

The picture presented so far is one of rising absolute and constant relative rates of mobility in the long period of post-war prosperity which came to an end in the mid-1970s. Did mobility patterns change with the end of the long boom and the beginning of a new period of political economy in which growth was halted, unemployment rose, deindustrialization accelerated, and economic management became 'Thatcherism'? John Goldthorpe and Clive Payne have provided an answer by analysis of mobility questions included in the study of the 1983 general election. Their conclusion is unequivocal: 'that the stability of relative rates or chances of inter-generational class mobility, which our analyses of the 1972 data suggested went back to the 1920s, has *not* been disturbed to any appreciable degree in the first decade after the ending of the post-war era.'

But what of absolute rates? Has recession resulted in a freezing of mobility and especially the upward mobility of working-class and lower-middle-class sons into the middle-class professions, salariat, or 'service class'? The evidence, on the contrary, is that absolute rates of upward and of total mobility have continued to rise. A comparison of the 1972, 1983, and 1992 samples using our three-fold class schema is given in Table 6.3. In 1972, 16 per cent of the men of working-class origin had found their way into the middle class: by 1983 the percentage had risen to 23.6 and by 1992 to 31.0. Again in 1972 over 61.2 per cent of those of working-class parentage were themselves in working-class jobs: by 1983 the percentage had fallen to 52.6, and by 1992 to 47.4.

Still more recent work on the general election studies of 1987 and 1992 serve only to confirm the thesis that the underlying

Table 6.3 Class distribution of respondents by class of father, 1972, (1983), and [1992] inquiries

Father's class	Respondent's class (percentages by row)		
	Middle class	Lower-middle	Working class
Middle class	57.7 (62.0) [59.1]	23.2 (22.2) [22.3]	19.1 (15.8) [18.6]
Lower-middle	31.2 (34.2) [41.6]	31.9 (34.3) [32.8]	37.0 (31.5) [27.5]
Working class	16.0 (23.6) [31.0]	23.7 (23.8) [21.6]	61.2 (52.6) [47.4]

mobility regime, neither completely open nor rigidly caste-like, remains stable despite drastic changes in both the occupational structure and the opportunities for education offered to women and to ethnic minorities. Except for the continuing expansion of the middle (service) class, the two other main classes (and their sub-divisions) have shrunk further and the unemployed (including the long-term unemployed) have remained at the high level they reached by contrast with the period before the 1972 Oxford Mobility Study. In short, there is no reason to change our interpretation even though we recognize increases in absolute rates of mobility and equalization of educational opportunity by gender and ethnicity.

This continuing evidence into the 1990s of *both* stable relative class chances or 'constant social fluidity' *and* increasing absolute rates of net upward mobility is clearly damaging to the degradation of work hypothesis of the labour process theorists, and is supportive of the optimistic liberal theory of the technologically led expansion of middle-class opportunities. Yet we must pause and heavily qualify the award of this particular prize in theoretical debate. We must consider unemployment.

In 1972 unemployment was virtually negligible. In 1982 and subsequently it was 'double digit': there was an unemployment rate of over 12 per cent, and more than a million people had been out of work for at least a year. The unemployed could reasonably be viewed as an additional stratum of the working class (thus modifying the picture of the shrinking of the latter) which should objectively be analysed as a 'destination status' in mobility tables. Moreover, more recent studies confirm what was generally known, that unemployment is a characteristically (though not exclusively) working-class risk.

Thus, while the expansion of the professional and technical middle class remains a feature of late twentieth-century Britain, as it was in the long boom from mid-century, unemployment has also emerged as a structure of negative opportunity which tends to *polarize* mobility chances, especially of those who begin in the working class. The Thatcherite period did not reverse the trends of widening access to the middle class, but it raised the stakes in the selective process. The class prizes and the risk of prolonged social deprivation both increased. We have, in short, reached a more polarized society.[17]

Mobility and education to 1972

The search for an explanation of these patterns of mobility naturally leads us to schools and credentials. Table 6.4 summarizes the educational career of each of the nine groups we distinguished in the 1972 study. It amalgamates the experience of those who had passed, at various times, through the expanding system of schooling in England and Wales from before the First to after the Second World War.

The educational profiles of our nine mobility categories, apart from yielding recognizable stereotypes of Britons, show a reg-

Table 6.4   Education and mobility (percentages)

	Private primary schooling	Selective secondary schooling	School exams	Some FE qualifications	Univ. degree
Stable middle class	32.0	88.4	82.0	33.1	29.8
Middle to lower-middle	24.9	65.1	53.6	17.2	5.7
Middle to working	3.8	33.5	15.1	7.0	0.5
Lower-middle to middle	11.7	67.9	62.1	34.1	13.5
Stable lower-middle	7.5	44.3	27.1	5.6	1.0
Lower-middle to working	3.0	21.9	8.1	1.8	0.1
Working to middle	1.6	63.1	58.5	32.3	12.8
Working to lower-middle	2.0	32.2	20.2	3.9	1.1
Stable working	0.6	14.7	4.6	0.4	0.1
TOTAL	5.8	34.8	23.9	10.3	4.3

ular patterning of the relations between education and mobility. It can be seen from the underlined rows of Table 6.4 that the educational norms for each of the three social classes, as represented by those who had had stable membership, are positively related to social class both of origin and destination. Thus the stable middle-class men are composed of 88 per cent with selective secondary schooling, and 30 per cent with a university education, compared with 44 per cent and 1 per cent for the stable lower-middle class, and 15.0 per cent and 0.1 per cent for the stable working class. In other words, those who find jobs in the higher occupational categories have more education and more qualifications. This will surprise no one.

Looking at the other six categories of those who have moved from their birth position, it is equally clear that mobility involves realignment of social class membership according to educational qualifications. Thus, those who have moved upwards have, in the process, exceeded the educational norms of their origin group, and those who have moved downwards have had less educational advantage and attained fewer education qualifications. This pattern is absolutely regular. But there are some details worth remarking. If we look at the destination classes it appears that those who move up from below do not, on average, have as much educational qualification as those who have been stable in the destination class in question. Similarly, those who move down still have a rather higher educational profile than the stable members of the class they join and, which follows from our remarks on the upwardly mobile, a still higher one than those who have joined the same destination class from below.

Putting these two tendencies together, that is, the association of education with social origin and also its association with mobility, what we then find is that exchange between the social classes is also a partial exchange of the educationally qualified. For example, those who had moved from the middle class to the working class included only 1 per cent of graduates, while those who moved from the working class to the middle class included 13 per cent of graduates. There is thus, in the process of mobility, exchange not only of individuals but of social investment of education and qualifications which maintains a differential distribution of social qualities between the social classes. I would lay particular emphasis on this aspect of the reproduction of the stratification system. Intergenerational mobility serves to reconstitute the general pattern of distribution of attributes of the different social classes.

At the same time this evidence on education and mobility in Britain shows that neither a division into social classes nor into mobility groups completely differentiates the population by their education. It is just as important to notice that the great majority of those born into the middle class did *not* go to private primary schools or to universities as it is to notice that those who were either born into, or made their way into, the middle class were more likely to have had these educational experiences than those who came from, or went to, either the lower-middle or the working class.

Education and inequality

If these are the mobility patterns and their educational correlates, how are we to explain them in relation to familial and educational development? My account of social reproduction in Chapter 5 was a description of the supply of children. But the supply of children in turn constitutes a demand for education which, though fashioned by the principle of stratified diffusion, and made to fluctuate quantitatively by changes in the birthrate, has risen qualitatively throughout the century. The demand has been met by a state policy of educational expansion. And this policy, advocated originally by Victorian liberal optimists, has always been seen as the promise of new and higher levels of both material prosperity and elevated culture for the nation, happily accompanied by more equality, since to raise the supply of educated labour would result in a reduction of its relative price.

For the period up to the mid-1970s the Oxford Mobility Studies enable us to assess the extent to which the Victorian vision was realized.[18] That assessment has to be less than the hopes of the reformers, though it also contains no support for

those 'Black Paper' writers who would have us believe that
educational standards declined.[19] Expansion there was, and with
it a cumulation of cultural capital. The outstanding feature of the
state selective secondary schools, which developed after the
1902 Education Act, was always that the majority of their pupils
were 'first-generation' recruits to advanced education.

Nevertheless, we have been forced to the depressing conclusion that over the first three-quarters of the century, the
unequal relative educational chances of boys from different class
origins were remarkably stable, and that the conventional picture of a steady trend towards equality was an optimistic myth.
The metaphor of the column with which we began in Chapter 5
does, apparently, work for education if not for fertility.

What, then, is the connection between school and work?
Launching a 'great education debate' in 1976, the Prime Minister, James Callaghan, called for a closer link between education
and the needs of industry. He was entirely right if he meant that
there is a rather tenuous connection between educational and
occupational changes in modern Britain. At first glance it might
appear otherwise. Both the output of qualified people from the
educational system and the intake of professional, managerial,
and white-collar manpower into the workforce have risen year
by year, especially in recent decades.

But there has been no automatic supply/demand relation between education and the labour market. They have proceeded
independently of each other and no simple conclusion can be
drawn along the lines of praising or blaming the schools for the
level of efficiency or national income or unemployment or any
other aspect of the economy. Of course, for an individual, job
choice and protection against unemployment are improved the
longer he stays in school and the more she collects educational
certificates. But the wealth of the nation, the range of occupational opportunities, and the level of employment for British
society as a whole are determined by quite other forces, such as
monetary policy, the international market, and the collective
attitudes towards work and leisure which prevail at any given
time. Education alone cannot create either wealth or welfare.

The seminal research in this regard has been done by Sig Prais and his associates at the National Institute of Economic and Social Research[20] and the policy discussion crucially focused by David Finegold[21] and David Raffe.[22] The correlation between effective training and productivity has been demonstrated by Prais in precise comparison between Britain, Germany, and other continental countries. Britain's low supply and low demand for skills have been traced by Finegold to short-termism, insufficient investment, and inadequate incentive on the part of employers and employees. And, despite past expansions and present declarations, Britain's laggardly participation in the education and training of 16- to 18-year-olds has been demonstrated by Raffe.

The Oxford Mobility Study enables us to trace the educational experience of boys in four successive decennial birth cohorts—1913–22, 1923–32, 1933–42, and 1943–52. From the beginning of the century until the 1960s the crucial point of educational selection was at eleven-plus. At this age all children took tests of intelligence and attainment. From this result the most fateful decision was whether children went to a grammar or technical school, or to an unselected elementary or (after 1944) secondary modern school. The proportion of children attending grammar schools increased in every decade. Even for those born between 1943 and 1952 the supply of grammar school places kept pace with the growth in total population, although not with the growth in the middle classes. The proportion of grammar school children from all classes went on increasing right up to the mid-point of the century, the relative rates being highest for the working class, but the absolute increases being highest for the middle class. Then for the first post-war generation, the working class managed to protect its gains, while the now expanded middle classes lost some of theirs, though without falling back to the position they held a generation earlier. Hence, with respect to the grammar school, there were increased chances in general throughout the period and some narrowing of class differentials, both relative to the average, and relative to each other. The technical school picture, however, is very different. After the 1944 Education Act these schools began to disappear. The expansion of the grammar schools in the post-war period and before the comprehensive movement got under way in the 1960s was largely at the expense of the technical schools. What the working class gained through the expansion of the grammar schools, they largely lost through the decline of the technical schools. Thus, comparing the 1913–22 with the 1943–52 birth cohort, one hundred working-class families sent an extra eight boys to grammar school, but they also sent eight fewer to technical schools.

Meanwhile, after the 1944 Act, the emphasis of expansion gradually shifted to the later stages of secondary schooling, and to post-secondary provision. Here the class-differentiating forces continued to operate. The rewards for success and survival were high, and the result was that the amount spent on the education of children of different origin, far from equalizing chances, helped to maintain class inequality. Over the period as a whole, those born into professional and managerial families had three times as much spent on them as those born into the families of agricultural labourers. Those who went to selective secondary schools, private schools, and on to post-secondary education, especially in universities, were also relatively more expensively raised. The upshot was, as I pointed out in Chapter 2, that although there was a slight tendency to greater equality of investment in the school education of boys from different classes, the development of post-secondary education more than counter-balanced this equalizing effect because it was disproportionately used by boys from the middle class.[23]

We can illustrate these processes in twentieth-century Britain by focusing on the university graduate, as revealed in the national sample of men aged 20–64 in England and Wales in 1972. We can ask a simple question: How many men had university compared with other possible kinds of education? Again, while noticing the obvious risk of over-simplification, nine types of education can be distinguished and these are shown in Table 6.5. Three types of schooling are combined with three types of experience after school to produce this ninefold classification.

They ascend, in conventional British evaluations of the desirability of different educational experiences, from a non-selective schooling in an elementary, secondary modern, or comprehensive school with no education after school, to a private education in a direct-grant or 'public' school followed by full-time attendance at a university. The first category accounted for 25.3 per cent of men in 1972, and the last for 1.6 per cent. The typical Englishman or Welshman had had a non-selective education in a state school plus some further education, usually in the form of apprenticeship or training within a firm, or part-time attendance at a technical college or night-school, or some combination of these. In the population as a whole 41 per cent were typical in this sense. The next most important group were those with some sort of selective education in a technical, central, or grammar school. The smallest groups were those who started at a non-selective school, but found their way to a university, and those who had secondary schooling in the private sector (including direct-grant schools) without any education beyond school. Both of these groups constituted less than 1 per cent of the whole.

University men from all three kinds of school background amounted to 5.2 per cent of the male population in 1972. The comparable figure for those who have had a selective secondary education within the state system was 26.8 per cent and for those who went to independent schools 6.2 per cent. Of those born between 1907 and 1912, 1.5 per cent were graduates and the

Table 6.5 Types of education (each category expressed as percentage of the whole)

School	No further education	Further education	Full-time university	Total
Non-selective	25.3	41.0	0.7	67.0
Selective state	4.6	18.3	3.9	26.8
Private	0.7	3.9	1.6	6.2
				100.0

proportion rose steadily with a spurt (the expansion associated with the Robbins Report of 1963) for those born after 1947 to bring it up to 10.4 per cent. Private secondary schooling increased from the early years of the century but not either fast or steadily, reaching a high point for those born just before the Second World War. Selective secondary education provided by the state followed a roughly similar course but involving proportionately four times as many people. Thus, though this is the century of educational expansion, university graduates remained in 1972 only a twentieth of the adult male population, and those with a selective education were barely a third.

That university graduation leads to occupational advantage is perfectly clear from the second column of Table 6.6. Nearly nine out of every ten of the university men found their way into the professional and managerial classes. But this is not the most interesting view of the distribution if we are looking for a meritocratic social order or some universal process of 'certification', labelling people for appropriate employment. The third column of Table 6.6 tells us more. The graduate element was still strongest at the top but nearly three-quarters of the top class were not graduates.

Perhaps the graduate criterion underemphasizes the bond between education and occupation. So we return finally to the nine educational categories of Table 6.5 and show them again in

Table 6.6   Occupational distribution of university men

Registrar-General's class	Percentage distribution of university graduates by class	Percentage of each class who are university graduates
I	39	27
II	48	10
III Non-manual	8	3
III Manual	3	Less than 1
IV	2	Less than 1
V	0	Less than 1

Table 6.7 for the top class of professionals (the number above the diagonal in each cell) and the bottom class of unskilled workers (the number below the diagonal in each cell). The bond is clear and strong. The typical professional is a grammar school boy with education beyond school, though not in the university. The typical unskilled worker went to an elementary or secondary modern school and no further. What presumably is happening is that the occupational hierarchy is gradually being regraded upwards in formal educational terms.

Educational reform has moved on since 1972. How far then has the picture presented by the Oxford Mobility Study been modified by subsequent events? A recent attempt at an answer may be found in the *Oxford Review of Education*, 1993. (19.2)

The structure of access to education has shifted since the end of the 1940s. Before the Second World War the main European preoccupation with educational equity was focused on entry to secondary schools. This was the decisive point of selection in traditional education systems and remained so, for example, when OECD staged its first major review and conference on the

Table 6.7 Education and occupation

Registrar-General's Class I (top diagonal of cells)
Registrar-General's Class V (bottom diagonal of cells)
Percentage of the occupational class with defined educational background

School	No further education		Some further education		University	
Non-selective	1.3		18.8		3.8	
		61.0		30.4		0.0
State selective	1.2		41.5		14.6	
		5.2		2.5		0.5
Private	0.0		10.1		8.8	
		0.0		0.5		0.0

issue of equity in 1961 at Kungalv in Sweden.[24] But in the past two or three decades, with secondary schooling becoming universal, attention has perforce shifted on to entry to higher education or, more accurately, entry into some form of post-compulsory schooling, a stage of mass tending to universal provision, whether classified as training or further or higher education. Crucial selection now occurs at the transition out of secondary education. The underlying idea of meritocratic society gives tertiary schooling a new significance.

The 'meritocratic' question itself remains in debate. Definition and measurement apart, it cannot be maintained that qualifications from schooling exactly determine market rewards. Other factors, including luck and the function of prices as signals of profitable shortages, may be in play, though a typical path analysis usually shows the highest coefficient for some measure of education where income or occupational status is the dependent variable. Market rewards accrue from occupational as well as educational experience and have no necessary relation to merit. The concept of merit is, however, more apt for analysing access to advanced forms of education than for measuring the justification or defensibility of variations in income.

Within the frame of fairness or desert, the balance of social interest has also shifted in the ensuing period of spectacular educational expansion. Rightly or wrongly the major focus of traditional concern was with social class as the largest obstacle to mobilizing the productive power of nations and realizing a more acceptable social equity in the distribution of opportunity. More recently attention has shifted to gender and to ethnicity. Class, gender, and ethnicity are now the three giants in the path of aspirations towards equity, though awareness of other obstacles, including rurality and religion, has persisted. And most significantly, there are strong signs, in discussion as well as in research, of heightened awareness that educational achievement and life-chances generally are fundamentally shaped by the structure of family upbringing. A picture of advanced industrial countries is beginning to emerge which links economic growth to regimes of low fertility. The two features of modernized society are correlated in some way with the decline of the nuclear family, at least in the Western world. Research by demographers and sociologists is therefore directed on to more concentrated analysis of family background. We see some reflections of this underlying transformation of industrial society in considering the trends in access to higher education of the genders, the classes and the ethnic minorities.

Trends in Britain

The *Oxford Review of Education* papers carry the analysis further, at least in the sense of bringing the description up to date. We must, however, note cautiously that they use different definitions of what is meant by access. Most refer to any form of higher education aimed at a degree or equivalent qualification: but one restricts its attention to the universities and another is concerned only with the Scottish universities. Moreover, the papers employ a variety of methods of measuring equity. There are good reasons and a rich tradition in the social sciences of concern with exact methods here if only because of preoccupation with answering questions about social justice. It is relevant to recall A. B. Atkinson's assertion that all measures of inequality involve social as well as statistical judgements.[25] Interpretation is always necessary.

We draw attention here to these methodological variations for two other particular reasons. One is to underline the errors inherent in using sample surveys to estimate the state of populations. There are differing sampling errors. Second, there are different classifications (such as ethnic minority status), and, especially in combination, the two variations may mislead. Thus Modood's[26] important and bold finding that all ethnic minority groups in Britain outdo the native whites in their admission proportions to higher education might be modified by shifts in definition or sampling ratios. Indeed we know from Cheng and Heath[27] that Irish-born admissions are lower than whites: but Modood includes the Irish-born among the white population and thereby underestimates the white performance.

Nevertheless it may be asserted that social scientists are in accord in their broad appraisal of 'what is going on' in British higher education. Gender inequalities have decreased rapidly

over the past two decades and feminist advocacy has moved
somewhat towards inequality of access to the higher echelons of
the professions and business management. The expansion of
higher education has propelled many more women into new
opportunities but with a skewed distribution towards the less
prestigious courses and institutions.

With respect to ethnicity it appears that very considerable
advances have recently been made in the accessibility of degree
courses. It may even turn out on further evidence that ethnicity
per se is not a barrier: only the asymmetric fit of race to class
produces apparent inequality of access, and the case for positive
discrimination may be solely on behalf of the disadvantaged
working class. To be sure, the white working-class child has had
increased absolute chances of going on into some form of higher
education, though in competition with women and those from
the ethnic minorities. But class inequalities, measured in relative
terms, have apparently remained stable for the past three generations. Muriel Egerton's analysis[28] confirms several other studies and also confirms the continuation of stable class inequality
established far earlier in the century by the Oxford Mobility
Study.

It emerges that expansion has had and is having two further
effects of some relevance to the general question of equality of
access. Expansion has been disproportionately in favour of
cheaper and less prestigious forms of institution offering degree
courses or their equivalents. Women have become more concentrated in the ex-polytechnics and the colleges concerned. It is
also noticeable that ethnic minority recruitment has tended to
become concentrated on particular colleges and universities.

How then do these British developments appear in the wider
context of advanced industrial countries generally? In the context of the European countries it appears that the period after
the Second World War saw a growth in enrolment, a diversifi-
cation of curricula, and a crisis in relation to the labour market
destination of alumni (from both the education and the training
systems and at both the secondary school and the tertiary college level) in the mid 1970s. The post-war period came to an end

in the economic and political turmoil of that time. Then there was a phase of reconstruction in the 1980s in which access and selection were increasingly influenced by manifold difficulties in the political economies of Europe, including public expenditure and unemployment and the rise or resurgence of economic-liberal doctrines of state management. Put crudely, the 1980s were the decade of the market and the expansion of higher education had to proceed under conditions of fiscal constraint which led to much redefinition of the structure and purposes of the university. Conspicuous among these developments was a pronounced weakening of the traditionally close link between the academic secondary school and educational institutions. The upper secondary school in all countries became, in effect and instead, a free-standing institution rather than a conveyance of selected minorities from common elementary schooling to élite advanced education. Most secondary pupils now leave at 18 years, many postponing entry to higher education, others choosing part-time or full-time attendance at some other form of tertiary education, and still others going straight into employment.[29]

None the less, entry to higher education in Europe and in most developed countries is still generally straight from school, sometimes from a particular type of school at which the student has concentrated on academic subjects. Italy has a very special-ized structure, particular types of school leading to certain higher education categories. In the United Kingdom, as in Japan and USA, the examination required for higher education entry can be taken at any type of establishment which provides for post-compulsory schooling. In other countries (and in Northern Ireland and some other parts of the UK), children may be selected for entry to different types of secondary education although there is provision for transfer at later stages: the higher education entry examination is then usually taken in the more academic schools.

Each country has a specific national education qualification which forms the main basic requirement for entry to higher education. The qualification generally covers at least five subjects, some compulsory, and usually including mathematics, the native language, and one modern language. England, Wales, and Northern Ireland are unusual in limiting the number of subjects more narrowly and thus specializing earlier. At least five passes at GCE are required for degree level courses, of which two must be of Advanced level, although most candidates for entry attempt three A-level subjects and already have at least 6 O-level passes. Special arrangements exist for mature students, and this growing provision is discussed by Nina Wakeford as a new development in Britain which is designed to offer a novel avenue of access to those who had not passed to higher education in the traditional way.[30] Entry to higher education depends mainly on gaining the appropriate entry qualification, although limits on places may mean that a further selection process takes place either for certain types of course, or for certain institutions which experience strong demand from students. In the United Kingdom, entry to all institutions is competitive.

More generally in Europe the state has increasingly controlled entry to higher education since Napoleonic times, either through defining examination content and standards or through varied means of student financial support or through special schemes of encouragement for particular social categories of student by positive discrimination or, more usually, by setting up barriers to entry. Some countries like Belgium, France, or Germany use one uniform national examination. Sweden attempts the ranking of students by marks weighted according to the courses taken and work experience (which tacitly introduces age as a selective barrier). The American system of standardized attainment tests is not used in Europe. Positive discrimination in favour of candidates with working-class backgrounds has been used in Hungary, Poland, and the former Czechoslovakia, though examination performance has also been part of the entrance procedure. Entrance examinations have been widely used with higher requirements in medicine, science, and law. Such procedures obtain in the highly prestigious institutions such as Oxford and Cambridge in England and the Grandes Écoles in France, but also in the East European Communist states where, at the same time, at least a quarter of the places have been reserved for working-class students. Even the lottery is not unknown. In the Netherlands and Germany the problem of excessive demand has been overcome by its use. A lottery has been operated in which an individual's chances have been weighted by marks attained in the secondary school-leaving examinations.

Nevertheless the automatic right of entry to the university, which is the privilege of those who obtain a baccalaureate or the *Abitur*, still gives admission in France and Italy, though not to other forms of higher education. The consequences are seen in high failure or drop-out rates in the first two years of undergraduate study. Some countries, like Belgium or Spain, never granted the prerogatives of the *Abitur*. In France, however, in spite of several university reforms, including the Loi Savary of 1984, the right of entry of a *bachelier* has never been modified. Of course, the highly selective Grandes Écoles continue to cream off the best 15 per cent of the candidates. And the *numerus clausus* has been increasingly applied in France and Germany so that we can now describe the right as nominal. It gives all qualified people a place; but it does not guarantee a place in any particular faculty of any particular university.

In summary, it appears that the evolution of the admissions system since the Second World War moved the point of selection upwards from the upper secondary school and its examinations to the admissions offices of the institutions of higher education. The traditional system was essentially controlled by teachers in universities. Control now is much more in the hands of politicians and budgetary administrators. Diversity is to be found at both the secondary and tertiary levels and the unique role of the baccalaureate, the *Abitur*, and their equivalents in other European countries as the *rite de passage* to university education, is no more.

Instead there have developed alternative modes of entry to a diverse set of post-compulsory educational and training institutions with the parallel development of vocational equivalents to A level, the baccalaureate and the *Abitur*. In France there is a technical baccalaureate with 12 options as well as the traditional one with 8 sections and a proposed 30-option practical baccalaureate which, it is expected, will be taken in one form or another by 80 per cent of the secondary school-leavers by the end of the century.

In all countries most students first enter higher education aged between 18 and 21. However, older students are also admitted everywhere; in Germany a quota of places is reserved for them. Reasons for starting first study in higher education later in life are many; some students pursue lower-level further education full time or enter employment; others may retake entry examinations and so increase the range of institutions which will accept them.

Britain's tertiary system was distinctive in the period before 1990 in that it was binary. There was a short, high-cost and efficient sector of restricted but socially open universities attended full time for three years; and a diversified, localized, part-time vocational sector with rather tenuous connections to the universities.

It may turn out that a principal historical feature of post-war higher education in Europe was the elaboration of alternatives to the university. As part of an ambitious programme of expansion, 'doubling in a decade' as the progressive slogans of the 1950s had it, the terms of entry and the definition of what was to be learned in a university were altered all over Europe. The old stereotype of entry through completion of the baccalaureate or equivalent leaving certificate from a *lycée* or other upper secondary school into a full-time course of three or more years in pure science or pure arts was to be transformed into a large variety of courses, typically vocational or preparatory to professional training, and offered in a wider range of institutions, residential and non-residential. The development of mass higher education was dawning in Europe, increasing participation to significant proportions of the young and, in effect, replacing the older idea of the university in Europe by a much more expansive and, as many would argue, a diluted conception of tertiary rather than higher education.

Social Selectivity and Stratification

Walter Muller's study of nine European countries, because based on the Casmin data sets, pertains largely to the earlier post-war years.[31] Blossfeld's data show the experience of young people in the 1980s as well as in the earlier years of the century.[32] The results of the two studies are complementary and consistent. They confirm that German higher education expanded from a low point immediately after the Second World War and that in the process there was a reduction in social selectivity for the population as a whole and for women but no serious change in the relative chances of children from the disadvantaged classes. Tertiary education remained linked characteristically to the superior and professional end of the service class with respect to recruitment and also to placement in an occupational career. This is the essential shape of meritocratic development in Europe and the role of the university within an expanding and elaborating system. The picture is complicated, not least by variation between countries in demography, the structure of the economy and the historical peculiarities of national arrangements for access to the stages of education, their curricular content, the type and availability of student financial aid, and the articulation between educational qualifications and entry to professions and trades. Thus, for example, where a country has had a large agricultural sector as in France or Poland, the significance of educational selection has been minimized for the sons of farmers. Where, as in the British Isles, education has been relatively loosely connected to qualifications in the labour market, it has been possible for relatively democratized access to the universities to emerge. Muller's analysis thus reveals the remarkable contrast between France and Britain that, adjusting for the difference in the shape of the occupational structure, those who acquired a higher tertiary degree had service class origins of 55 per cent in France and only 35 per cent in England. So, at least in the earlier post-war years, the system of selection in France gave the offspring of the service classes—compared to children from other social backgrounds—better odds of surviving up to the highest educational level than they had in other countries. For his nine European countries Muller finds that, beginning at a less than 10 per cent proportion of the pupils in primary school, the service class children grew to a cross-national average of about 45 per cent among those who attained a higher tertiary degree.

England, Muller tells us, did not stand alone at the lower end of social selectivity but shared its relatively egalitarian position with Scotland and Northern Ireland. He also points to an interesting contrast between Germany and France. By the end of compulsory schooling the proportion of service-class children was highest in France and remained so through the successive stages or 'transitions'. In Germany the proportion of service-class children was lowest until the stage of an intermediate secondary degree, but then increased more than in most other countries until, at the end point of the educational career, Germany was placed in an intermediate position. Interestingly the two command economies or Communist countries included by Muller were not among the most egalitarian from the point of view of class opportunity. Hungary in particular is near the top of the league for distributing most certificates of higher education to the higher social classes.

Like Blossfeld, Muller identifies two important processes common to the countries which have inherited the European university. First, educational systems are organized so as to allow ever decreasing fractions of a student cohort to survive at each successive stage of education and, second, dropping out is socially selective though with decreasing severity. The outcomes are an interplay between these two processes. On the one hand the policies of expansion gradually move the systems of higher education through mass towards universal provision and *a fortiori* towards equality. On the other hand the selective forces continue to shape the composition of the student body.

Muller's study of an earlier period shows that already the European countries differed strongly in the extent to which they provided opportunities for obtaining educational qualifications to each successive cohort of young people. His data were collected in the early 1970s and the analysis relates to those aged 30 to 64, i.e. born between 1910 and 1947. They therefore had left their schools or universities mostly before 1970. Only a small proportion of them were affected in their educational careers by the reforms of the 1960s and 1970s in the West European nations but, it must be noted, educational change in East Europe had been initiated earlier. Thus, for our earlier years, Muller shows a pattern which is essentially binary. The British Isles and Sweden had a similar survival pattern from which Germany, Hungary, Poland, and France differed. The sharpest contrast was between France and Germany. In Germany 85 per cent of pupils were surviving beyond compulsory schooling, in France only 30 per cent. Hungary and Poland had the highest survival rates up to the end of a full secondary education. Yet, given the differences in survival rates between nations in early schooling, the remarkable feature of the systems as a whole is their similarity of outcome at the upper end. At that point only France is distinctive with its exceptionally low fraction of the population obtaining a degree from an institution of higher education.

Within the context we have sketched, Muller draws attention to particular features of class selectivity. In Germany, Hungary, and Sweden the upper service class appears to have given its children rather superior chances of educational survival. This finding fits with the observations of historians of the *Bildungsbuergertum*, a social stratum of civil servants, professionals, and teachers in higher education, which has traditionally shared a set of common values associated with the experience of higher education and a relatively higher determination to pass on high standards of educational ambition and achievement to their children. The *Bildungsbuergertum* was probably most distinguished as a status group in Germany, but also existed in other countries that were influenced by the German tradition of higher education, such as Sweden and the Austro-Hungarian monarchy. English society in the early twentieth century was distinctive in not having such a broad and educationally defined upper class. Entry to the upper echelons of British society was not so clearly restricted to educational channels.

In Britain the 1970s saw little progress towards the democratization of leisure which a modern system of higher or continuing education should represent. Instead the end of the decade saw governments, whether of the Left or of the Right, groping for solutions to external checks on economic growth, while the minority of the educated began to be more sophisticated about the nature of education as a positional rather than an investment or a consumption good, and the majority remained in blighted ignorance that education had anything seriously constructive to offer to either private or public life.

The Robbins Report (1963) confirmed the fact of expansion in the 1950s and heralded further expansion in the 1960s and 1970s. What then about the 1980s and 1990s? The number of students enrolled in degree courses has risen every year since Robbins; but the more interesting questions are: what kinds of students in what kinds of institutions and what proportions of their contemporaries in the population at large do they represent?

From 1963 to 1990 expansion continued in such a way as to obliterate Robbins as a numerical landmark. Absolute numbers of students in the higher education system rose every year. In 1962 the total number of full-time students was 216,000. By 1989/90, including home and overseas students, part-timers in universities, the Open University, the polytechnics and other colleges offering advanced courses, it was 1,086,300.

Apparently therefore Britain has had, and indeed still has, a straightforward record of successful development of its investment in higher education through fluctuating economic fortunes. In fact the story is less simple and more interesting. Less simple because the numbers have risen at varying rates. More interesting because the definition has widened from the original concept with which Robbins began. Higher education, in successive steps, has invaded further education. The stereotyped view of higher education as a three-year residential system of high quality learning for young men has been overtaken. The definition moved gradually, and continues to move, towards an American concept of higher education as all post-compulsory or post-secondary schooling.

The statistics cited begin with full-time or sandwich-course students and end with all full-time and part-time students in a wide range of colleges in addition to those in the universities. The White Paper (Higher Education: A New Framework, Cm 1541, May 1991) described the higher education system in the United Kingdom as one in which the polytechnics and colleges (including Scottish central institutions) took 53 per cent of the student total, with the Open University taking 4 per cent and the universities 42 per cent. Underlying this description lies the commitment to mass provision of post-compulsory opportunities towards which educational reformers have been slowly moving for at least a century.

At the universities it may be seen from Table 6.8 that full-time student numbers rose from 119,000 in 1962/3 to 352,600 in 1990/1. But the annual rate of increase was by no means steady. It averaged 12 per cent between 1962/3 and 1972/3 during which time the former Colleges of Advanced Technology were incorporated and the new greenfield universities of the 1960s opened their gates. These were direct consequences of the Robbins surge. But advance slowed down in 1972/3 and turned to retreat after 1981 when severe funding cuts were imposed. There was

Table 6.8 Universities in Great Britain— staff and students 1962–1991

Year	Full-time students (000)	Staff/ Student Ratios
1962–3	119.0	
1972–3	239.4	8.2
1982–3	295.4	9.5
1986–7	301.3	10.0
1990–1	352.6	11.6

Source: Education Statistics for the United Kingdom.

absolute decline from 1982 to 1985 when economic slump gave
way to boom, from which point growth accelerated each year to
1990, recapturing the expansion rates of the late 1960s and the
early 1970s.

Diversification

At this point we are in a position to see the evolving institutional
and opportunity pattern of developments since Robbins. The
general pattern of expansion is disaggregated in Table 6.9 for the
period from 1970 to 1989.

It is confirmed that the total enrolment rose but the composition of the student body crucially shifted. The traditional pattern
of higher education—the full-time male undergraduate in a
university—was the one that rose most slowly, by 20 per cent.
The alternative forms expanded more rapidly. For example, the
number of part-time female students at polytechnics or colleges
of higher education rose by 758 per cent and Open University
enrolment of undergraduates rose by 368 per cent, from 19,000
in 1970 to 60,500 in 1981 and 89,000 in 1989. Thus for the traditionalist, the experience of higher education has been one of
dilution, presented as expansion. For the reformer, on the con-

Table 6.9   Expansion of higher education in United Kingdom
by type of establishment, sex, and mode of attendance, 1970–
1990

		Universities			Polytechnics & Colleges			Open University		
		1970/ 1971 (000)	1989/ 1990 (000)	% rise	1970/ 1971 (000)	1989/ 1990 (000)	% rise	1970/ 1971 (000)	1989/ 1990 (000)	% rise
Full-time	Men	167	200	20	107	170	59	—	—	—
	Women	68	151	122	114	169	48	—	—	—
Part-time	Men	18	31	72	110	159	45	14	47	236
	Women	6	23	283	12	103	758	5	42	740

Source: Education Statistics for the United Kingdom (HMSO).

trary, access has widened to offer opportunities appropriate for a modern economy and an increasingly well-educated citizenry. For the traditionalist more looks worse. For the reformer more means different.

Demographic and educational trends

Demographic and educational factors underlie the trend of higher education numbers. The total number of 18-year-olds in the UK peaked at over a million in 1965, fell to 800,000 in 1973, rose again to nearly a million in 1981, and then fell to nearly the 1973 level in 1990. These wide, even wild, oscillations were, however, evened out by the rising productivity of the secondary schools. The percentage of the age group in England with two or more A levels in GCE rose from under 8 per cent in 1962/3 to approaching three times that proportion by the late 1980s (20.9 per cent of boys and 22.2 per cent of girls in 1988/9).

For full-time students in higher education as a whole there has been an increase in the age participation ratio (defined as the proportion of home students under 21 years to the 18-year-old population of Great Britain in the year of entry). Before the Second World War it had been less than 3 per cent. Just before Robbins in 1962/3 it was 7.2 per cent. It rose steadily until 1972/3 but then the ratio fell (to 12.7 per cent in 1977/8) and did not climb back to the 1973 level again until 1984 when it rose to 15.2 per cent and further to 20.3 per cent in 1990. According to DES calculations the Age Participation Index (virtually the same as APR, i.e. the number of home initial entrants to full-time higher education as a proportion of the 18- to 19-year-old population) was 13.7 in 1984 and reached 19.3 in 1990. The interesting movements in this index from 1978 to 1989 are displayed in Figure 6.1 for men and women separately and distinguishing universities from other higher education institutions. The index is projected to increase to 28.1 in 1995 and 32.1 in 2000 (Appendix 2 of Cm 1541). There is, in short, a declared intention of continuing expansion to include more than ten times the post-war proportion of young people by the end of the century. It had already risen by a factor of seven by the beginning of the 1990s.

Gender and social class

The expansion of opportunity for women may be regarded as a further exemplification of the same general pattern. The proportion of all students who were women was less than a quarter before the Second World War, began to rise significantly after the mid-1960s, and became 42.8 per cent in 1989. Those who consult the facts will accordingly have mixed emotions. In the ex-polytechnics sexual equality of opportunity is established. And, as is clear from Table 6.9, the growth in full-time university undergraduate places has accommodated more women both absolutely (83,000 extra women compared with 33,000 men) and relatively (122 per cent increase for women compared with 20 per cent increase for men). But the evidence of differential relative expansion is also there. Women have gained on men but their advance has been disproportionately in the newer forms of higher education. All part-time categories have risen faster for women than for men over the two decades.

For social classes the general tendency towards inequality of educational attainment persists. General Household Survey data show that, measured in relative terms, the proportions of those entering higher education from manual working families

Figure 6.1   Age Participation Index, Great Britain, 1978–1990

have scarcely shifted by comparison with those from the professional and managerial classes. For degree-holders in 1974 whose fathers were professionals or managers, the ratio was 2.75, i.e. they were graduating at nearly 3 times the rate that would obtain if degree-holding were randomly distributed. At the other extreme the children of semi-skilled and unskilled workers had a ratio of 0.28 and the children of skilled manual workers 0.52. By 1985 these ratios had moved to 2.05, 0.36, and 0.50 respectively. The numbers of entrants to higher education from manual social origins had risen absolutely but not relatively to their numbers in the population. This is cold comfort for those who seek the 'classless society'. Moreover, the movement from grants towards loans inaugurated in 1989, and the logic of education as a 'positional good', might well produce greater class inequality in British higher education in the future.

Nevertheless the story remains unfinished. Both economic fortunes and political pressure moved in the later 1980s. On the economic front a much disputed restructuring of the economy with an also disputed movement towards integration with continental Europe had educational consequences. The achievement of competitive advantage impelled renewed educational expansion. Invidious international comparison in the preparations for '1992' excited almost hysterical reorganization of training arrangements and reinforced pressure towards vocational education at all levels of schooling. From different standpoints and with different assumptions both the Conservative and Labour parties and the reformed Liberal Democrats began to share the view that a mass system of higher education was inevitable for twenty-first century Britain. In May 1991 the Conservatives, following the other parties, announced the beginning of the new educational era. Mass higher education would accommodate one school leaver in three (an extra 300,000 students over the next eight years), polytechnics could become universities, the funding bodies would be dismantled and 'a single intelligence' would replace them, though with separate establishments in England, Scotland, and Wales. In the event, the student targets for 2000 were achieved in 1993.

It must be immediately added that plans for funding the new expansion remained vague. The drive towards increasing reliance on tuition fees remained as a governmental stimulus of market forces. The government will also encourage universities and colleges to seek funds from the private sector, particularly from industry and commerce, benefactors and alumni. A fair share of public expenditure is guaranteed to higher education but the final emphasis is on further efficiency, which the embattled dons realistically interpret as a levelling down of standards and still further reduction of staff/student ratios. The struggle will doubtless go on as Europe seeks ways to renew economic growth. But one thing is sure. The binary line has lost its official status and a post-binary system has begun in Britain.

Meritocracy

What, then, in the light of this description of the developments in education and an analysis of their relation to political aims or moral ideals, are we to make of the liberal optimisms of the twentieth century? Expansion there has been. It remains unfinished today; and along with this has been the creation of much cultural capital. But the anticipated greater equality of access to the national heritage has not fully materialized. Thresholds have certainly been raised and the area of free secondary education has been expanded under the auspices of the state. But the further activity of the state in expanding educational opportunity beyond the statutory leaving age has provided additional opportunities which have been seized disproportionately by those born into advantageous class circumstances. The overall result, on the various measures we have brought to bear, is that inequalities of class opportunity changed their form but retained their substance despite, if not indeed because of, a heavy investment by the state in enlarged educational opportunities.

In defining equality of educational opportunity, however, we have so far accepted the assumption that the characteristics of the average member of different classes were similar with respect to their claim and capacity to profit from whatever educational opportunity society provides. We must now question this assumption and explicitly consider a modification of it. Merit is commonly held to constitute a claim on social rewards and opportunities over against the claims, for example, of citizenship or rank or market power. Expressions of the liberal tradition in advanced industrial countries have characteristically justified the granting of opportunities to merit on grounds of efficiency in industry, government, and administration. As governmental bureaucracies developed in the nineteenth century, selection of entrants on merit increasingly replaced patronage, nepotism, and purchase. In Britain this movement can be traced to colonial administration, especially in India. It had a metropolitan milestone in the Northcote-Trevelyan reforms of the Civil Service. Merit in this context was educationally defined and the examination emerged as an instrument for detecting potential capacity for the performance of an expanding range of occupational positions.

This is what is meant by the general sociological thesis of a transition from 'ascriptive' to 'achievement' criteria in occupational selection. The theory of meritocracy evolved from this liberal movement and the definition attached to it by Michael Young is summarized in the label or slogan 'IQ plus effort'. Neither the Oxford mobility data nor subsequent studies yield measures of the complex amalgam of mind and character which would fully represent any of the possible definitions of merit. They are confined to a definition in terms of measured intelligence and even here the IQ distributions between classes are estimated. Moreover, simplification apart, the meaning of measured intelligence in the context of explaining and justifying educational selection procedures is highly contentious.[33] There is an unresolved debate as to how far measured intelligence is cause and how far effect of class membership. There is continuing disagreement as to how far, if at all, past social selection has, in association with assortive mating, produced *genetically* distinct classes.

The significance of class comparisons of IQ scores must accordingly be limited and tentative. Nevertheless both the method and the result of the Oxford study is of some interest.

The method consists of three steps. First, the social class composition of types of school can be estimated from the 1972 survey. Second, the share of places in each type of school which would accrue to each social class if allocations were made strictly on IQ scores can also be calculated. For this second step an assumption has to be made as to the appropriate rank order of each type of school and the assumption chosen is that public schools take the highest band of IQ. Then third, the actual shares are compared with the hypothetical IQ or 'meritocratic' shares obtained by each class in each type of school. The result turns out to be that the real world and the hypothetical meritocratic world are pretty similar. Moreover, this closeness of fit has been characteristic of secondary schooling for the past half century.

However, a crucially different result emerges when the same kind of analysis is applied to education beyond the statutory school-leaving age. Here the queue is reconstituted to give the universities the first slice of measured intelligence, the colleges of education the second, and part-time further education the third. When the quota which would have been allocated to each class in each birth cohort on IQ measurement is set alongside the actual allocation, it emerges that there was class equality of opportunity on meritocratic assumptions for some form of post-secondary education. But in the case of the most sought-after form of education beyond school—the university—there was still class inequality between the middle class and the other two classes. Privileged, that is non-meritocratic, access to the universities rose to its highest point among those born between 1933 and 1942, and then fell back, but not quite to the point recorded for the first cohort of those born between 1913 and 1922. Lower-middle-class boys born after the Second World War were relatively disadvantaged compared with their predecessors after the First World War, while working-class boys stayed at much the same level of relative disadvantage in the 1960s as they had been after the First World War, and with even more disadvantage in the years between. Thus, paradoxically, if the university is regarded as the crowning edifice of the state's policy of educational expansion, it is ironic to notice that this is the development which accords least with the meritocratic principle.[34]

Conclusion

The long words of politics—capitalism, socialism, communism, and democracy—have many and ambiguous meanings. So, too, has the educational system appropriate to a modern society. Education prepares children for society, transforming biological organisms into social personalities. Its capacity is essentially not to create but to re-create society, not to form structures of social life but to maintain the people and the skills that inform these structures. Education as a means of social change is secondary. It is not impotent because, *pace* Marx/Engels, man's social consciousness to some degree determines his social existence. Yet that social existence must be the starting-point for reforming educational policies of the past which come out of a class society, evolving perhaps towards one of classless inequality, complicated by the peculiar British history of political independence, of cultural homogeneity, and of primacy in the development of an urban-industrial civilization.

Ideologically, the national histories of education seem also to have echoed the themes with which we are concerned in this book—liberty, equality, and fraternity—against the constraining forces of structure and culture in each country. In Britain, the constraints have been those of a class society which gave rise, in the nineteenth century, to a mass system of elementary education imposed from above. Liberty gave ideological justification to the privileges of the minority in the public schools and the Oxford colleges, and later to an enlarged minority through selective secondary schools and universities. For the mass it was essentially freedom for a selected few to escape—a policy of selective educational embourgeoisment. This, at the same time, was the liberal approach to equality, taking the form of policies of equality of opportunity. Liberty also increasingly penetrated the infant school in that brief period in the life of a child in which there is some protection from the exigencies of educational selection. Thus, the twentieth-century debate in education has been dominated by a liberal solution which links equality to liberty but, with the exception of the comprehensive school movement, neglects the link to fraternity.

7 ORDER AND AUTHORITY

Order, Order, the House will come to Order
(Betty Boothroyd)

It is always possible that the United Kingdom of England, Scotland, Wales, and Northern Ireland could disintegrate. If for a moment we look beyond native British pieties and take instead the wider perspective of contemporary world history, the prospect of an approaching insular disestablishment becomes conceivable. Integration between nations and ethnic disintegration within them is the common pattern of current economic and political development all over the world. The British find themselves drawn simultaneously into the European Economic Community and into Scottish and Welsh separatism. The very different political and economic circumstances of the former Soviet Union, of China, and of Africa reveal on a larger scale in each case the same story. Enlarging economic organization, with modernity as its aim, combined with sharp internal conflicts between Russian and non-Russian were significant factors in the break-up of the USSR, and a thwarted Russian nationalism still threatened Yeltsin's reform programme after the elections of 1993. Han and non-Han minorities struggle in the context of rapid industrialization in China, as do tribal groups including the 'white tribe' in Africa.[1] The British experience is not unique, Bosnia and Iraq are current examples of endemic ethnic conflict. Nor is conflict, despite a cultural bias against recognizing it, in any way odd. As I pointed out in Chapter 1, the coexistence of interests and scarcity make it more difficult to explain why societies hang together, rather than why they break up.

All the more, then, is it a puzzle that, at least since Culloden in 1746, despite the alarm and dramas of the revolutionary years of 1688 and 1848, the General Strike of 1926, and the violent picket lines of the miners' strike in 1984–5, and notwithstanding the Southern Irish breakaway in 1922, and the current so-called troubles in Ulster which we hesitate to name as civil war*, British history and the British state have been quite outstandingly tranquil. Ever since the battle between the Parliamentary armies and the forces of the Crown, three hundred and fifty years ago, the outstanding fact about Britain is domestic peace. Apologists throughout the modern age and down to our own day have never tired of words like 'decency', 'tolerance', and 'restraint', and phrases like 'respect for tradition', 'innate conservatism', 'the law and the constitution', and so on through a political and social lexicon of approval for consensus and condemnation of 'extremism'. By contrast, unlike those of consensus, the ugly words of political conflict never rid themselves of their inverted commas. 'Capitalism' and 'communism', 'bourgeoisie' and 'bureaucrat', 'dialectic' and '*démarche*', 'liberation' and 'liquidation': these remain alien visitors to an unfanatical tradition of political discourse. Not only in tourist brochures is the essential England still depicted as curling wood-smoke from a Cotswold cottage against an autumn sky.

Why? How did the nation that led the Industrial Revolution somehow contrive this changelessness? How did it retain monarchic and medieval symbols of unity, absorb first a bourgeoisie and second a proletariat, turn Hadrian's Wall and the Edwardian castles into tourist attractions, and contain the eisteddfod (which, I am told, is a medieval invention of the nineteenth century) and the kilt as quaint atavistic regional colourfulness, signifying politically nothing? And why, if it is so, are these ancient manifestations of war, bloodshed, force and oppression, so long turned into harmless symbols of pacification and gentleness, now re-emerging as signals of separatism and hostility? These are the final questions for this book: the problem of fraternity which has been latent in my discussion of liberty and equality, the problem of social order which has underlain my chronicle of class, status, and party.

One thing is obvious. Neither Marxism nor economic liberal-

* The announcement of ceasefire by Gerry Adams and Sinn Fein in 1994 is yet another step in the complex search for order in British society.

ism by itself explains the central problem of order. Neither tradition ever developed a serious theory of nationalism. For the Marxist nationalism is a secondary force, more or less useful in the march of history towards world revolution, given greater or lesser emphasis according to whether the theorist prefers Lenin or Rosa Luxemburg.[2] Liberal theory, too, has a central concept of one world, evolving as rationality displaces mercantilism and other superstitions towards free trade, Gatt agreement, and comparative cost advantages. Both theories come out of the early development of capitalism, both vastly overestimate the possibility of economic solutions—the Marxists by assuming that the economic power of the capitalist class is all that stands in the way of a harmonious society of free and equal men, needing no political state to organize their brotherhood; the economic liberals, by assuming that the free market generates just distribution, needing only minimal government to guard its contractual perfection.

I want to argue that there are native traditions of social and political theory, which can be of more use to those who search for a solution. If the position which I support must be labelled, its name is *citizenship*. It is a tradition of radical reform in which democracy is both a means and an end and which seeks to attain a maximum of equality between individuals in a free society. If the first enemy of social peace in Britain is the persistence of inequality, then we look to such writers as T. H. Marshall who, as I suggested in the third chapter, avoids both the Marxist and the liberal error. He stands in a tradition much influenced by Durkheim and Weber. He brings us back to politics as the arena in which the conflicting claims of class and status are fought out. As David Lockwood has pointed out,[3] his theory of citizenship offers the most cogent answer to the problem, originally posed by Durkheim, of the basis of solidarity in modern societies.

Social integration in modern society

Writing in 1893,[4] Durkheim distinguished two forms of solidarity. The first type he called 'segmental', and the second 'organic'. In pre-literate societies, solidarity is mechanical, based on substitutability and resemblance. Individuals have experience and feelings common to all. The social units of society are also similar in form and function, each family being much like any other family in the society, and each community like every other community. As society advances, it comes to depend increasingly on the division of labour. Individuals are differentiated in their feelings. They are bound together now, not by consciousness of kind, but by their interdependence, their complementarity. The question then becomes: what is the social base for organic solidarity in modern societies? Durkheim's general answer need not detain us. But before we leave him, we can note that he made an acute observation concerning late nineteenth-century Britain.

It may very well happen, that in a particular society a certain division of labour—and especially economic division of labour—may be highly developed, while the segmental type may still be rather pronounced. This certainly seems to be the case in England: major industry, big business, appears to be as highly developed there as on the continent, while the segmental system is still very much in evidence, as witness both the autonomy of local life, and the authority retained by tradition.

Local autonomy and the strength of tradition are two clues to the maintenance of social integration in Britain, despite marked inequalities of class and status. Both of these sources of national unity have been heavily damaged in the 1980s and 1990s with Thatcherite attacks on local authorities, professions, and unions, and with popular disenchantment with the monarchy and Parliament. And we can add the further Durkheimian point (though one he did not specifically apply to England) that 'all external inequality compromises organic solidarity'.[5] Writers like Barbara Wootton, R. M. Titmuss, and Alan Fox have carried further T. H. Marshall's approach to a direct analysis of the relation between inequality and social integration, and I shall return to them.[6]

Societies in general are made and broken by like interests leading to cohesion or competition, and by unlike interests which bind people together or bring them into conflict. But there is another principle of social organization—domination—which has become increasingly important in modern societies in the form of the authority of rationally created rules. Authority always has two sides, force and faith: the faith of the ruled that the rulers have the right to make rules by which people must live (for example, that they must pay such-and-such amounts in taxes), and the force that the rulers have at their disposal to compel compliance with the rules. In modern societies, by far the most important source of authoritative rules is the state, and the definition of the state, at once most simple and most useful, is that it has a monopoly of ultimate force in the territory it claims. But societies are not identical with states, as the example of Scotland clearly shows. The integration of a society is based less on force and more on faith—that is, on cultural affinities of language, custom, belief, and history, which give the members a consciousness of kind and kin with each other, and a sense of cultural boundary from other peoples. These bonds are more enduring so that states and empires have risen and fallen more rapidly than have societies: a nation and people can live, politically or militarily speaking, underground through many generations of foreign rule. Faith converts force into authority and consent.

But this distinction between force and faith, though essential to understanding of social cohesion in societies and states, does not complete the analysis. What sociologists call legitimation (which gives authority to those who wield power) involves the modern state not only in enforcing and administering law but also in elaborate processes of non-coercive integration, including the display of national symbols, appeals to traditional sources of authority, selective presentation of policy, and action in terms of what is or is judged to be the preferred values of the electorate, and so on through the whole range of relations of communication between government and governed over which the state can exercise more or less control or influence.[7]

Hence faith may vary in its social bases. It may be engendered or maintained by the power of classes, status groups, or parties to influence the consciousness of those they dominate. Consequently, some may wish to distinguish a third force, and to label it 'fraud'. Fraud typically resides in the power of ruling groups to exercise calculated control over communication, and thus to impose ideas and beliefs on the majority in the interests of the minority. In this way, organized religion, schooling, and the mass media may serve to hold a society together, continually reinforcing and disseminating its established ideologies. In practice, integration by fraud is intrinsically fragile. False faith is more characteristically an unintended consequence of unequally shared power. Conspiracy theories of society cannot be convincingly applied to Britain, and those writers like Frank Parkin who interpret the problem of social order as essentially that of legitimating the control of a dominant class, none the less recognize a variety of social mechanisms, such as religious ritual, the teaching of school history, or opportunities for social mobility, as not deliberate creations of that dominant class.[8]

The forces of fusion

Despite many examples of the insecurity of consensus, no Hobbesian collapse of civil society has so far marred modern British history. On the contrary, force and faith in their varied manifestations have played their part in what has been historically, a remarkably United Kingdom. The twentieth-century inheritance was, on balance, heavily weighted towards fusion rather than fission. Some of the unifying influences are easy enough to discern. The British state, centred on the Crown in Parliament, held undisputed sway over England, Scotland, and Wales for two centuries and, more important, naval power controlled an Empire eventually covering one-quarter of the land surface of the whole earth. Britain in 1900 was still the greatest of imperial nations, a major workshop of the world, and miraculously secured at the same time by a still impregnable insularity. British society was itself the apex of a world-wide imperial dominion, and London the financial centre of world trade.

This powerful combination of industry and empire obviously afforded huge wealth and wide opportunity to its controllers. Wealth and opportunity were most unequally shared within the society, between classes, sexes, and regions. But continuing, if decelerating and unsteady, expansion, itself a supplement to integration, was further and massively reinforced by the custom and culture of a most peculiar island. It was a culture of patrician liberalism. The aristocracy and the gentry maintained a dominance over both society and state from the overthrow of absolutist monarchy in the seventeenth century, and right through the imperial and industrial developments of the next two hundred years. The continuity of cultural symbols—a constitutional monarchy, a tame but titled Second Chamber, a democratized but dignified Oxford and Cambridge—was made possible by these economic and military forces and, in turn, gave venerated changelessness to the continuous adaptiveness of a dominant class—an adaptiveness which included pathways to the control of British institutions by people of Scottish or Welsh origin. Neil Kinnock and John Smith have led the Labour party, Macmillan and Ramsay MacDonald as well as Lloyd George have been prime ministers, and Lord Reith was the head of the BBC.

So, as Tom Nairn has put it, and is saying, in effect, what Durkheim said:

the pioneer modern liberal-constitutional state never itself became modern: it retained the archaic stamp of its priority. Later the industrialization which it produced, equally pioneering and equally worldwide in impact, never made England into a genuinely industrialized society . . . And therefore no recovery from industrial 'backwardness' has been possible, precisely because no second revolution of the state has taken place in England: only the state could have engendered such a recovery, by revolution from above—but the old patrician structure of England's political system, incapable of such radical action, has also resisted every effort at serious reform up to the present day.[9]

But, I would add, if economically weak, it was made socially strong by the culture of the gentleman.

Nairn's historical analysis has to be taken seriously. Economic liberalism as a theory of free markets in the service of economic growth is older in England than the bourgeois industrialist manufacturer. The English land-owning classes had developed it long before the Industrial Revolution.[10] The aristocracy and the gentry absorbed the bourgeoisie in the nineteenth century. This gave to the twentieth century a stratified society which, though resembling the Marxist description of polarized class society if one looked at the Northern industrial towns, was also a status hierarchy of apparent agelessness. It was rooted in a medieval agrarian past. It provided a governing class descended from pre-industrial times to which was added, especially in the Southern counties, those whose wealth and status derived from the Empire, and from the finance capitalism of the City of London.

In short, Edwardian Britain was a country of inequality, but a strongly knit nation. A legacy of feudal aristocracy had, in the course of overseas imperialism and domestic industrialization, been accepted by both bourgeoisie and proletariat. No wonder, then, that Lord David Cecil saw the sunset over his grandfather's deathbed as also the twilight of British greatness. For the fusion I have briefly sketched was gradually to be dissolved by corrosion at home and abroad. The industrial competitors abroad—America and Germany—had already ended Britain's pre-eminence. In a century of relative, though not absolute, decline there was a period of exceptionally high prosperity in the 1950s and 1960s. When that interlude ended, domestic discontents fanned by economic stagnation, class and status inequalities, and later in the 1980s the recrudescence of economic liberalism as Thatcherism, were less and less easily contained by the traditional remedies of political liberalism, gentlemanly culture, and civic incorporation. A formidable toll of human energy and resource now has to be mobilized in order to control a country hitherto frequently held up as an exemplar of urbane peace. For example, in Northern Ireland there are 31,000 British soldiers, making a ratio of one to every forty-five of the population. This is a ratio not very different to that of teachers to schoolchildren before the Second World War. In the English mining communities in 1984 and 1985 the massive use of police forces against massed pickets was an outstanding feature of the miners' strike.

Nevertheless, there have been strong forces making for integration. If only because we are so accustomed now to gloomy

discussion of Britain's economic decline, we should remind ourselves that it is a country which has enjoyed economic growth
during this century. The national bookkeeping of economists
suggests a quadrupling of real income per head since 1900. And
even if growth faltered in the last quarter, prosperity is still the
condition of the great majority. The average person is unquestionably better fed, better clothed, better housed, and enjoys a
longer, healthier, and more leisured life than his Edwardian
predecessor. Clearly allegiance to a society is more secure when
these ameliorations are in train, that is, when the generations see
a darker past and a brighter future.

We also do well to remind ourselves of the integrating aspects
of war. It is a paradox of external conflict that it promotes
equality and fraternity within the nation. This is true especially
of modern 'total' war. If all must be called upon to fight for their
country, all must be brought to believe that they have a stake in
it. Both World Wars brought renewed promise for the future.
They reinforced patriotic sentiment.

> But ever 'twixt the book and his bright eyes
> The gleaming eagles of the legions came.[11]

This was a possible reverie for a young clerk in England in the
First World War and even the Second, before the bomb dropped
on Hiroshima. The two Wars also softened class divisions and
reduced inequality. In 1945, much more than in 1919, there
was intense feeling among working men and women that the
promises of English culture were about to be redeemed in their
own lives. As they had sung in the shadows, so now they sang
Edward Carpenter's secular hymn in the light: England is risen
and day is here. Even the Falklands war of 1982 and the ex-
pedition to Kuwait and Iraq in 1990/1 manifestly raised national
morale.

The forces of fission

Yet, although war and prosperity may tend to integrate, other
twentieth-century experiences have had an opposite effect. For
one thing, economic growth has had a cyclical character. Earlier

slumps were increasingly forgotten in the full employment decades of the 1950s and 1960s. But their failure seriously to disturb
the social and political order in the 1930s is testimony only to the
power of cultural integration. As we have seen, when he came
to Jarrow in 1933, J. B. Priestley marvelled that men in such
economic conditions, not under the constraint of military force,
but on the contrary politically enfranchised, should nevertheless
have accepted their lot.[12] That they did has to be explained
largely by the strength of a consensual political culture. It inculcated belief in progress towards a more civilized society and
nourished the faith that as their cause was just, so their victory
was certain. Neither the consensual culture nor the belief in
progress has been as strong in the face of the renewed experience of mass unemployment in the 1980s and 1990s.

Again, industrial productivity in the twentieth century has
been accompanied by growing alienation of labour. On his inter-
war journey, Priestley reports the opinion of a craftsman that 'all
our labour troubles did not come from a quarrel about distribution of the profits, but from a deeper cause, the crushing of the
workman's self respect by mechanical labour in which he could
not find himself'.[13] And the author returns to the theme in reflecting on a Leicester sock-making factory. He remarks the
'great distinction between the fortunate few who are outside the
machine and are capable of making changes in it and the great
mass of ordinary work people, mostly women, who are inside
the machine, simply part of it. This distinction is so great that
you feel that the two sets of people ought to belong to two
different races.'[14] Of those 'inside the machine' he observes 'they
are not bullied or even nagged at; their very weaknesses are
elaborately taken into account; their comfort is considered, but
between the time when they "clock in" and "clock out" their
central human dignity which entitles them under our democratic
system to a vote as good as anybody else's, has no real existence,
except in that dream of life which occupies their minds as their
fingers fly to do their own mysterious little task.'[15]

But above all—the factor of paramount importance—has
been the essentially unprincipled inequality of distribution of

wealth and income. The stubborn persistence of distributional inequality of wealth and income is such as to need no further documentation. What it does need, however, is emphasis on the polarizing character of its movement. It is true that, at least until recently, the implications of inequality have manifested themselves in the economic rather than the political sphere. Within the economic sphere, however—in industrial relations and the management of incomes policy—inequality has been corrosive. The manifestations have not been those of class warfare but rather, as John Goldthorpe has argued, 'in a situation of anomie; that is . . . a lack of moral regulation over the wants and goals that individuals hold'.[16] Consensual politics have been maintained partly by the remarkably restricted comparisons within and between classes which Runciman has analysed,[17] and partly by the political culture of democracy which I reviewed in Chapter 4.

However, the development of the social rights of citizenship generates conflict as well as consensus in such a way as to *exacerbate* anomic conditions. This unintended by-product of an otherwise integrative force takes at least three forms. First the egalitarian principle intrinsic to citizenship challenges normative approval of market inequalities. Class and citizenship are at war in the twentieth century. Second, citizenship also undermines traditional status hierarchies which, though strongly rooted in British culture, are conventionally, not legally, based. Citizenship is therefore a basis for dissent from the established social order. Feminist movements have been conspicuous beneficiaries of these protesting sentiments. And third, the extension of citizenship rights into the industrial sphere—a movement towards various forms of industrial democracy—gives unions, and especially local groups of workers and their shop stewards, increased protection and power to pursue their market and work interests relatively undisciplined by traditional constraints. Attempts since 1979 to shift the balance of industrial power away from the unions by new legislation have met angry if ineffective opposition in part because the citizenship ideal is thereby outraged.

So, the partial development of the principle of citizenship, under circumstances where competing distributional principles deriving from class, status, and citizenship still contend for pre-eminence, may reduce rather than increase organic solidarity. The consequences have been increasingly evident in the recent history of industrial relations. They are most dramatically illustrated in the growing bitterness of race relations in the major English cities.[18]

One feature of 'Thatcherism' is the successful exploitation of an ancient traditional belief that the economic and the political spheres should be kept separate. It is always an open question, of course, how far economic inequality, alienation, and anomy take on political forms of expression. They may be individualized or localized. Rising rates of divorce, separation, crime, vandalism, and hooliganism are possible outcomes: and these have risen markedly in recent decades. The connections, I must emphasize, are not proven. None the less, whatever the reason for the escalation of anti-social activity, there can be no doubt that they in turn reduce confidence in the political and social order. The legitimacy of government and administration is thereby threatened. The apparently increasing frequency of corruption in government and administration—or perhaps simply the wider publicity it receives from investigative journalism—further diminishes civic trust. The role of the media in publicizing scandal among holders of high office in politics and industry or entertainment cannot be of negligible effect. Whether it be David Mellor or Robert Maxwell or Asil Nadir or Cecil Parkinson or Alan Clark being 'economical with the truth', the drip drip of hostile gossip gradually wears away the stone of social confidence. Police corruption, politician's venality, industrialists' greed, or priests' sexual irresponsibility all corrode the civic culture, and spectacular financial gains for individuals, however justified, invite a broadening of reference groups through the rapid and repeated dissemination of news. We cannot measure exactly the strength of these forces, and I fully appreciate that political corruption is normal rather than abnormal in the history of states. Nevertheless, solidarity in Britain in the nineteenth and early twentieth centuries depended heavily on political trust to counterbalance resentments naturally born of inequality.

Shifting balance of cohesion and conflict

Twentieth-century experience, then, has been mixed. Before the First World War, discontents springing from class divisions and stultifying industrial labour were checked by limited working-class expectations and the strong alliance of aristocrat and bourgeois. Meanwhile, the old traditions of civil liberty in which modern citizenship is rooted, though providing the legal basis for the development of class inequalities, had also begun to extend into political enfranchisement and into a set of social rights which later came to be called the Welfare State. The organization of the working class was also built on the same foundations of citizenship. These integrative forces were, however, only weakly struggling into existence, and they carried their own threats to the established order. There was also, especially on Clydeside, a serious syndicalist current flowing away from the more moderate mainstream of the trade unions, the co-operative societies, and the infant Labour party. The war itself suspended opposition and brought a primitive form of war socialism, some reduction of wage differentials, and steps towards the emancipation of women.

Return to 'normalcy,' as it was then termed, shifted the balance again towards, but not quite back to, the pre-war situation. Religion had lost some of its restraining power. The expected boundaries of self-fulfilment were pushed back, educational horizons began to widen, and many intellectuals were vehemently critical of bourgeois life and values. This was the period of fellow-travelling. Nevertheless, this weakening of cultural control never showed signs of being turned into a threatening political movement. British radical politics centred on the Labour party. Bitter industrial struggles scarred the 1920s, but the rise of the Labour party after the First World War to replace the Liberal party was its incorporation into the politics of consensus, not very different from that described in the nineteenth century by Walter Bagehot. Then the slump years of the early 1930s temporarily overlaid the basic politics of belief in progress with hopelessness, fatalism, and fragmentation—a deadening and defeatist interpretation of events was universally shared: economic depression was seen as externally imposed rather than politically soluble.

Then again, partial recovery and the Second World War eased the tensions and renewed the national promise. Liberty, equality, and fraternity all made progress during the war and post-war years. Labour party philosophy dominated politics and there were even five early post-war years of a Labour government in clear majority—winning the solid allegiance of most of those who came of age in the 1930s and 1940s.[19] The Labour victory was never, of course, total, even among its natural supporters—the industrial working class. But, in any case, the following thirteen years of Conservative government were years of full employment, and of educational and occupational opportunity for a significant minority of the new generation of the working class. Belief in an emergent meritocracy was developing in this period, despite the evidence of continuing class inequality of conditions for fair competition, which are necessary for meritocratic principles to replace hereditary or ascriptive ones as the normative basis for an unequal society. It was a time of high net upward mobility and of slowly burgeoning mass affluence. Governments derived legitimacy, deservedly or not, from the *absolute* improvement of conditions and opportunities, not from any amelioration of relative inequality between classes, ethnic groups, or the sexes. The tide of political consensus flowed strongly for twenty years or more.

The tide began to run out towards the end of the 1960s. By this time the Empire was gone. Ideologically, all that was left was Powellite English nationalism. Economically, what remained was the overseas-oriented financial capitalism of the City, which drained talent and attention away from the needs of an ageing and sluggish industrial economy. Hope and glory faded from the land, weakening both national and local cohesion. Internal tensions became more anxiously acute with economic stagnation, quickening inflation, and rising unemployment.

Meanwhile the trade unions, fostered by the further development of citizenship rights, had become more powerfully entrenched, more able to press sectional against national interest. Indeed their successful expansion into the white-collar occupations further enlarged the sphere for competitive sectionalism in bargaining over wages and conditions. And, as I argued in Chapter 4, the incorporation of the Labour leadership both in Parliament and in the TUC, undermined the allegiance of the rank and file, reducing the 'governability' of those officially organized into the working-class movement.

There were also ideological movements in these post-war years with strongly divisive effects. The authority of churches and chapels declined still further. Schoolteachers and parents became less effective conveyors of cultural values and traditional pieties as they too lost confidence in their right and their ability to be so. Scandals from the Profumo affair (1963) onwards dealt repeated blows to the British reputation for incorruptible government. Names like Burgess and Maclean or Blunt gradually destroyed the myth of patriotic, upright, and gentlemanly rulers schooled at Eton and Cambridge. The Poulson revelations of widespread racketeering in the Labour strongholds of the North-East were especially damaging to popular respect for the authority of both the Town Hall and Whitehall. There was a marked contrast between the moralistic Primitive Methodist Labour leaders, like Peter Lee, steeped in the proprieties of constitutional liberalism, and the political bosses like Dan Smith and Andrew Cunningham who replaced them, with their public relations networks and their eventual exposure and long gaol sentences for criminal behaviour in public office. And the adversary culture of students, intellectuals, journalists, and media men grew more strident in the 1960s. The expansion of the universities permitted the growth of social science, which emerged after 1965 as a powerful vehicle for radical criticism of established society. (Social science faculties in the expanding universities grew at three times the rate of the other faculties in the 1962–7 quinquennium.)

Then, in the 1970s, came the sudden wave of nationalism in Scotland, echoed by weaker but still significant separatism in

Wales. Even the detachment of Northern Ireland became a
possibility. These three countries, Scotland with 5½ million,
Wales with 2¾ million, and Ulster with 1½ million population, are
few in numbers compared with the 46 million who dwell in
England. All four peoples are intermixed, geographically and by
intermarriage, to a considerable degree, but are also to a greater
or lesser degree opposed to the political and cultural dominance
of the London metropolis. Minorities within them aspire to political independence and, in Ulster, social tension is further and
tragically compounded by conflict between the Protestant majority and the one-third minority of Catholics who receive violent, if not wholly welcomed, support from the Irish Republican
Army (IRA) operating in part from Eire, south of the partition
border.

   In consequence, the United Kingdom faced an uncertain
future, variously assessed and actively debated. One extreme,
unrepresentative view was that

it depends upon one's conception of the United Kingdom. There are
those who believe that this rump of the former empire will last for ever,
in an essentially unchanging evolution. Their number includes virtually
all England, and a still formidable mass of allies in Scotland, Wales, and
Northern Ireland. On the other hand stands the growing opposition—
within sight of being a majority in Scotland—which accepts the verdict
a great part of the outside world passed on Britain long ago: that it is a
matter of time before it founders. Its post-empire crisis is long overdue,
and not even to be regretted. What else is likely to revive this polity of
stultified anachronism and complacent privilege?[20]

Nairn published this judgement in 1977. The results of the general election of 1979 sharply contradicted his assessment of
Scottish attitudes. But the underlying problem, more soberly
stated, of social cohesion in a United Kingdom remained and
was confronted by a new challenge. Thatcherism brought to an
end the post-war period of consensus politics just as the crisis of
West European economies ended the long post-war boom. A
new period of political economy began with explicit attack on
what Stuart Hall calls the historic class compromise. Neo-liber-
alism was to reassert the rule of the market and with it the

restoration of class power. Political legitimacy was to be sought through authoritarian populism. Conviction politics and the confrontation of the enemies of the state, at home as well as abroad, were to be the basis of a renewed nation.

Regional differences of ideology remain and political party support shows a spectacular patchiness of red, blue, and yellow. There are still, in the 1990s, deep rooted attitudinal differences even if they have narrowed somewhat since the 1980s.[21] The English Midlands, London, and the South are more trustful of the market than are Scotland, Wales, and Northern England. No doubt attitudes there, especially towards unemployment, are rooted in the history of differential economic growth and prosperity.

There was also some reversal of the political divide in that support for the Conservatives rose a little in Scotland and the North of England while falling in the rest of the country in the 1992 general election. Not too much can be read into these trends except perhaps that a long-term upturn in the Northern economy might reunite the nation.

Frailty of authority

Whatever the balance of faith and force, cohesion and conflict, the frailty of authority is a characteristic feature of large and complex modern societies. Three types of authority are distinguished in sociology. One of these, the rational-legal in Max Weber's inelegant phrase, bids to dominate the modern world in the form of *bureaucracy*. What is rational and legal about this type of authority is that it claims to apply to particular cases. Its deeper justification comes, at least in Britain, from the fact (or at least the theory) that the general rules are arrived at by democratic legislation. Its legitimacy rests ultimately on the preferences of the majority. The danger is that bureaucrats all too easily and frequently break the chain from popular will to executive decision.

There is a second type of authority—*charisma*—the personal authority of the inspired leader who is trusted by his followers. His word is the criterion of truth and worth. This type of auth-

ority also has its frailties. It can be de-legitimized by failure to
'deliver the goods'. Public opinion polls reflect its instability.
Those who aspire to it, like Neil Kinnock or Margaret Thatcher
in their different ways, must face the ordeal of their annual party
conferences, and elections. And there is a third type—tradition.
Today's orders are justified on the grounds that we have always
done it that way. It is ancestral wisdom. But I hardly need to
explain the frailty of traditional authority in our world of rapid
social change. In the village where I grew up, custom decreed
that all adults, within limits well understood, could and should
act *in loco parentis*. There was an intergenerational authority,
legitimized by culturally stored solutions to unchanging problems. But in the shifting populations of large cities, young people
are less ready to accord respect to their elders. 'Grandad'
becomes a term of contempt. This is the absence of intergenerational authority.

   It seems almost, once one's thoughts begin to run on these
lines, that the newspapers, the radio, and the television are
concerned with nothing else than authority, its legitimation, the
conditions for its exercise, and the causes of its rupture. Members of Parliament defy the Speaker, young men assault old
women in the street, prisoners rebel against warders in the gaols,
condemned members of the Irish Republican Army refuse to
recognize an Irish court, Asil Nadir runs off to Cyprus.

   By way of contrast, I recently saw a copy of a passport signed
by Lord Palmerston in 1851.[22]

We, Henry John Viscount Palmerston, Baron Temple, a Peer of Ireland,
a Member of Her Britannic Majesty's Most Honourable Privy Council,
a Member of Parliament, Knight Grand Cross of the most Honorable
Order of the Bath, Her Majesty's Principal Secretary of State for
Foreign Affairs, request and require in the Name of Her Majesty all
those whom it may concern to allow Mr. Edward Holyroyd, his wife,
Mrs. Holyroyd, two daughters and three sons, travelling on the Continent, with a man and a maid servant, to pass freely without let or
hindrance, and to afford them every assistance and protection of which
they may stand in need. Given at the Foreign Office, London, the 10th
day of July 1851.

Notice the symbols of authority here. And, perhaps even more telling, the confident description of social hierarchy from Her Majesty down through the Viscount to Mr Holyroyd and thence to sons and daughters, and finally a man and a maid servant.

Honi soit qui mal y pense, says the heraldry. No matter that, three years before, Marx and Engels in the Communist Manifesto of 1848 had, with no less confidence, announced the impending fall of the capitalist state, the overthrow of imperial authority by the rising revolutionary proletariat.

We have since seen the twentieth-century rise and fall of *new* authorities—the TUC, and the Parliamentary Labour party—from Downing Street, Manchester, to Downing Street, London, to become what journalists described in the 1970s as the natural government of the country. In the early 1990s, despite the indications of opinion polls, they seem remote from governmental power. The annual conferences are a much cherished opportunity for the rank and file to belabour their masters on the platform, rather as we know many primitive tribes have annual rituals in which the chief is ceremoniously reviled and insulted by licensed warriors before the assembled people. Behind the rituals less open struggles proceed for power which can be translated into authority. We have witnessed Thatcher and Kinnock come and go in this context. It is also characteristic of the Russian and Chinese regimes that there have been bitter struggles for succession to the places emptied by death among the founding gerontocracy.

I choose these diverse examples partly to emphasize that the problem of authority is ubiquitous in human relationships, extending from the encounter in the street through those small human groups which are sufficiently bound by rules for us to call them institutions, like the family, or the youth club, or the office, and on up to the great political organizations of party and Parliament.

From all these instances, we can discern the three basic forms of authority—rational-legal, charismatic, and traditional—combining and contending with one another. And we can further see that social change makes each of them uncertain as legitimate sources for stable and peaceable relations between people. The examples emphasize that authority is not a synonym for law. The adults in my village had no legal authority over children: but they had the authority of long-established tradition. Neither law nor traditional authority is absolute. The young 'mugger' flouts the law. Certainly Mao exercised enormous charisma in his progress from young revolutionary in Yenan Province to the chairmanship in Peking. But charisma too has no universal writ. It may be routinized, as with Christ's authority in the institution of the papal succession. But Mao's charisma, if it did not die with him, at least could not prevent a power struggle among the survivors.

Charisma is historically like the wind which bloweth where it listeth. Churchill is thought of in Britain as having had this type of authority. He gained it at a moment of desperate external threat to a country at war. External threat does, in fact, accelerate the process whereby many are called and few are chosen. Mrs Thatcher, too, seemed to gain charismatic legitimacy during the Falklands war of 1982 and was thus rescued from an unpopularity which was undermining support for her and her party. By 1990 charisma and competence looked very different as Ian Gilmour has shown.[23] The passing of the post-war period has carried with it a chronic political atmosphere of threatened collapse. But let us be clear that the possibility of new and dramatic leadership, which infirmity invites, is highly dangerous. Charisma is no necessary friend of democracy—*explicitly* not if it comes from the political extreme Right, and *actually* not if it comes from the extreme Left, for all its ideological clothing in rhetoric proclaiming the will of the people.

Bureaucracy

Alienation from the state apparatus is an equally widespread popular experience. Bureaucracy, like bourgeoisie, serves more often as a term of abuse than as a descriptive category. Gordon Tullock[24] has described it as a 'comprehensive criticism of politicians and civil servants for being more interested in feathering their own nests than serving the public'. Professor Tullock argues that civil servants are just like other men and that therefore 'they will make most of their decisions in terms of what benefits them, not society as a whole'. And, 'as a general rule, a bureaucrat will find that his [interests are best served] . . . if the bureaucracy in which he works expands'.

In the late 1970s the two large Civil Service unions, alarmed by what their leaders described as a 'hate campaign against civil servants', had distributed a pamphlet to MPs and other unions defending the incumbents of public offices against exaggerated rumours of their pay and pensions, and against misrepresentation of their conduct towards citizens. The Civil Service unions had also protested against cuts in public expenditure in general and public service jobs in particular. No one ought to need reminding that forced unemployment is a private tragedy and a public failure, but anyone could be forgiven, after following the public announcements of Labour and Conservative governments after 1970, for thinking that there had been a sharp reduction in the number of officials. And this was specially marked in the case of local government with its alleged reorganization for greater economy and efficiency. In fact the opposite was the case.

The Manpower Watch Survey—made jointly by central and local government—records that, between March 1975 and March 1976—a much publicized 'No Growth' period—there was an *increase* in English and Welsh local government staff of over 30,000. On a longer view it is clear that governments of either colour presided over continuous bureaucratic growth. There were 1¼ million local government employees in 1960. It was 2 million when Labour displaced the Tories in 1964. They added over 400,000 before the Conservatives came back in 1970 determined to turn the tide. But the tide flowed on. By 1975 there were 2,875,000 despite the fact that 77,000 were transferred to the NHS and Water Services in 1974 and so did not appear in the 1975 total. By 1978 there were 5 million central and local government officials, compared with 17.5 million in the private sector. No wonder that the 1979 Conservative government redoubled its resolve. There was a decrease of almost 15 per cent in the total number of industrial and non-industrial civil servants in the United Kingdom between April 1979 and April 1984, bringing the number down to 592,700. But the much larger local authority manpower was only marginally reduced (from 2,347,700 to 2,267,400).[25] Later in the 1980s the trend towards privatization, including the purchasing of services from the private sector, obscures the continuing upward tendency of bureaucratization.

Taking a still wider view it can be seen that in the twentieth century the occupational structure has shifted its centre of gravity from basic productive employment to the tertiary sector of services and administration. One measure of the change is that between 1911 and 1966 white-collar numbers went up 176 per cent, while manual jobs rose only 5 per cent and actually decreased after 1931. Another indicator is that between 1951 and 1981 the managers and administrators grew from 5.4 per cent to 10.1 per cent of the economically active population, and the trend is continuing into the 1990s, balanced by contracting classification into manual work.

These figures reflect an increasingly organized world in which bureaucracy is the dominant working principle. Though the word 'community' also spatters its pages, the contemporary newspaper habitually looks out, sees organizations everywhere, and tells us in a more or less sensationalist way how people enter them in pursuit of their interest only to lose themselves.

In common speech, of course, the word 'bureaucracy' is an established term of abuse. The word 'bureau' referred originally to the cloth covering the desks of French government officials in the eighteenth century. With its suffix added it came to refer to the rule of government, and a host of '-ocracies' have since been added to the vocabulary of politics as commentators have searched desperately to find the ultimate seat of power in modern society. The pejorative term then spread throughout Europe during the nineteenth century, at first to ridicule the high-handed arrogance of officials in absolutist regimes, and later more generally as a whip for the backs of unresponsive organizations, tortuous methods of administration, and large-scale enterprises (whether of government, business, religion, or recreation) in which power was concentrated into the hands of the administrative few. In our own time nothing has warmer response in the British media than undocumented reference to 'Brussels bureaucrats' even though support for EEC member-ship grew from 53 per cent in 1983 to 76 per cent in 1990.[26]

There is, on the other hand, a technical, social-scientific use of bureaucracy to describe a type of social organization deliber-ately devised by men for the rational and efficient pursuit of defined purposes. No one saw more clearly than Max Weber that bureaucracy and large-scale organization were the fundamental phenomena of modern political, social, and economic life. And Weber's account of bureaucracy, from one point of view, reminds us of its virtues. Bureaucracy, he noted, was distinguished from other forms of human authority and control by its routinized rationality, its capacity to attain a high degree of efficiency, its stability, the stringency of its discipline, and its reliability. It is a matter of national pride in Britain that it showed the world how to escape from the corrupt control of administration by the privileged into uncorrupt and dedicated public service recruited on merit in open competition, by the Northcote-Trevelyan and Gladstonian reforms; and that was the acceptable face of bureaucracy.

It is true that Weber at the same time saw the tragedy of the highly organized world into which industrialization would take us—a world of disenchantment, robbed of magic and mystery. Even charisma, the gift of grace, would be routinized within it and freedom and individuality could be destroyed by it. Nevertheless, in company with both the Leftists and the Right-ists of his age, Weber identified modernity with the spread of bureaucratic administration:

This is true of church and state, of armies, political parties, economic enterprizes, organizations to promote all kinds of causes, private as-sociations, clubs, and many others. However many forms there may be which do not appear to fit this pattern, such as collegial representative bodies, parliamentary committees, soviets, honorary officers, lay judges, and what-not, and however much people may complain about the 'evils of bureaucracy', it would be sheer illusion to think for a moment that continuous administrative work can be carried out in any field except by means of officials working in offices. The whole pattern of everyday life is cut to fit this framework. For bureaucratic administration is, other things being equal, always from a formal technical point of view, the most rational type. For the needs of mass administration today, it is completely indispensable. The choice is only that between bureaucracy and dilettantism in the field of administration.[27]

Adherents of different ideological traditions than that of Weber's liberalism echoed his celebration of the inevitable march of bureaucracy as well as his ambivalence towards it. Sheldon Wolin[28] has written a subtle and scholarly account of the origin of this view in all political camps. Whatever differences there were in diagnosis and prescription, most of the major writers have been agreed on the general formula for developing wealth, welfare, and social order—organization. Thus for the nineteenth-century French conservative, de Maistre, the organization of society into a vast hierarchy of authority would reinstitute stability and peace under the command of king and pope, assisted by a public-spirited aristocracy. For his compatriot, Auguste Comte, there would be an organized hierarchy of savant-priests. For yet another compatriot, Emile Durkheim, the organization of society had to be on the basis of professional and producing groups. For the proponents of managerial élitism in the twentieth century the best organization of society is one under the control of the professional managers and administrators who alone possess the requisite knowledge for maintaining social equilibrium in the age of successive technological revolutions.

Weber himself remorselessly drove home the inference from the indispensability of bureaucracy that it made no difference whether an economic system was organized on a capitalist or a socialist basis. And he adds:

though by no means alone, the capitalistic system has undeniably played a major role in the development of bureaucracy. Indeed, without it capitalistic production could not continue and any rational type of socialism would simply have to take it over and increase its importance. Its development, largely under capitalistic auspices, has created an urgent need for stable, strict, intensive, and calculable administration. It is this need which gives bureaucracy a crucial role in our society as the central element in any kind of large-scale administration.[29]

Bureaucracy, I would stress, in theories of the Right and the Left, has been seen as an instrument not only for efficiency but also of social control. There is accordingly an élitism of the Left as well as of the Right. Lenin is perhaps the outstanding example. In Professor Wolin's phrase 'organization was to mass in Lenin's theory what idea had been to matter in Plato's: that which imparted form to the formless'. Lenin was the first to seize the implications of transferring politics to the plane of organization. He taught that politics had meaning only within an organizational setting. The trick was not to destroy the political but to absorb it into organization to create a new compound. The irony is that his prescription for revolution has also been used to preserve giant capitalism. Democracy has no meaning in such élitist thought except in so far as it is consonant with the imperatives of organization. Thus Lenin wrote:

Bureaucracy *versus* democracy is the same thing as centralism *versus* (local) democracy as opposed to the organizational principle of the opportunists of Social Democracy. The latter want to proceed from the bottom upwards ... The former proceed from the top, and advocate the extension of the rights and powers of the centre in respect of the parts ... My idea is 'bureaucratic' in the sense that the Party is built from the top downwards ...[30]

Lenin's theory was the basis for Communist organization. But the historical roots of British socialism were never like that. Democracy came to Britain from the bottom upwards. The urban working classes of the nineteenth century were uprooted newcomers to the growing provincial industrial towns who responded to their circumstances with extraordinary social inventiveness to give Britain in the first half of the twentieth century its most characteristic popular organizations—the co-operative store, the trade union, and the Labour party, as well as the dance hall, the football club, and the Friendly Society. The first and the greatest three of these were experiments in democracy. This urban proletariat created its own local, communal welfare societies. Nothing could have been more democratic than the constitution of the co-op, nothing more fraternal than the miners' lodge. Nowhere could we find a more sturdy institutional protection for individuals against becoming a mass to be manipulated. Then, with political organization as its instrument, the Labour movement, dominated by the statist tradition of reform as propounded by the Webbs and the Fabians, set out to nationalize democracy and welfare; to translate fraternity, equality, and liberty from the local community to the national state.

What has been the outcome? In 1973, very near to the end of his life, R. H. S. Crossman gave an account, in the form of a review, of the Labour movement as he had experienced it. It was in essence a lament for the eclipse of voluntarism by bureaucratic organization—a disappointment in Westminster and a despair in Whitehall:

From the 1920s on, the normal left-wing attitude has been opposed to middle-class philanthropy, charity, and everything else connected with do-gooding. Those of us who became socialists grew up with the conviction that we must in this point ally ourselves with the professionals and the trade unions and discourage voluntary effort particularly since it was bound to reduce the number of jobs available to those in need.

I am now convinced that the Labour Party's opposition to philanthropy and altruism and its determined belief in economic self-interest as the driving dynamic of society has done it grievous harm. For ironically enough the Party, trade unions, and the Co-operative were all a hundred years ago inspired by a profound and passionate altruism—a belief in a new Jerusalem—linked with an urgent sense of duty—a conviction that it was an essential part of socialism to practise what one preached by volunteering to help comrades in distress.[31]

So the movement which had invented the social forms of modern participatory democracy and practised them in union branch and co-op meeting, thereby laying a Tocquevillian foundation for democracy, was ironically fated to develop through its political party the threats of a bureaucratic state. Of course, there were those who protested against these emerging tyrannies with the authentic voice of a deeply rooted English socialism. Norman Dennis has written, for example, a completely convincing demolition of British planning practices, from the standpoint of democratic socialism in the English tradition which I have described.[32] There is an authentic anti-statism of the Left.

Planning is, of course, associated with left-wing politics and the illogical 'therefore' is frequently added that criticism of it is comfort to the Right. But the 'hidden hand' is also 'a planner' with the market as its instrument. This form of 'planning', however, is vitiated by unequal distributions of power, wealth, and income between citizens; it does not accurately reflect the preferences of citizens in community as opposed to individuals in a market. Studies of planning do often turn out to be a more or less sophisticated attack on socialism and a plea to 'return to the market'. With Dennis, however, the criticism is directed to the planner's indifference to egalitarian notions of income and power, and his ignorance of the preferences and values of the community he is appointed to serve.

On what grounds can we accept or reject the theory or principle by which a bureaucracy is guided in its action? Sociologists call these grounds the 'legitimation' of the organization and its activities. Max Weber pointed out that organizations differ greatly when they come to decide whether what they are doing is 'morally right' and based upon 'the correct and relevant data'. One type of organization accepts the word of its leader on both these matters. This is charisma, the personal authority of the inspired leader—the sayings of the leader are the criteria of both truth and worth. A second type of organization rests its activities upon a piety for what has actually, allegedly, or presumably always existed and upon a belief in the everyday routine as being the inviolable norm of conduct. This is organized authority based on tradition. Thirdly, there are organizations to which Weber gave the term bureaucratic, which appeal to the rule of general laws applying to all within the jurisdiction of the organization without regard to differences of race, age, family background, or social condition. The legitimacy of such an organization's authority does not depend upon the actual benefits given to particular persons, but upon the legality of the general rule which has been purposely thought out and enacted. Authority here is based on formal as distinct from substantive justice.

This said, it is immediately apparent how enormously ambitious is the claim, scientific and moral, for a bureaucratic organization.

The task is relatively easy, and successful bureaucratic routine administrations have emerged, where the same service can (and especially where it must) be provided day after day in an identical way to large numbers of people. This is the case with, for example, gas, water, and electricity supplies, and transport and postal services. Bureaucratic administration is also appropriate, if more problematic, in the production of houses when, because of chronic shortage, large numbers of identical dwellings must be produced. It may even be appropriate to the demolition of houses where a few formal characteristics—for example, whether the house is at all damp, or possibly where a measurable amount of dampness is present—enable an official to distinguish unequivocally between a slum house and a non-slum house. But when we come to the service of more subtle and varied human needs in medicine, social security, or education, difficulties multiply and a fourth type of legitimation appears which is increasingly important in the modern world. The activities of an organization are not 'proved' right and good because they are the command of a charismatic leader, or because of tradition, or because they can be subsumed under some general rule, but because they are so certified by the trained members of the organization whose special function it is to evaluate the particular issue. This is professional authority. Decisions, characteristically in the form of 'advice', are made by those who have been appointed to a 'sphere of competence' on the basis of qualifications attested by a professional group of peers.

As long as the group of professionals make claims only in the technical sphere, and as long as they merely say 'this is the given task, we know the most economical means of accomplishing it', the organization will show many acceptable bureaucratic characteristics. But it is also possible for professionals to make claims in such a way, or to such an extent, that their legitimation resembles that of the inspired leader. These claims to legitimation typically take the form of a kind of group charisma. Each case is adjudicated not by an appeal to strictly formal conceptions unambiguously established, made public, and safely recorded 'in the files', but by informal judgements rendered by the personal incumbent of the professional status in terms of concrete ethical or practical valuations. These valuations may be quite opaque to those outside the profession. The professional, by definition, is absolved from justifying his decision; he does not need to reveal his basis in theory or fact or value.

Thus the legitimacy of professional bureaucratic decisions must be judged in two ways. The first is scientific. Decisions ought to be made in the light of ascertainable knowledge. No one can read Dennis's account of planning in Sunderland and retain confidence in the professionalism of planners. Nor is this an isolated local example. Here, speaking more generally, and with examples from many branches of public policy, is R. H. S. Crossman again:

But I was even more worried, particularly when I became a Minister and was able to see a good deal for myself, by the inexplicable decisions under which I found our social services to be operating, decisions which in themselves were inhuman and stupid. And yet as I knew full well they had been made by intelligent, well-intentioned people. How could it be possible that now we had abolished the amateurism of philanthropy and placed the administration of our welfare state in highly professional hands such decisions could be made?[33]

The second way of judging professional bureaucracies emphasizes the capacity of ordinary people to reach rational decisions about matters which directly affect them. But even more it emphasizes the moral proposition that the exercise of personal discretion is itself a social and personal good. When such discretion has to be abbreviated, as is unavoidable on countless grounds, the case of those who desire to impose restrictions must be well based in fact and convincing in terms of political, social, and moral argument. Otherwise we are all too likely to forget, in a fog of pseudo-science, that, as Dennis likes to say, 'the citizen is usually his own best expert'.

Conclusion

The outlook, some may conclude, is gloomy—the huge private businesses we have created, and the public servants we invented to realize justice, freedom, and equity will become our tyrannical masters. Even the ombudsman will turn out to be another professional bureaucrat.

What, then, is to be done? The characteristic response by the centre to peripheral unrest is further efforts at incorporation. The various forms of community development projects, initiated and controlled from Whitehall under the Urban Programme, exemplify the pattern.[34] Central direction is resented by local activists. For example, the grand national design for developing and applying a response to poverty through more effectively delivered and integrated local services degenerates into a complicated pattern to conflict between the centre and the locality, and within the locality between competing interest groups. It would be idle to pretend to an easy answer. But if there are answers, they might more readily be found in our own heritage of democracy and socialism. Our hard-won civil liberties need new defence from a radical overhaul of administrative laws. We have an unfinished programme of greater economic and social equality. But the social integration which is needed to underpin it all cannot survive the national organization we have erected.

In this context Thatcherism, if it maintains its strategy of excluding organized labour from the political process and insisting on a 'new realism' in the economic market-place, threatens the basis of social order. The renowned gentleness of British society may be jeopardized. Fraud bids to supplant faith, if necessary by the use of force. Modern states are increasingly authoritarian. Techniques of surveillance and of opinion management are increasingly built into public and private bureaucracies. In Britain, E. P. Thompson has pointed in alarm to the exploitation of the Official Secrets Act, telephone tapping, and the manipulation of the Press in the interests of the ruling party by ministerial and departmental leaks.[35] The Ponting affair of 1985 and the supply of arms to Iraq investigated by the Scott Inquiry of 1993 symbolize Thatcherite government. Secrecy and restriction of information successfully resist the demands of open democratic government.

In the post-Thatcher period of the 1990s bureaucracy has taken a new turn as the instrument of government designed to impose market discipline on previously public professional bodies alleged to be inefficient. The National Health Service is the best known and most heatedly debated example. It now appears that the fastest rate of growth within the NHS in the early 1990s was not among medical staff but among administrators. A less well-known example is that of the universities. They have expanded between 1970 and 1991 to take over a million students. In the process staff/student ratios have declined (from 8.2 to 11.6), tenure has been abolished, an increasing minority of teachers and researchers are on insecure, short-term contracts, and average salaries have fallen in real terms by at least a third. The only exception is the trend of prosperity for administrators, especially those who run the former polytechnics.[36]

Weber saw only one escape from bureaucratic tyranny—a return to small scale. Subsequent writers following this line have been dismissed as proposing economic absurdity, as did William Morris in *News from Nowhere*, or medieval romanticism, as did G. K. Chesterton in *The Napoleon of Notting Hill Gate*. But at least this type of response to the modern conditions of state power and manipulative social integration, with its recognition of the failure of emotional bonds in large impersonal structures of authority, points forward rather than backward to the possibilities of solidarity through democracy.

If neither charisma nor rational legality is an adequate base for a viable authority, the only other recourse is to tradition, or rather to that strand of political tradition in Britain which is democracy. Democracy is the consensus of free men and women, free to assemble, to express opinion, to persuade, and to elect, but, having done so, willing to accept the will of the majority, whose rule will be tempered by consideration for the minority among whom they may at any time find themselves. Democracy so defined is always prone to exhibit the classic dilemma of conflict between the values of liberty and equality. Potential conflict, in a society with high unemployment, ethnic minorities, regional inequalities, and emergent claims to equality for women, is a strong challenge to democracy in contemporary Britain.

8 A DEMOCRACY OF CITIZENS

The only way to meet the challenge of those who would dismiss any successful prospect for Britain is to turn from analysis of our present discontents to an attempt to chart the way to a brighter future. This does not mean abandoning objectivity. The determining of social ends should always be disciplined by study of the means to reach them: and that has been the burden of the earlier chapters. Exhortation alone is futile, whether to altruism or to tolerance or to recognition of the equal claim of others to share in the bounty afforded by society. The problem is to discover, to establish, and to strengthen those social institutions that will encourage and foster the kinds of relations between people that are desired.

I have asserted that liberty, equality, and solidarity are the three fundamental values in terms of which societies are to be judged. None of these ideals is fully realized in Britain. The question, then, is how each may be more fully realized. Simultaneous maximizing of them is not possible. It is a matter of finding the best balance between the revolutionary triad. Yet I believe that advance towards all three is possible, and that the limits of that advance depend upon the development of a democracy of citizens.

No theory of inevitable future history is involved in this view. Its underlying assumptions about 'human nature' and social possibility are, to be sure, reformist in a strong sense and morally committed to both libertarian and egalitarian ends and to the democratic means of their attainment.[1]

For those who accept this tradition of social thought the past is a constraint: the future is an opportunity. That in essence is the theory of change that has underlain my discussion in this book.

The peculiar constraints of British history have emerged. It is a country in which the unequal powers and advantages of a ruling minority have survived from agrarian through industrial towards post-industrial society with remarkable continuity. A long series of accommodations has been negotiated, the privileged exchanging concessions to new interests for agreement by the newcomers not to undermine the fundamentals of the inequality of the status quo.

A political culture of individualism and moderation permitted, and at each step was reinforced by, tentatively accumulated social bargains. British culture accordingly has its characteristic vocabulary of 'decency', 'the law and the constitution', 'Her Majesty's loyal Opposition' and 'custom and practice' alongside the popular suspicions of all ideals and ideologies as 'extremist'. It is a culture of gradualism, pragmatism, and appeal to common sense. The pursuit of individual liberty and sectional interest is assumed as an unproblematic law of nature. The 'national interest' is a dubious concept outside the emergency of war. Hegelian notions of an organic supra-individual entity are incomprehensible. Ancient struggles for liberties against kings and popes and potentates are seen as consensus against over-ambitious government. Localism has been the natural source of authority. Individualism restricts the political power of the state and simultaneously turns the work place into the theatre if not of class warfare then at least of adversarial, arms-length bargaining over wages and job regulation. Economics and politics are thus divided by economic liberalism while the state has maintained a remarkably successful appearance or mythology of impartial even-handedness between the classes in their economic struggles. Meanwhile gradually widening opportunities, the dispensation of honours, and the slow concession of welfare rights have together adapted the status system as a continuing support to political legitimacy as well as a cushion against the harsh divisive inequalities of class.

The new Conservatism

This, on the whole, cohesive structure has faced increasing challenge since the 1960s and the end of the post-war period.

Economic depressions after the first oil crisis of 1973 followed their characteristic British variant—response was slower, unemployment greater, and slump longer than in the Western European economy as a whole. Balance-of-payments crises and inflation always reopen the past negotiations over the shares of the economy which should go to the complex competitors of capital and the sectional interests of labour. Class conflict is intrinsic to capitalism. In Britain the social balance has always been precarious but rescued by the culture of accommodation I have described.

Confirmation of the Maastricht treaty in 1993 marked a new phase in British debate as between the legitimacy of local, national, and federal government. The national interest in the EEC context becomes more meaningfully if painfully expressed as subsidiarity, identifying the locus of a struggle between ancient principles. There are passionate opponents of European political integration on both the Thatcherite Right as well as on the Left. The future of nationalism and of Westminster power are at stake. It is perfectly possible that in future Westminster will be humbled by, in effect, an alliance between local authorities and the Commission in Brussels.

These crises, on which British consensus came near to breaking-point in the early nineteenth century, have reappeared in the late twentieth century. The new Conservatism—'Thatcherism'—resuscitated economic liberalism. The Thatcher government from 1979 resolutely set out to exclude organized labour from participation in political management, returned to a renewed emphasis on the separation of the economic from the political sphere, and did not flinch from imposing mass unemployment and failing welfare services, ostensibly as the necessary price for combating inflation and raising productivity, actually because of a conviction that the old class compromise had to be swept away if a new strong and prosperous country was to be built.

Whether or not these policies of economic liberalism will continue to be pursued in the later 1990s and, if so, whether they will eventually strengthen the British economy, remains highly disputable. What is certain is that they are a radical departure from traditional Conservative compromise. They spell danger. If successful and leading, as promised, to a return to full employment, then frustrated and resentful trade unions could renew the sectional scramble and 'pay off old scores' against management. If unsuccessful, they could encourage extremism of the Right and the Left as the legitimacy of parliamentary government is undermined. A government which pursues class war unsuccessfully is likely thereby to destroy parliamentary democracy.

Neither a triumphant return to national wealth and power through capitalist free enterprise nor a comprehensive national collapse supervened by a Fascist or Communist dictatorship are likely outcomes. But, short of total post-Thatcherite success or lack of it, there is an alternative, but no less dispiriting, possibility of stability which is best described as a new polarization: not the class polarization envisaged by Marx for nineteenth-century industrial capitalism, but a no less fundamental dichotomy between the haves and the have-nots in a post-industrial society. It is all too readily conceivable that a political democracy with an emerging economy of increasingly white-collar employees, individualistic, privatized, and market-oriented, could be stable. The majority of the qualified, employed, and house-owning citizens could use the state to protect their interests against politically unorganized and socially fragmented minorities of the unqualified and unskilled. Control of such an unequal community would be feasible through minimal welfare and efficient police.

This is no fictional nightmare. The elements and tendencies of a new polarization can be assembled all too easily from the preceding descriptive chapters. The rich have become richer and the poor poorer in Britain since 1979. Opportunities for a career in management, enterprise, or profession are still increasing but alongside the mounting risks of serious deprivation in protracted unemployment and dependency on impoverished social services. Success in the formal economy is complemented, not substituted, by success in the informal economy.[2] The stakes of individual success or failure in school and in work are rising. Yet the odds of success or failure are lengthening along lines of

social division—between the inner city and the prosperous suburb, between the North and the South, the white majority and
the ethnic minorities, the privately and the publicly schooled. In
short, not a simple division into two nations but a complex
polarization of increasingly embittered inequalities.

It is even possible that such a society could be politically ruled
by a Labour government or some combination of the recon-
structed Left. Underestimation of the extent to which economic
liberalism has captured the modern political vocabulary is all too
easy. Socialism has become a self-damning word. There is no
reason to suppose that the old meaning—that is the pre-political
meaning of socialism as against individualism—has lost its grip
on popular consciousness. There is clear evidence that the NHS
remains a valued national institution and the fear or suspicion
that such politicians as Peter Lilley or Michael Portillo are pursuing a half-hidden agenda of demolishing the Welfare State is
likely to drive the Conservative party still further into unpopularity. But, on the other hand, virtuous declaration to opinion
pollsters as to the desirability of higher taxation for Welfare
State purposes did not in fact dislodge Conservative government
in 1983, 1987, or 1992.

If care and compassion for the weak is the mark of a good
society, it is the least likely feature of an order of economic
liberalism. Such an order forms classes, and liberty goes to those
with power and advantage with respect to the market and the
state apparatus. Such an order has the further insidiously self-
fulfilling property of justifying inequality by blaming the poor
for their poverty and encouraging the strong to save themselves
individually at the expense of the weak. Such an order relies
ultimately on individual contract enforced by the minimal state:
it has no place within it for what the European tradition of
reform and revolution has labelled fraternity.

Solidarity

The notion of fraternity in political discourses is a metaphorical
reference to this ideal of a moral community, covering all the
relationships, conjugal and consanguineous, that are entailed in

the family. Indeed, it has sometimes been argued, and with force, that the fraternal metaphor impoverishes this conception: that brotherhood is more diluted and more prone to enmity than any of the other relationships; and that, in the revolutionary creed, 'brotherhood has been selected as the image of perfection, not because it represents the family at its best, but because it is the family at its least familial'.[3]

Fraternity of this kind, in reality, rejects the family. But this is not my intention. On the contrary, while recognizing that family loyalties may limit or conflict with similar civic or community ties, I assume that the fraternal loyalty of the monk or the dedicated party member can and should be an overriding creed and code of conduct only for the few. Nor is this type of human association a necessarily superior expression of moral integration. The ethical value of such a fraternity, whatever the self-sacrifice which it may entail, depends upon the treatment it gives to those who by choice or circumstance are not part of the brotherhood.

Moreover, just as the harmonious family, nuclear or extended, bears value in its own right, so too can the limited political community, even though it restricts itself to something less than the ecumenical brotherhood of man. The United Nations, the European Community, the United Kingdom, England, Scotland, and Wales, can surely exist together. Of course, against those who advocate or allow particularistic forms of fraternity, the charge of 'contradiction' may be laid. Restricted definitions of community inevitably leave problems of external relations. Bounded human groups, by definition, always set such problems. But the proper reply, appealing to experience, is that the smaller group can cultivate the values to be applied in the larger. If these values are liberty and equality, then a practical meaning is given to the idea of the brotherhood of man. It is in this sense that I see fraternity, even though, and indeed because, it is rooted in small-scale organizations, as the precondition of liberty and equality. But, by the same token, the forms of fraternal association which can make up a fraternal society can vary, and communities can remain integrated while attaching different importance to liberty and equality.

However, there are two compelling arguments against the use of the term fraternity in the meaning and connotation it brings to us as a cultural inheritance. First, it is sexist. Its male and its narrowly familistic association is crippling to any future ideal of inclusion in a genuine community of citizens. Neither the addition of sorority nor any other tortuous use of kinship language can overcome the difficulty. A suitable alternative word is hard to find: 'socialist' or 'communitarian' are literally correct but ineligible for other reasons of connotation. The best alternative is 'solidarity', and I propose now to adopt it.

The second reason—nostalgia—is hardly less compelling. Fraternity, like community, so easily evokes a romantic version of the old respectable working-class district or mining-village as described by Jeremy Seabrook or Richard Hoggart. No viable policy can re-create that society even if it were desirable. Moreover, the use of the concept of community—as, for example, in 'community care' can all too easily be a disguise for forcing public responsibility on to vulnerable private individuals—in this case usually women. There is, I have argued, an authentic tradition of local collective self-help outside the state: and the best of the old tradition should indeed be retained and renewed. This means, for example, recognizing the value of what Christian socialists in the 1880s called the 'socialism of character', the belief that individuals acting both alone and in co-operation could raise the quality of themselves and their society.

Citizenship

The new Conservatism in Britain has opted for one of the two contesting alternatives for realizing the revolutionary ideals—capitalism and communism. Western industrial capitalism pioneered the market as the central mediating institution in the development of wealth and its distribution. But the market promotes neither solidarity nor equality. It was historically the means of escape from feudal community and has been the target of Marxist criticism as the mechanism of class inequality and of the substantive restriction of liberty. Industrial communism substituted a state bureaucracy for the market. But here, and especially in the Russian case, the liberal critic can point to the repressive fraternity of the party which controlled the state apparatus, and the sacrifice of political liberty in exchange for a far-from-perfect equality. Out of this contention the possibilities seem to be no more than a choice between two vast historical failures.

Is there another way? I think so. The third alternative, for Britain, is to take its own traditions of citizenship and democracy seriously in all their richness and inspiration. They offer the basis for a new solidarity without which both liberty and equality are impoverished. They offer also the political and social means of progress towards a newly integrated society. They were pointed to in Durkheim's emphasis on local autonomy and respect for tradition in late nineteenth-century Britain. They are best thought of as a *radical tradition*: a willingness to change institutions under changed circumstances. But they are the radicalism of the Left rather than the Right because they seek to realize more perfectly the values sought by past reform. John Major's citizenship charter or Douglas Hurd's 'active citizenship' are weak responses to the challenges of alienation and rising disorder. They are not in accord with calls for granting citizens' universalistic claims which add up to a Welfare State providing and entitling first-class public services. Nor do they fit with the 'social chapter' of the Maastricht treaty which seeks to protect workers and to aim for the restoration of full employment.

The relevance of capitalism and communism, in any event, has to be put in the context of actual and present British circumstances. These, briefly recapitulated, are the legacy of a 'first-world' development, post-imperialism, tentative integration with the European continent, and a resurgent economic liberalism. But they also include a tradition of solidarity which has supported the slowly developing institutions of civic, political, and social citizenship. In Britain, political solidarity is citizenship. Its seeds were sown in the civil liberties of the seventeenth and eighteenth centuries. Its roots grew in the social inventiveness of the urban working class of the nineteenth century, and in the traditions of public service which were developed by the liberal elements of the professional middle class. These have been the finest expressions of British membership one of another, but the Labour movement has faltered in its attempt to nationalize the local welfare societies of an exploited class, and the ideal of public service has been diluted in its transformation to an overpowerful bureaucracy. So the political organization of citizenship, which is democracy, and the social organization of citizenship, which is community, continue to be thwarted by class interests and bureaucratic subversions.

What, then, are the prospects for a third way, through solidarity as citizenship, between the first and second worlds of capitalism and communism? The Thatcherite answer is to dismiss the 'third way' as the failed and fudged compromise of Butskellism. Capitalist conviction is the path to a prosperous future. Against this movement, it must immediately be conceded, there is still no unified powerful and coherent political movement for a third way. True, the communist alternative is even less likely to succeed by popular persuasion. But the very failure of its advocates has served mainly to weaken the political organization of the social-democratic Left, to deepen suspicions of 'socialism' as unpatriotic, and to reinforce popular disbelief that the party of nationalization and central planning has a practical solution to the problems of mass unemployment, civic disorder, and national integrity. There is, in other words, no obvious and immediately mobilizable new radicalism with a programme to match the complexity of our cumulated problems. Blair's resurgent Labour Party is the most hopeful sign so far.

Indeed, the greatest danger is precisely the offer of simple solutions to our complicated plight. We have an economy that does not release our energies, a polity that does not secure our trust, and a culture which does not sufficiently attract our affections. Simple solutions can only lead to political tyranny, whether from the Right or the Left. Either would destroy that fundamental element of our social life and tradition in which we can take pride—our long-developed and tenaciously held civil liberty. Our essential predicament is that the historical conditions which allowed this liberty also permitted divisive inequalities of class and status, a stratified society held together by imperial might abroad and deference and respect for shared religious and cultural values at home. But external empire and internal social control have been losing their power to pacify without violence, leaving market success and political bureaucracy, in all their weaknesses, to justify a still markedly unequal society.

Past failures to achieve fair and equal social distribution have driven some to apathy, others to a belief in a violent seizure of power and the imposition of an authoritarian social order, and still others to denial of the possibility or even desirability of an egalitarian society. These are the roads to tyranny. Our experiences of industrial, nationalist, and racial conflict continually demonstrate the need for a new sense of equality to replace old class-restrictive liberties and status-crippled fraternities. We have still to provide a common experience of citizenship in childhood and old age, in work and play, and in health and sickness. We have still, in short, to develop a common culture to replace the divided cultures of class and status.

Equality

Our society cannot stand on such shifting foundations. To strengthen them, we need principles and practices of social distribution which are acknowledged to be just by the great majority. And in a world of growing visibility of reference groups, these principles will be seen as just only if they actually are just. The implication is that in a political democracy which secures our liberties, the paramount principle of distribution must be equality. Equality of opportunity is not enough. It is a state of affairs we have still not reached but which is, in any case, a step towards a society that could be more ruthlessly stratified than the one we live in now. Nor is it enough to eliminate all irrelevant discriminations of skin colour, sex, cultural background, or family upbringing. We need full equality of the basic material conditions of social life. If poverty remains in Britain this is not because the technical means to its abolition are missing: it is because of an inadequate sense of moral implication in the lives of compatriots. It is a failure not of economic production, but of political distribution. The guarantee of the material essentials for freedom from want does not require even a radically egalitarian policy. The altruism nurtured in the kind of family experienced by the majority, extended by standards of schooling that most parents expect, and embodied in the political definitions of citizenship which were proclaimed during and after the Second World War, would put an end to poverty, once and for all.

Nor is the end of poverty a Utopian dream. Mrs Thatcher told the House of Commons in December 1983 that 'people who are living in need are fully and properly provided for'. A glance at the government's own statistics on the income of children, or an evening walk from the House of Commons to Waterloo Station shows that beggars have returned to a society which imagined that unrelieved poverty had disappeared into older unhappy memory. In any case, a subsequent national poll showed that most of the nation (57 per cent) did not agree with her. The researchers, Joanna Mack and Stewart Lansley, went further and asked their national sample to say whether they would be willing to pay extra income tax for poverty relief where poverty was what the respondents themselves had defined as minimum necessities for living in contemporary Britain.[4] Three-quarters were willing to pay a penny more on the standard rate. An increase of 5p on the income tax would have been enough to lift one-third to one-half of the poor above the level which the majority of the nation defined as minimally decent. Admittedly, five-penny philanthropists did not quite muster a majority. But they included 30 per cent of the Conservative, as well as 42 per cent of the Labour voters; and, most impressively, they included 44 per cent of the richest 10 per cent of citizens—the very people who have stood to gain most by the contrary policies of the new Conservatives.

Beyond this readily attainable minimum of a fair society, R. H. Tawney's conception still stands: because men are men, social institutions—property rights, and the organization of industry, and the system of public health and education—should be planned, as far as is possible, to emphasize and strengthen, not the class differences which divide, but the common humanity which unites them.[5]

Unless they are shown to be relevant to needs, inequalities based on differences of personal quality are no argument against equality. Nor is the familiar argument that incentives necessitate inequality to be taken as a fundamental law of human economic nature. The incentives they assume are the products of present values and interests which arise from our existing institutions, and institutions can be changed. In a solidaristic society it could reasonably be expected that any extra rewards to effort and capacity that might be necessary for an efficient division of labour would leave the basic structure of equal citizenship unimpaired.

The outstanding example of an established solidaristic institution, one in which the most elevated familial ideal is extended voluntarily to the stranger, is the British blood donor system, which R. M. Titmuss has compared with the marketing of blood in the United States and other countries to demonstrate that large-scale solidarity is a human practicality and not merely a Utopian exhortation. From his study of American practice, Titmuss concluded that:

the commercialization of blood and donor relationships represses the expression of altruism, evades the sense of community, lowers scientific standards, limits both personal and professional freedoms, sanctions the making of profits in hospitals and clinical laboratories, legalizes hostility between doctor and patient, subjects critical areas of medicine to the laws of the market place, places immense social cost on those least able to bear them—the poor, the sick, and the inept—increases the danger of unethical behaviour in various sectors of medical science and practice, and results in situations in which proportionately more blood is supplied by the poor, the unskilled, the unemployed, negroes, and other low-income categories of exploited human populations of high blood yielders.[6]

We do not have to assume with Titmuss that, in social institutions, there is a Gresham's law of ungenerosity. But we can recognize the opposite and integrating principle, which is to seek the community of citizenship in all public organizations. To do so is to encourage, through public policy, those social motives which the blood transfusion service brilliantly exemplifies.

Family

From this point of view there is nothing more important than the policy pursued by the state towards the family. Families have unequal shares of material and cultural capital. The remedy is positive discrimination. The material base for parenthood does not measure up to democratic standards of fairness. It is true that, no thanks to government, babies began in the post-war period to be born rather more in the better-off and less in the worse-off homes. Fertility was coming to be positively correlated with family income—a reversal of the previous absurdity. But mothers, and especially working-class mothers, are still at once the most hard-worked and the least-rewarded members of our working population. They are an essential element of the social division of labour but, unlike nurses, teachers, social workers, and the like, are excluded from the paid occupational division of labour. They deserve an income which reflects their service to society. They deserve publicly provided facilities in street child centres and nursery schools to relieve their isolated labours in raising the under-fives. The family is our best carrier of the basic education of each new generation of citizens. An enlightened social policy should recognize this and define the experts and specialists, the schools and the child services, as agents for the support, not the replacement, of family upbringing. The implication is that we must challenge the usurpation of authority by experts (whether they appear as teachers or as administrators) and grant full citizenship to the amateur parents against the professional pedagogues. This is what is meant, for instance, by the community school. Not parent governors as tokens in a ritual, but genuine parental and community government of schools.

Education for citizens

What kind of educational policy would put solidarity into more even balance with liberty and equality? The liberal approach through slow and limited expansion is not enough. The equality of plenitude is probably an unattainable dream. We are unlikely to see the Utopia, which William Morris envisaged in *News from Nowhere*, of a consensual restriction of consumer demands together with happy coincidences between demand and voluntary supply of services. Nor can there be firm reliance on the American hope for unrestricted supply through technological advance leading to rates of economic growth which out-distance consumer expectations. In reality, a balanced educational policy would have to deal with the equality of scarcity—which means educationally the problems of transformation from élite to mass, rather than mass to universal higher education. Such a policy is therefore bound to hurt the established vested interests of privileged minorities. Moreover, to reassert an unpalatable truth, equality can never be attained through educational policies alone.

But making the large assumption that a society which wanted equality would put through the necessary fundamental reforms for the equalization of participation in the work place and the community, the structure of schooling would be that of recurrent education, and rights of participation in it would be those of citizenship rather than those of the market-place. The selective function of education for a hierarchy of occupational positions would be transformed into one of differentiation for a complex and fluid array of jobs having roughly equal material rewards. Selection would thereby become strictly educational.

The allocation of resources to education in such a system would not substitute flat equality for the present unequal reinforcement of advantages already distributed to families in a hierarchy of class and status. It would follow the principle of positive discrimination directed against all arbitrary or accidental, and therefore unfair, disadvantages. This would mean less for the universities and more for the nurseries, less for Solihull and more for Newham, less for the 18- to 21-year-olds and more for the over-65s. The basic citizenship right to a given amount of time free from work would be universal, and its increments would accrue to everyone and not simply to those in the rising generation. This basic citizenship principle would then be linked to, and modified by, that of positive discrimination through carefully worked out and constantly revised formulae for translating measures of disadvantage into extra educational benefits in so far as these were not more appropriately dealt with through income, employment, and housing policies.

In the interests of solidarity both the organization and content of education would be centred on the idea of community schools. At all levels education would be locally governed within the national framework of citizenship rights and positive discrimination. The form of educational government would be participatory democracy, within which the role of the professional teacher would be that of community servant with all this implies for teacher training, the practice of educational administration, and the claims of teachers' unions. 'Free schools' would find their place in such a community organization, and might, incidentally, offer a more effective service of experiment and innovation than was ever given by the 'public schools'.

The idea of the community school has to be given a geographical meaning, especially for the under-5s, parents, and over-65s. In part, this would be to recognize the hidden costs of alienation, anomy, rootlessness, and isolation which are exchanged for the benefits of physical mobility. In part, it would be to recognize the costs in inhumanity of grandiose economic and political structures. In part, it would be to assert that in so far as there is a 'logic of industrialism', it does not necessarily involve the rates of migration which are presently experienced, and far less the destruction of local social networks by mindless urban planning. Educationally, it would be to assert the learning potential of all

social relations and to deny the arbitrary attribution of monopoly to the formal teacher in the class-room. Culturally, it
would be to assert the worth of local life, its distinctiveness, and
its commonalities with other places and other times, and to deny
that local experience only fosters parochialism and excludes
universalism.

Higher education would become adult education, and in that
sense immediately be made universal. Its organization would
also be dominated by the idea of the community school, and its
development would realize the principles of recurrent education. There would thus be a greater variety and flexibility of
provision in community colleges and local institutions, as well as
through the mass media and the Open University. Access and
student finance would be provided through sabbaticals and
arrangements for retirement, as well as student fees.

Industrial democracy

Democracy is not a long tradition. It was a usurper at the end of
the eighteenth century, fighting a previous tradition of feudal
custom. As I pointed out in Chapter 4, it was slow in coming. It
has yet to be fully realized beyond the formalities of the polling
booth in those spheres of life, particularly the work place, where
it lays claim to be applied.

I am not, of course, suggesting that democracy can be applied
mechanically to all forms of human association. What I am
suggesting is that it can be the ultimate court of appeal for our
secular lives. Families cannot be full democracies: they are not
bands of brothers, and the lesser responsibility of childhood is
an inescapable fact: but they can be, and can be judged as,
nurseries of responsible citizenship. Schools and universities
cannot be democracies, whatever is said by the National Union
of Students. If you are a teacher and I come to learn, then your
knowledge must have authority over my ignorance: but again,
the school you run is successful precisely in so far as it brings
me to competent citizenship in the trade, profession, or subject
you teach me; and from that moment I can claim the right to
democratic relations with you.

That is all obvious enough. But Britain is far from laying the democratic foundation for traditional authority in all the spheres to which its modern evolution points. There are two spheres of life where this is conspicuously so—the nation state and industrial organization—two areas in which the democratic principle could be more firmly applied.

The starting-point in both spheres is that a modern society organizes itself by extremely specialized division of labour. But in national affairs Britain has overreached itself. It is tied into a huge apparatus of international markets. It has given over a great deal of its effective authority to international agencies through membership of the EEC, the development of multinational companies, and its trading relations all over the world. And the island occupies a specialist position within this complex through the London money market which we call the City. Britain is very far from being an autonomous economy and, quite apart from internal dissension, the extent to which its government can control inflation, price levels, and standards of life is feeble. To domesticate authority within its shores—and so to give its people a chance to run an effective democracy— would probably entail some cost to their general standard of living.

Some would prefer to pay that material price, assuming democratic justice in the distribution of the burden: and it must be pointed out in defence of this 'little Englandism' that no economist or politician in the current debate who seeks solutions within the international framework holds out any immediate prospect of relieving the misery of 3 million unemployed. That is one painful and inequitably distributed cost of persistence with the large and therefore effectively undemocratic system under which Britons live.

I said, 'quite apart from internal dissension'. That brings me to the other sphere in which greater democratization is possible, and here I would point to the analyses offered by Alan Fox. Fox's main attention in *Beyond Contract* is focused on the experience of work in the office, the factory, and the workshop. Work relations in the past have given low discretion and low trust to subordinates *vis-à-vis* their superiors. This was the triumph of the so-called scientific management which reached its most extreme form in the modern factory assembly line. The low-discretion syndrome, as Fox describes it, contrasts the rank-and-file production worker with the professional. The worker on the shop-floor has little sense of being an expert; of commitment to a calling; of autonomy on the job; of obligation to produce high-quality work, and he has little or no sense of identification with the organization in which he works.

Fox has also analysed the low levels of trust which lie behind the struggles between different groups of organized workers. Obviously a more democratically integrated society would organize its work by the opposite principles of high-trust relations, both vertically and horizontally. Professional work at its best requires and involves a high level of trust between people. Rigidly hierarchical forms of industrial authority produce at best the solidarity of the resentful. In this context the trends of occupational structure towards professionally skilled work are a vast opportunity for developing new forms of high trust in the workplace.

Industrial democracy is a vital element in the unfinished British programme of creating a society which commands willing and widespread allegiance. Britain has the strongest shop-steward organization in the world. Its indiscipline against corporatism is far more impressive than the corporative hierarchy of the Trades Union Council, which the mass media have been quick to portray as the modern demon. What is more important than shop-steward radicalism is that this shop-floor organization has been the most conspicuous form of democracy in contemporary Britain. Nevertheless, the low-discretion, low-trust principle still dominates work organization.

These tendencies could, however, be reversed. Reversal, of course, might carry its considerable price—and not only in terms of cars and television sets (at least in a transitional period). But estimates of that price must be examined with scepticism when they come from those with a private interest in maintaining the status quo. 'Scientific management' methods are not invariably the most efficient. Any argument that extension of high-trust relations must be at the expense of the expectation of affluence needs to be qualified by realistic appraisal of a country's particular conditions. However, there seems little doubt that some price would have to be paid. Moreover, there is little prospect of the bargain being eagerly sought either by those presently in authority (who have vested interests in their present power), or the workers, patients, consumers, and citizens (who are conditioned to prefer a bit more of what material benefits they already have). Only those who experience autonomy and relations of trust can fully appreciate their satisfactions.

Democratic devolution

Political organizations could be refashioned to mirror the values cultivated in home, school, and work place. The twentieth-century trends in government and industry have made size and complexity into serious obstacles to effective citizenship and threaten to replace it by oligarchic and bureaucratic power. The increase of economic co-operation over larger areas makes all the more urgent the devolution of decision. Bold advances towards a more developed citizenship—in Scotland for the Scots, in the work place for workers, in the school for parents, in the locality for the neighbour, and so on, could evoke popular support. John Osmond's eloquent plea for Welsh devolution, pointing to the way in which democracy should be rooted in community, is a persuasive contemporary example:

Man needs an anchor in a particular community. It is the source of that moral power which enables him to resist the monolithic State. The nation and the community in which he seeks his roots is not an end in itself: it is man's link with eternity. 'Cadw tŷ mewn cwnwl tystion', as Waldo Williams so movingly expressed it: man's relationship to the community is 'Keeping a home amidst a cloud of witnesses'.[7]

Conclusion

These familial, educational, and industrial examples cover only a small part of the total range of the institutions of production and reproduction, all of which need to be measured and reformed in the direction which leads to a society which is integrated, because it rests on an optimal balance of what is possible to make real our traditional revolutionary dreams. My review of past progress makes it all too clear that the journey to a society of citizens is no easy one. Stratification is stubbornly resistant to change: there is bound to be opposition. There are always those who place private interest above public welfare. Yet in a society of the kind I am advocating, patient persuasion has to be our principal weapon: for persuasion is democracy in action. Only if it is given constant priority can we both guard our freedoms and override the resistance of vested interest. Only then, but certainly then, democracy has the right to enforce its will.

The attainment of a new and sound basis for social order requires political will of a strength we have hitherto lacked. No one can guarantee that either the challenge will be accepted, or the response forthcoming. After a review of the British past and present, Alan Fox concluded:

None of this offers much cheer for millenarians, but there are consolations. Life in Britain retains many decencies, and most of them are connected with painfully constructed defences against the arrogances, impertinences and corruptions of power. These decencies are under threat from different directions. An independent-spirited, independently organised working class can sometimes bring its own minor threats, but as a bulwark against the major threats its record in Britain gives hope. In other ways, too, Britain will continue to be marked by its history and its heritage, and contained in that heritage are traditions that are creative, radical and reveal a love of country that stops short of bellicose assertiveness against others. They may surface again. It is too soon to declare 'the end of an old song' and consign Britain to the category of failed enterprises.[8]

That was true in the 1980s. For the twenty-first century it is also socially and politically possible. Its elements are in our social traditions and on our political agenda. Adversity itself is now sufficient to give social response to political initiative. Here again the initiatives have to be congruent with the end in view: and that means democratic politics. Democratic politics is essentially a system in which citizens actively mould the final decisions binding on all. It works only if liberty of thought and expression is ranked first among rights and the active exercise of citizenship first among duties. Political action is inevitably carried on by imperfect people in public office. Hence the constant need for alert and knowledgeable citizens, to defeat oppression and to prevent the public services from degenerating into organizations which serve the private interests of public servants.[9]

That, all too briefly, is my view of our best way into the future. We have no paradise lost, no paradise to be regained. Yet we can, if we will, take heart from the ancient story of the departure of our primal ancestors from the Garden of Eden:

> Some natural tears they dropped, but wiped them soon;
> The world was all before them, where to choose
> Their place of rest, and Providence their guide:
> They hand in hand, with wand'ring steps and slow,
> Through Eden took their solitary way.[10]

NOTES

Preface

1. M. Albrow, 'The Undergraduate Curriculum in Sociology—a Core for Humane Education', *Sociology*, 20/3, 335–46.
2. W. G. Runciman, 'Sociologese', *Encounter*, 25/6, 1965, 45–7.
3. P. Abrams, *The Origins of British Sociology 1834–1914*, University of Chicago Press, 1967.
4. P. Anderson, 'Components of the National Culture', *New Left Review*, 50 (July/Aug. 1968).
5. J. A. Banks, 'The British Sociological Association—The First Fifteen Years', *Sociology*, 1, 1967, 1–10.
6. A. H. Halsey, 'Provincials and Professionals: The British post-war sociologists', *Arch. European Sociology*, 23, 1982, 150–75.
7. M. Bulmer, *Essays on the History of British Sociological Research*, Cambridge University Press, 1985.
8. See note 14 below.
9. R. Dahrendorf, *The Modern Social Conflict: An Essay on the Politics of Liberty*, Weidenfeld and Nicolson, 1988.
10. B. Barry, 'The Continuing Relevance of Socialism', in R. Skidelsky (ed.), *Thatcherism*, Chatto and Windus, 1988.
11. A. Heath, R. Jowell, and J. Curtice, *How Britain Votes*, Pergamon Press, 1985.
12. A. Giddens, *The Constitution of Society*, Basil Blackwell, 1984.
13. *Horizons and Opportunities in the Social Sciences*, Economic and Social Research Council, 1987.
14. For an extended view of British sociology at the end of the 1980s see *British Journal of Sociology*, 40/3 and 4, 1989.

Chapter 1: To know ourselves

1. E. Gibbon, *The Decline and Fall of the Roman Empire*, J. M. Dent and Sons, Everyman edn., 1911–13, i. 5.
2. (1735–1801.) Professor of Civil Law at the University of Glasgow from 1761 to 1801.
3. (1723–90.) Professor of Logic at the University of Glasgow from 1751. He then held the Chair of Moral Philosophy from 1751 to 1763.

4. In *The Times*, 7 Oct. 1977.

5. W. Dibelius, *England*, Jonathan Cape (English edn.), 1930. (First German edn. 1922.)

6. Ibid. 18.

7. G. Orwell, *Collected Essays, Journalism and Letters*, ii, 1940–3, Penguin, 1970, 74–135.

8. J. P. Lehmann, *Remember You Are An Englishman: A Biography of Sir Harry Smith*, Jonathan Cape, 1977.

9. C. Crouch, *Class Conflict and the Industrial Relations Crisis*, Humanities Press, 1977, 3.

10. T. Hobbes, *Leviathan*, J. M. Dent and Sons, Everyman edn., 1914, 49–50.

11. M. Friedman, *Capitalism and Freedom*, University of Chicago Press, 1962.

12. I. Berlin, *Four Essays on Liberty*, Oxford University Press, 1969.

13. R. Dahrendorf, *The New Liberty*, Routledge and Kegan Paul, 1975. *The Modern Social Conflict*, Weidenfeld and Nicolson, 1988.

14. J. Rawls, *A Theory of Justice*, Clarendon Press, 1972.

15. R. H. Tawney, *The Acquisitive Society*, G. Bell & Sons, 1943. And *Equality*, Allen and Unwin, 1931, 4th rev. edn., 1952.

16. F. Hirsch, *The Social Limits to Growth*, Harvard University Press, 1976.

17. Ibid. 11.

18. Lord David Cecil, *The Cecils of Hatfield House*, Constable, 1973, 267.

Chapter 2: A class-ridden prosperity

1. See G. Marshall and J. Goldthorpe, 'The Promising Future of Class Analysis', *Sociology*, 26, 1992, 381–400.

2. This division of social organization derives from Max Weber. See H. Gerth and G. W. Mills, *Essays from Max Weber*, Routledge and Kegan Paul, 1948, 180–95. See also J. H. Goldthorpe and P. Bevan, 'The Study of Social Stratification in Great Britain in 1946–76', *Social Science Information*, 16 (3/4), 1977, 279–334. For a lively and recent general account of Weber, see S. Andreski, *Max Weber's Insights and Errors*, Routledge and Kegan Paul, 1984.

3. See F. Parkin, *Class Inequality and Political Order*, Paladin, 1972 (first published by MacGibbon and Kee, 1971).

4. R. Dahrendorf, *Class and Class Conflict in Industrial Society*, Routledge and Kegan Paul, 1959.

5. See G. Marshall, H. Newby, D. Rose, and C. Vogler, *Social Class in Modern Britain*, Hutchinson, 1988. Also A. Heath *et al., Understanding Political Change*, Pergamon, 1991, esp. chs. 5, 6, and 7. For a prognosis of future class analysis see Marshall and Goldthorpe, loc. cit., and R. E. Pahl, 'Does Class Analysis without Class Theory Have a Promising Future?: A reply to Goldthorpe and Marshall', *Sociology*, 27/2, 1993, 253–8.

6. For example, the Oxford Mobility Study, discussed briefly in Chapter 3 and more extensively in Chapter 6 below, has made a 36- and a 7-fold classification based on J. H. Goldthorpe and K. Hope, *The Social Grading of Occupations: A New Approach and Scale*, Oxford University Press, 1974. Note is also made below of the Registrar-General's classification of five social classes (with a further division of Class III into its non-manual and manual components). A short discussion of class schema may be found in G. Marshall and A. Swift, 'Social Class and Social Justice', *British Journal of Sociology*, 44/2, 1993, 187–211.

7. A. Heath *et al.*, op. cit., 67.

8. J. H. Goldthorpe and C. Llewellyn in their 'Class Mobility in Britain: Three Theses Examined', *Sociology*, 11/2, May 1977, 257–87. Table 2.1 is reproduced from this source.

9. *Social Trends*, 23, 1993, 52.

10. J. H. Goldthorpe, 'Women and Class Analysis: In Defence of the Conventional View', *Sociology*, 17/4, 1983; N. Britten and A. F. Heath, 'Women, Men and Social Class', in E. Gamarikow (ed.), *Gender, Class and Work*, Heinemann, 1984; A. F. Heath and N. Britten, 'Women's Jobs Do Make a Difference: A Reply to Goldthorpe'; and J. H. Goldthorpe, 'Women and Class Analysis: A Reply to the Replies', *Sociology*, 18/4, 1984.

11. *Social Trends*, 23, 1993, Table 4.8.

12. F. Parkin, *Marxism and Class Theory: A Bourgeois Critique*, Tavistock, 1979, 85.

13. J. Westergaard and H. Resler, *Class in Capitalist Society: A Study of Contemporary Britain*, Heinemann, 1975, 352.

14. Cf. C. Clark, 'The Economics of Housework', *Bulletin of Oxford Institute of Statistics*, 20/2, May 1955, 205–11.

15. For details and guidance through the difficulties of measurement see A. H. Halsey, *British Social Trends Since 1900*, Macmillan, 1988; and *Social Trends*, a publication of the Government Statistical Service which is an invaluable source of material data on British social structures.

16. See J. Mack and S. Lansley, *Poor Britain*, Allen and Unwin, 1985.
17. Royal Commission on the Distribution of Income and Wealth, *Report*, No. 5 (Third Report on the Standing Reference), Cmnd. 6999, HMSO, 1977. *Social Trends*, 23, 1993, Chart 4.22: international comparisons (table 4.23) show that rises and falls in rates of unemployment were:

	1976	1981	1986	1991
UK	5.6	9.8	11.2	8.7
Germany	4.4	4.4	10.4	4.3
France	6.4	7.4	11.2	9.5
USA	7.6	7.5	6.4	6.6

18. *Social Trends*, 15, 1985, 87.
19. A. B. Atkinson, Keynes Lecture, 1991, British Academy.
20. See R. M. Titmuss, *Essays on the Welfare State*, Unwin University Books, 1958, 34–55. For an analysis of redistribution through the welfare state since the mid-1970s see J. Hills (ed.), *The State of Welfare*, Oxford University Press, 1991.
21. Westergaard and Resler, op. cit., 118.
22. Ibid. 119.
23. *Social Trends*, 15, 1985, 89.
24. J. B. Priestley, *English Journey*, Heinemann, 1934, Penguin edn., 1977, 296.
25. W. G. Runciman, *Relative Deprivation and Social Justice*, Routledge and Kegan Paul, 1966. Runciman uses the word power to mean what I refer to as party.
26. W. W. Daniel, *The PEP Survey on Inflation*, PEP Broadsheet 553, July 1975.
27. W. J. Wilson, *The Truly Disadvantaged*, Chicago University Press, 1989.

Chapter 3: The reconstitution of status

1. See G. D. H. Cole, *Studies in Class Structure*, Routledge and Kegan Paul, 1955, 65. His ch. 3, 'The Social Structure of England', is a good brief summary of changes in the structures of class and status from the middle of the nineteenth to the middle of the twentieth century.
2. R. Roberts, *The Classic Slum*, University of Manchester Press, 1971, Penguin edn., 1973 (to which my references apply).
3. Ibid. 30.

4. Ibid. 160–1.

5. Ibid. 23–5.

6. B. Webb, *My Apprenticeship*, Penguin edn., 1971, 171.

7. R. Hoggart, *The Uses of Literacy*, Chatto and Windus, 1957, and his autobiography (3 vols., 1990–2): i: *A Local Habitation*; ii: *A Sort of Clowning*; iii: *An Imagined Life*. See also his *Townscape with Figures. Farnham—Portrait of an English Town*, Chatto and Windus, 1994.

8. See J. H. Goldthorpe *et al.*, *Social Mobility and Class Structure*, Oxford University Press, 1980.

9. D. V. Glass (ed.), *Social Mobility in Britain*, Routledge and Kegan Paul, 1954.

10. G. D. H. Cole, op. cit., 58.

11. J. Westergaard and H. Resler, *Class in a Capitalist Society*, Heinemann, 1975, 324–33.

12. W. G. Runciman, *Relative Deprivation and Social Justice*, Routledge and Kegan Paul, 1966.

13. For an excellent short account, see ibid., ch. 5. See also R. M. Titmuss, *Problems of Social Policy*, HMSO and Longmans, 1950.

14. It is often assumed that Weber's conception of status is also trivialized by liberal writers, who have identified it with the prestige of occupations. On this see F. Parkin, *Class Inequality and Political Order*, Paladin, 1972, 29–32. But I think that the underestimation of class in this tradition is the more fundamental error.

15. See T. H. Marshall, *Citizenship and Social Class*, Cambridge University Press, 1950: this lecture was republished and a 'forty years on' commentary added by Tom Bottomore in 1992 by the Pluto Press. For a brief appreciation of Marshall, see D. Lockwood, *Sociology*, 8/3, 1974, 363–7, and my fuller treatment, 'T. H. Marshall Past and Present', *Sociology*, 18, 1984, 1–18. See also T. Geiger, *Society in the Melting Pot*, Kiepenheuer and Witch, German edn., 1950.

16. G. M. Trevelyan, *English Social History*, Longmans, Green, and Co., 1944, 351 (quoted in T. H. Marshall, op. cit., 15).

17. T. H. Marshall, op. cit., 15. Marshall goes on to remark that the most celebrated actor in this drama was John Wilkes and, as he puts it, 'although we may deplore the absence in him of those noble and saintly qualities which we should like to find in our national heroes, we cannot complain if the cause of liberty is sometimes championed by a libertine'. Perhaps Marshall was thinking particularly of the

occasion when Wilkes was arraigned before a posse of outraged peers of the realm, one of whom declared, 'Wilkes, you will die on the gallows or of the pox': 'That depends, my Lord,' Wilkes replied, 'on whether I embrace your principles or your mistress.'

18. This was made up of social security, £441; education, libraries, science, and arts, £314; health and personal social service, £281; housing, £195; environment services, £104; law, order, and protective services, £80; food and transport subsidies including concessionary fares, £45. (*Hansard*, 10 Nov. 1977, Written Answers, Column 186.)

19. A. Fox, *History and Heritage: The Social Origins of the British Industrial Relations System*, Allen and Unwin, 1984, ch. 4.

20. A. Giddens, *Profiles and Critiques in Social Theory*, Macmillan, 1982.

21. F. Parkin, *Class Inequality and Political Order*, Paladin, 1972, 30.

22. T. H. Marshall, *Sociology at the Cross Roads*, Heinemann, 1963, 87 and 115.

23. Ibid. 217.

24. Ibid. 61.

25. Ibid. 129.

26. Ibid. 135.

27. Ibid. 61.

28. A. Giddens, op. cit., 172.

29. A. Fox, op. cit., ch. 9.

30. A. Giddens (op. cit., 177–8) draws attention to the extension of surveillance techniques by the modern state and points out that the resulting threat to civil rights in both Western and socialist countries needs urgent analysis, has had little attention from Marxist or liberal political theory, and can be aided by Marshall's precise specifications of the nature of civil, political, and welfare rights.

31. R. Dahrendorf, *The Modern Social Conflict: An Essay on the Politics of Liberty*, Weidenfeld and Nicolson, 1988.

32. *Social Trends*, 23, 1993, 16.

33. Ibid. 17.

34. M. Banton, *Race Relations*, Tavistock Publications, 1967.

35. E. J. B. Rose, *Colour and Citizenship: A Report on British Race Relations*, Oxford University Press, 1969.

36. United Kingdom National Report on the Future of Migration, OECD, Feb. 1986.

37. J. Solomon, *Race and Racism in Britain*, Macmillan, 1993, 75.

38. C. Husbands, 'Why has there been no extreme right in Great Britain?' *LSE Magazine*, Spring 1992, 4–8.
39. J. H. Goldthorpe, 'Social Inequality and Social Integration in Modern Britain', in D. Wedderburn (ed.), *Poverty, Inequality and Class Structure*, Cambridge University Press, 1974.
40. Ibid. 221.

Chapter 4: The fortunes of party

1. J. S. Martin and J. Spear (eds.), *The Changing Labour Party*, Routledge, 1992.
2. See C. Crouch (ed.), 'The Place of Participation in the Study of Politics', *British Political Sociology Year Book*, iii, *Participation in Politics*, Croom Helm, 1977, 1–17.
3. The relevant legislation was enacted in 1855–6.
4. R. Price and G. S. Bain, 'Union Growth Revisited: 1948–74 in Perspective', *British Journal of Industrial Relations*, 14/3, 1976, 339–55. See also their 'The Labour Force' in A. H. Halsey (ed.), *British Social Trends Since 1900*, Macmillan, 1988.
5. T. H. Marshall, *Citizenship and Social Class*, Cambridge University Press, 1950. See also N. Dennis and A. H. Halsey, *English Ethical Socialism*, Oxford University Press, 1988.
6. K. Marx, *Contribution to the Critique of Hegel's Philosophy of Right* (1844), in K. Marx and F. Engels, *On Religion*, Foreign Languages Publishing House, Moscow, 1957, 42.
7. Those juvenile thoughts, I appreciate, were neither humble nor meek.
8. A. Fox, 'Corporatism and Industrial Democracy: The Social Origins of Present Forms and Methods in Britain and Germany'. Paper prepared for the *International Industrial Democracy Conference*, July 1977 (Social Science Research Council), Cambridge, UK. The papers were published by the Social Science Research Council in 1978. Fox's general work, *History and Heritage: The Social Origins of the British Industrial Relations System*, Allen and Unwin, 1984, incorporates the earlier work.
9. Ibid.
10. See G. M. Young, *Stanley Baldwin*, Rupert Hart-Davis, 1952, 93–4.
11. Ibid. 95.
12. See R. T. McKenzie and A. Silver, *Angels in Marble: Working Class Conservatives in Urban England*, Heinemann Educational, 1968; E. A. Nordlinger, *The Working-Class Tories*, MacGibbon and Kee,

1967; W. G. Runciman, *Relative Deprivation and Social Class*, Routledge and Kegan Paul, 1966. J. H. Goldthorpe *et al.*, *The Affluent Worker*, 3 vols., Cambridge University Press, 1968–9; B. Hindess, *The Decline of Working-Class Politics*, MacGibbon and Kee, 1971; B. Jessop, *Traditionalism, Conservatism, and British Political Culture*, Allen and Unwin, 1974.

13. The Communist party used to be described by Ernest Bevin as no less the enemy of the working class than the Tory party.

14. D. Butler and D. Stokes, *Political Change in Britain*, Macmillan, 2nd edn., 1974, 182.

15. A. F. Heath, R. Jowell, and J. Curtice, *The British General Election 1983*, Pergamon Press, 1985. *Understanding Political Change: The British Voter 1964–87*, Pergamon, 1991.

16. Heath *et al.*, *British General Election 1983*.

17. B. S. Rowntree and G. R. Lavers, *Poverty and the Welfare State*, Longmans, 1951.

18. J. H. Goldthorpe *et al.*, op. cit.

19. *Report of the Committee on Financial Aid to Political Parties* (Chairman, Lord Houghton of Sowerby), Cmnd. 6601, HMSO, 1976, on the basis of replies from 91 constituency Labour parties, estimated that individual membership by 1974 was down, not to two-thirds of a million, but to less than one-third of a million. The research organization, PEP, put the figure still lower at 250,000 (D. Leonard, *Paying For Party Politics*, PEP 1975). In February 1977 the Gallup organization drew a representative sample of 315 local party organizations and asked the agent, secretary, or chairman to estimate the number of individual members in his own constituency Labour party. Since the respondent's estimate was taken at its face value, the Gallup result is probably an overestimate. Even so, in Northern England, on these figures a full half of the constituency parties were reported to have 500 members or fewer, and only 12 per cent more than 1,000 members.

20. D. Hayter, *The Labour Party: Crisis and Prospects*, Fabian Tract 451, Sept. 1977. In only 4 per cent of the Gallup constituencies was the ratio of individual members of the Labour party to Labour voters better than 1 in 10. In half the seats it was worse than 1 in 30, and it was worse than 1 in 30 in no less than 68 per cent of the constituencies in Labour-held seats in the Midlands, the North, and Scotland. The overall average was 1 to 26: the average for Labour-held seats in the Midlands, the North, and Scotland was distinctly

worse at 1 to 35 (C. Martin and D. Martin, 'The Decline of Labour Party Membership', *Political Quarterly*, 48/4, 1977, 464). By 1977 the inability of constituencies to finance them meant that Labour had only 86 full-time agents, the fewest since 1946. About half of the constituency parties were without youth branches in the mid-1970s; even among the party members themselves who were in the age range 15–25, only about 1 in 8 were members of the Young Socialists. (Labour Party National Executive Committee Report 1977, p. 20.) For more recent figures see Patrick Seyd and Paul Whiteley, *Labour's Grass Roots*, Oxford University Press, 1992.

21. It should be noted that party membership (however defined) has fallen for the Conservatives and the Liberals as well as Labour since 1980.

22. See articles in *Guardian*, 19 Nov. 1993 by Will Hutton, *et al.*

23. R. Roberts, *The Classic Slum*, Penguin, 1973.

24. D. Caute, *The Fellow Travellers: A Postscript to the Enlightenment*, Weidenfeld and Nicolson, 1973.

25. S. and B. Webb, *Soviet Communism: A New Civilisation*, 2 vols., Longmans, Green, and Co., 1935, 2nd edn., 1937.

Chapter 5: Between the generations

1. D. Bell, *Toward the Year 2000—The Trajectory of an Idea*, Beacon Press, 1969, 643.

2. M. Young and P. Willmott, *The Symmetrical Family*, Routledge and Kegan Paul, 1973, 19 ff. For trenchant criticism of this view of economic growth, see F. Hirsch, *The Social Limits of Growth*, Harvard University Press, 1976, 167 ff.

3. In a BBC Third Programme broadcast (1953), to which Lord Briggs kindly drew my attention.

4. R. Roberts, *The Classic Slum*, Penguin, 1973, 74 n.

5. A. Macfarlane, *The Origins of English Individualism: The Family, Property and Social Transition*, Oxford University Press, 1978.

6. A. Waley, *The Analects of Confucius*, Allen and Unwin, 1938, 83.

7. E. R. Leach, *A Runaway World?*, BBC Publications, 1968, 44.

8. E. F. Rathbone, *The Disinherited Family*, Edward Arnold, 1924, p. ix, Introduction.

9. For a detailed analysis of the history of reduction of fertility in Britain, see M. Teitelbaum, *The British Fertility Decline*, Princeton University Press, 1984.

10. E. A. Wrigley and R. S. Schofield, *The Population History of England 1541–1871: A Reconstruction*, Edward Arnold, 1981.

11. R. M. Smith, 'Fertility Economy and Household Formation in England over Three Centuries', *Population and Development Review*, 7/4, 1981, 595–622. Also H. J. Hajnal in 8/3, 1982, 449–94.

12. D. E. C. Eversley and W. Kollman, *Population Change and Social Planning*, Edward Arnold, 1982, and J. Ermisch, *The Political Economy of Demographic Change*, Heinemann, 1983.

13. These are graphically described by Lord Briggs in *Victorian Cities*, Odhams Press, 1963, Pelican edn., 1968.

14. See M. Teitelbaum, op. cit.; J. Habakkuk, *Population Growth and Economic Development since 1750*, Leicester University Press, 1971; J. A. Banks, *Prosperity and Parenthood: A Study of Family Planning among the Victorian Middle Classes*, Routledge and Kegan Paul, 1954; and J. A. Banks, *Victorian Values*, Routledge and Kegan Paul, 1981.

15. J. Habakkuk, op. cit., 69.

16. D. Coleman and J. Salt, *The British Population: Patterns, Trends, and Processes*, Oxford University Press, 1992.

17. Ibid.

18. N. Oldfield and A. C. S. Yu, *The Cost of A Child*, CPAG, 1993.

19. F. Engels, *The Origin of the Family, Private Property, and the State*, 1884. Repr. in Marx and Engels, *Selected Works*, vol. ii, Foreign Languages Publishing House, Moscow, 1951, 205.

20. R. M. Titmuss, 'The Position of Women', in *Essays on 'The Welfare State'*, Allen and Unwin, 1958.

21. E. F. Rathbone, op. cit., p. viii, Introduction.

22. M. Wynn, *Family Policy*, Penguin, 1972.

23. F. Field, M. Meacher, and C. Pond, *To Him Who Hath*, Penguin, 1977.

24. J. Bradshaw, in Oldfield and Yu, op. cit.

25. *Social Trends*, 23, 1993, 56.

26. For a vivid description, see N. Dennis *et al.*, *Coal Is Our Life*, Eyre and Spottiswoode, 1956.

27. *Observer*, 14 Sept. 1984.

28. K. Kiernan, 'Men and Women at Work and at Home', in R. Jowell *et al.* (eds.), *British Social Attitudes*, 9th Report, 1992/3.

29. J. Cheetham, *Unwanted Pregnancy and Counselling*, Routledge and Kegan Paul, 1977, 2.

30. N. Dennis and J. Erdos, *Families without Fatherhood*, Institute of

Economic Affairs, 1992.

31. N. Dennis and A. H. Halsey, *English Ethical Socialism*, Oxford University Press, 1988.
32. J. Elliot and H. Richards, 'Children and Divorce: Behaviour Before and After Parental Separation', *International Journal of Law and the Family*, 5/3 (1991), 258–76.
33. *Social Trends*, 8, 1977, 116, table 6.33.
34. R. Hoggart, *The Uses of Literacy*, Chatto and Windus, 1957.
35. Ibid. 95.

Chapter 6: Mobility and education

1. V. Pareto, *Mind and Society*, Harcourt Brace, 1935, iii. 2053, para. 20.
2. K. Marx, *Capital*, J. M. Dent and Sons, Everyman edn., 1936, iii. 586.
3. See H. Braverman, *Labour and Monopoly Capital: The Degradation of Work in the Twentieth Century*, Monthly Review Press, 1974. Also R. Crompton and K. Sandman, *Gendered Jobs and Social Change*, Unwin, 1990.
4. See D. Bell, *The Coming of Post-Industrial Society*, Basic Books, 1973, and J. Gershuny, *Social Innovation and the Division of Labour*, Oxford University Press, 1983.
5. A. B. Atkinson, A. K. Maynard, and C. G. Trinder, *Parents and Children: Incomes in Two Generations*, Studies in Deprivation and Disadvantage, SSRC/DHSS, Heinemann, 1983.
6. See B. S. Rowntree and G. R. Lavers, *Poverty and the Welfare State*, Longmans, 1951. Also, for a general picture of Britain at mid-century, see P. Hennessy, *Never Again: Britain 1945–51*, Jonathan Cape, 1992.
7. See D. V. Glass (ed.), *Social Mobility in Britain*, Routledge and Kegan Paul, 1954.
8. See J. H. Goldthorpe (with C. Llewellyn and C. Payne), *Social Mobility and Class Structure*, Oxford University Press, 1980, 2nd edn., 1987.
9. See A. F. Heath, *Social Mobility*, Fontana, 1981, 2nd edn., 1994.
10. The use of 'ten years after entry to the job market' as the 'destination' point had the advantage of standardizing the measure of mobility for each individual in the sample. It also may be expected to reflect the impact of education on mobility more clearly than a destination point which comes later in a man's working life. But this

procedure yields a smaller amount of recorded movement into the middle class than is obtained by using 1972 occupation as the destination point. This is because the older men have a longer period in which to reach 'occupational maturity' which, for this population, means greater proportions with middle- and lower-middle-class jobs. See also A. H. Halsey, A. Heath, and J. Ridge, *Origins and Destinations*, Oxford University Press, 1980.

11. J. H. Goldthorpe and C. Llewellyn, 'Class Mobility in Britain: Three Theses Examined', *Sociology*, 11/2, May 1977, 257–87.

12. G. Payne, 'The Lieutenant Class', *New Society*, 41/772, July 1977, 118–20.

13. See A. H. Halsey, 'Towards Meritocracy: The Case of Britain', in A. H. Halsey and J. Karabel (eds.), *Power and Ideology in Education*, Oxford University Press, New York, 1977.

14. J. H. Goldthorpe (with C. Llewellyn and C. Payne), 'Trends in Class Mobility', in J. H. Goldthorpe (with C. Llewellyn and C. Payne), *Social Mobility and Class Structure in Modern Britain*, Oxford University Press, 1980, ch. 3.

15. This method is now routinely used in log linear modelling of mobility.

16. R. Erikson and J. Goldthorpe, *The Constant Flux*, Oxford University Press, 1992.

17. A. H. Halsey, A. F. Heath, and J. M. Ridge, *Origins and Destinations*, Oxford University Press, 1980.

18. A. F. Heath, *Social Mobility*, Fontana, 1994.

19. For a summary of the debate see *Oxford Review of Education*, 10/1, 1984.

20. S. Prais (ed.), *Education, Training and Productivity*, National Institute of Economic and Social Research, 1990; Also his Keynes Lecture 1993 (forthcoming from the British Academy).

21. D. Finegold, 'Breaking Out of the Low Skills Equilibrium', *Briefings: National Commission on Education*, 5, Heinemann, 1993.

22. D. Raffe, 'Participation of 16–18 year olds in Education and Training', *Briefings: National Commission on Education*, 3, Heinemann, 1992.

23. H. Glennerster and W. Low, 'Education and the Welfare State: Does It Add Up?' in J. Hills (ed.), *The State of Welfare*, Oxford University Press, 1991, 20–87.

24. A. H. Halsey (ed.), *Ability and Educational Opportunity*, OECD, 1961.

25. A. B. Atkinson, *The Economics of Inequality*, Oxford University Press, 1974.
26. T. Modood, 'The Number of Ethnic Minority Students in British Higher Education: Some Grounds for Optimism', *Oxford Review of Education*, 19/2, 1993, 167–82.
27. Y. Cheng and A. Heath, 'Ethnic Origins and Class Destinations', ibid. 151–66.
28. M. Egerton and A. H. Halsey, 'Trends by Social Class and Gender in Access to Higher Education in Britain', ibid. 183–96.
29. T. Husen, A. Tuijnman, and W. D Halls, *Schooling in Modern European Society*, Report of the Academia Europaea, Oxford University Press, 1992.
30. N. Wakeford, 'Beyond Educating Rita: Mature Students and Access Courses', *Oxford Review of Education*, 19/2, 1993, 217–30.
31. W. Muller and W. Karle, 'Social Selection in Educational Systems in Europe', Paper presented to the meetings of the International Sociological Association Research Committee on Social Stratification, XIIth World Congress of Sociology, Madrid, 9–13 July 1990.
32. H. P. Blossfeld, 'Changes in Educational Opportunities in the Federal Republic of Germany', *EUI Working Paper*, SPS, No. 90/4, 1990.
33. For a review of the current state of the debate on this issue see M. Schiff and R. Lewontin, *Education and Class*, Oxford University Press, 1985, and A. H. Halsey (ed.), *Heredity and Environment*, Methuen, 1977.
34. See A. F. Heath, C. Mills, and J. Roberts, 'Towards Meritocracy? Some Recent Evidence on an Old Problem', in C. Crouch and A. Heath (eds.), *Social Research and Social Reform*, Oxford University Press 1992. Also J. O. Jonnson and C. Mills, 'Class and Educational Attainment in Historical Perspective', *British Journal of Sociology*, 44/2 (June 1993), 213–47; part 2 of the article appeared ibid. 44/3 (Sept. 1993), 403–28.

Chapter 7: Order and authority

1. See N. Glazer and D. P. Moynihan (eds.), *Ethnicity: Theory and Experience*, Harvard University Press, 1975, and J. G. Reitz, *The Survival of Ethnic Groups*, McGraw-Hill, 1980.
2. On which see T. Nairn, *The Break-Up of Britain: Crisis and Neo-Nationalism*, New Left Books, 1977, 82 ff.
3. D. Lockwood, 'For T. H. Marshall', *Sociology*, 8/3, Sept. 1974, 363–7.

4. E. Durkheim, *The Division of Labour in Society*, transl. G. Simpson, Free Press, Glencoe, 1947.

5. Quoted by J. H. Goldthorpe in 'Social Inequality and Social Integration in Modern Britain', in D. Wedderburn, *Poverty, Inequality, and Class Structure*, Cambridge University Press, 1974, 232.

6. B. Wootton, *The Social Foundations of Wage Policy: A Study of Comparative British Wage and Salary Structure*, Allen and Unwin, 1955; R. M. Titmuss, *The Gift Relationship: From Human Blood to Social Policy*, Allen and Unwin, 1970.

7. For an excellent discussion of legitimation and ideology in Britain see S. Hall and M. Jacques (eds.), *The Politics of Thatcherism*, Lawrence and Wishart, 1983.

8. See, for example, F. Parkin, *Class Inequality and Social Order*, Paladin, 1972.

9. T. Nairn, op. cit., 22.

10. See H. Perkin, *The Origins of Modern English Society 1780–1880*, Routledge and Kegan Paul, 1969, 187.

11. Herbert Asquith, 'The Volunteer', in *Poems of To-Day*, 2nd series, originally published separately 1922.

12. J. B. Priestley, *English Journey*, Heinemann, 1934, Penguin edn., 1977.

13. Ibid. 65.

14. Ibid. 126.

15. Ibid. 127.

16. J. H. Goldthorpe, 'Social Inequality and Social Integration in Modern Britain', in D. Wedderburn, op. cit., 222.

17. See his *Relative Deprivation and Social Justice*, Routledge and Kegan Paul, 1966.

18. See J. Benyon (ed.), *Scarman and After: Essays Reflecting on Lord Scarman's Report, The Riots and their Aftermath*, Pergamon Press, 1984; C. T. Husbands, *Racial Exclusionism and the City: The Urban Support of the National Front*, Allen and Unwin, 1983; J. Harris and T. Wallace (with the assistance of H. Booth), *To Ride the Storm: The 1980 Bristol 'Riot' and the State*, Heinemann, 1983; and Trevor Jones, *Britain's Ethnic Minorities*, PSI, 1993.

19. P. Hennessy, *Never Again: Britain 1945–51*, Jonathan Cape, 1992, 156.

20. T. Nairn, op. cit., 194.

21. J. Curtice, 'The North–South Divide', in R. Jowell *et al.* (eds.), *British Social Attitudes*, 9th Report, SCPR, 1992, 159.

22. Kindly sent to me by Paul Cheetham.

23. I. Gilmour, *Dancing With Dogma: Britain Under Thatcherism*, Simon and Schuster, 1992, 104.

24. G. Tullock, *The Vote Motive: An Essay in the Economics of Politics, with Applications to the British Economy*, Institute of Economic Affairs, 1976.

25. *Social Trends*, 15, 1985, 65.

26. A. Heath and D. McMahon, 'Changes in Values', in R. Jowell *et al.* (eds.), *British Social Attitudes*, 9th Report, SCPR, 1992.

27. M. Weber, *The Theory of Social and Economic Organization*, trans. A. M. Henderson and T. Parsons, Oxford University Press, New York, 1947, 337.

28. S. S. Wolin, *Politics and Vision: Continuity and Innovation in Western Political Thought*, Allen and Unwin, 1961.

29. Weber, op. cit., 337.

30. Quoted by, from Lenin, *Selected Works*, ii. 447–8, 456.

31. R. H. S. Crossman, 'The Role of the Volunteer in a Modern Social Service', in A. H. Halsey (ed.), *Traditions of Social Policy*, Blackwell, 1976, 278. For an interesting contrary view of the popular ideological base of the Labour movement see D. Selborne, *Against Socialist Illusion: A Radical Argument*, Macmillan, 1984.

32. N. Dennis, *People and Planning: The Sociology of Housing in Sunderland*, Faber, 1970; *Public Participation and Planners' Blight*, Faber, 1972.

33. R. H. S. Crossman, loc. cit., 268.

34. See D. Donnison, *Urban Policies: A New Approach*, Fabian Tract 487, 1984.

35. E. P. Thompson, *Writing By Candlelight*, Merlin, 1980, 113–33.

36. A. H. Halsey, *Decline of Donnish Dominion*, Oxford University Press, 1992, ch. 6.

Chapter 8: A democracy of citizens

1. An elaboration of this ethical socialist position may be found in N. Dennis and A. H. Halsey, *English Ethical Socialism: from Thomas More to R H Tawney*, Oxford University Press, 1988.

2. R. E. Pahl's *Divisions of Labour*, Blackwell, 1984, is all the more interesting because social research has led him to subscribe to this aspect of the new polarization thesis from an initial standpoint which was virtually opposite.

3. Ferdinand Mount, 'The Dilution of Fraternity', *Encounter*, 47/4, Oct. 1976, 20.

4. J. Mack and S. Lansley, *Poor Britain*, Allen and Unwin, 1985.

5. R. H. Tawney, *Equality*, Unwin Books, 1931 edn., 50.

6. R. M. Titmuss, *The Gift Relationship: From Human Blood to Social Policy*, Allen and Unwin, 1971, 245–6.

7. J. Osmond, *Creative Conflict: The Politics of Welsh Devolution*, Routledge and Kegan Paul, 1977, 251. W. Williams, 'Pa Beth Yw Dyn?' (What is Man?), in *Dail Pren* ('Leaves of a Tree'), Gwasg Gomer, 1956, 67. The quotation is in response to the question raised in the poem: Beth yw gwladgarwch? (What is patriotism?). The poem is essentially about man's search for identity. 'Adnabod' (recognition) is only attained between man and man when the common root is discovered:

> Beth yw adnabod? Cael un gwraidd
> Dan y canghennau
> (What is recognition? To find one root
> Beneath the branches.)

8. A. Fox, *History and Heritage: The Social Origins of the British Industrial Relations System*, Allen and Unwin, 1984, 452.

9. On this see N. Dennis, 'Councillors, Officers and Public Participation', in R. Rose (ed.), *The Management of Urban Change*, Sage Publications, 1974. See esp. pp. 169–70: 'England has created for herself a civil service of municipal officers entirely subordinated to the popular will in law and in fact . . . The control of the expert by the amateur representing his fellow citizens is the key to the whole of our system of government.' When one considers that the literature of English local government, early and late, is full of such statements, it is apparent that, if councillors can be coped with and controlled with ease and with their acquiescence, there is little to be feared from participants with no *locus standi*, or whose *locus standi* is in no way comparable with that of the local government councillor. Indeed, from the point of view of 'correct' decisions being arrived at in the field of urban renewal, in so far as these lie within the jurisdiction of the English local authority, there is a great deal to be said for deflecting attention from the local government councillor. If he did not exist he would be regarded as an impossibly hopeful panacea, extravagantly Utopian, by exponents of 'power and the people'. His weaknesses and the weaknesses of his position are either shared by or exacerbated among any alternative contenders for influence on behalf of residents in areas of

urban renewal. They have none of his strengths. While it is true, therefore, that officers are able to operate with a good deal of confidence on the assumption that the 'correct' decision will be made by councillors, they can be even more confident that neighbourhood councils, residents' panels, and any other arrangements yet suggested which aspire to the councillor's functions without giving them the councillor's power, will also, save in the most exceptional circumstances, have their views accepted if they are 'correct', and if they are not, ignored. Like the roar going round Sunderland when Roker Park is full, the officers can chant in chorus: 'Easy! Easy!'

10. J. Milton, *Paradise Lost*, Book XII, ll. 645–9.

FURTHER READING

General

To read more deeply into the subject of this book is a twofold task. On the one hand it involves further study of theories derived from the social sciences, and on the other hand it calls for wider knowledge of the social, economic, and political history of Britain in the twentieth century. This learning includes acquiring new language. Gordon Marshall's *Dictionary of Sociology*, Oxford University Press, 1993, will be an invaluable guide. Relevant sources of social and political theory are mentioned in the suggestions for further reading under each chapter heading below. As a general introduction there is S. M. Lipset, *Political Man: The Social Basis of Politics*, Johns Hopkins University Press, 1981. On the side of historical sources, a compilation of social trends from the beginning of the twentieth century to the middle of the 1980s is made in A. H. Halsey (ed.), *British Social Trends Since 1900*, Macmillan, 1988. Then from 1970, there is a convenient official source, *Social Trends*, published by the Central Statistical Office annually. This covers much the same ground as *British Social Trends Since 1900* from 1951 and has added further 'social indicators' of particular interest in each year, for example in No. 15 (1985) an essay on 'British Social Attitudes: The 1984 Report' by R. Jowell and C. Airey. This is itself a valuable new source which appears annually.

Economic Trends is a companion publication, and B. R. Mitchell and P. Deane, *Abstract of British Historical Statistics*, Cambridge University Press, 1962, contains a useful long-running series. D. Butler and G. Butler, *British Political Facts 1900–1994*, Macmillan, 1994, is a parallel and invaluable source of political information.

There are bibliographies of work on British twentieth-century history in C. L. Mowat, *Britain between the Wars*, Methuen, 1955; *British History Since 1926: A Select Bibliography*, Historical Association, 1960; and A. J. P. Taylor, *English History 1915–1945*, Oxford University Press, 1965. H. J. Perkin, *The Origins of Modern English Society 1780–1880*, Routledge and Kegan Paul, 1969; P. Hennessy, *Never Again: Britain 1945–51*, Jonathan Cape, 1992; and A. Marwick, *British Society Since 1945*, Allen Lane, 1982, are useful social histories of Britain, as is Noel Annan's *Our Age*, Weidenfeld and Nicolson, 1992.

To know ourselves

Further reading on the study of society in general, and of British society in particular, could well begin with the reviews of sociology in the *British Journal of Sociology*, Vol. 40, September and December 1989 and Vol. 41, 1990. Useful bibliographies are included.

K. Popper, *The Poverty of Historicism*, Routledge and Kegan Paul, 1957, is the best modern book on methodology, and C. A. Moser and G. Kalton, *Survey Methods in Social Investigation*, Heinemann, 2nd edn., 1971, gives an introduction to survey methods. M. Bulmer (ed.), *Social Science Research and Social Policy*, George Allen and Unwin 1986, is valuable. M. E. J. Wadsworth, *The Imprint of Time: Childhood, History and Adult Life*, Oxford University Press, 1991, illustrates how longitudinal surveys can be turned into illuminating social history.

The next step is to read more deeply into contemporary political argument. B. Barry, *Political Argument*, Routledge and Kegan Paul, 1965, is an excellent introduction. Since then Barry's publications have included *Democracy and Power: Essays in Political Theory 1*, Oxford University Press, 1991; and *Liberty and Justice: Essays in Political Theory 2*, Oxford University Press, 1991. See also J. Gray, *The Moral Foundations of Market Institutions*, IEA, 1992, and *Beyond the New Right: Markets, Governments and the Common Environment*, Routledge, 1993. M. Friedman, *Capitalism and Freedom*, University of Chicago Press, 1962, is a powerful exposition of libertarian theory. R. H. Tawney, *Equality*, Allen and Unwin, 1952, remains the best statement of egalitarianism: but see also W. Letwin (ed.), *Against Equality*, Macmillan, 1983. R. M. Titmuss, *The Gift Relationship: From Human Blood to Social Policy*, Allen and Unwin, 1971, is an eloquent plea for fraternalism which might be read alongside Ivan Illich, *Tools for Conviviality*, Fontana, 1973. B. Barry, *The Liberal Theory of Justice*, Clarendon Press, 1973, is a good summary and criticism of J. Rawls, *A Theory of Justice*, Clarendon Press, 1972. R. Dahrendorf, *The Modern Social Conflict*, Weidenfeld and Nicolson, 1988, is an excellent modern discussion of current social development from a liberal standpoint. F. A. Hayek, *The Constitution of Liberty*, Routledge and Kegan Paul, 1960, is a classic source. A. Macfarlane, *The Origins of English Individualism*, Blackwell, 1978, is indispensable for understanding of the British case.

Finally, H. Gerth and C. W. Mills, *Essays from Max Weber*, Routledge and Kegan Paul, 1948 (particularly Weber's essay on 'Class Status and

Party'), is an essential theoretical starting-point for the ground covered by the next three chapters.

A class-ridden prosperity

A general introduction to sociological research and writing on stratification in Britain is provided by H. Newby, *The State of Research into Stratification in Britain*, Economic and Social Research Council, 1982. The best recent study is G. Marshall, H. Newby, D. Rose, and C. Vogler, *Social Class in Modern Britain*, Hutchinson, 1988. Discussion of the general character of class in advanced societies is provided by A. Giddens, *The Class Structure of the Advanced Societies*, Hutchinson University Library, rev. edn., 1981; and F. Parkin, *Class Inequality and Political Order*, Paladin, 1972, and *Marxism and Class Theory: A Bourgeois Critique*, Tavistock, 1979. W. G. Runciman's *Relative Deprivation and Social Justice*, Routledge and Kegan Paul, 1966, is an important interpretation of the history of class and status in twentieth-century Britain in terms of the theory of relative deprivation. W. W. Daniel in his PEP *Survey on Inflation*, 1975, brings Runciman's 1962 survey up to date. J. Westergaard and H. Resler, *Class in a Capitalist Society*, Heinemann, 1975, presents a detailed account of British class structure from the Marxist standpoint. An outstanding empirical study of stratification in Britain is J. H. Goldthorpe, D. Lockwood, F. Bechhofer, and J. Platt, *The Affluent Worker*, Cambridge University Press, 1968–9. All three volumes are relevant: Vol. 1, *Industrial Attitudes and Behaviour*, 1968; Vol. 2, *Political Attitudes and Behaviour*, 1968; and Vol. 3, *The Affluent Worker in the Class Structure*, 1969.

For more detailed analysis of inequalities in income and wealth, there is A. K. Sen, *Poverty and Famines*, Clarendon Press, 1982, and A. B. Atkinson, *The Economics of Inequality*, Clarendon Press, 1975, which expounds the relevant methods of economic analysis. The most up-to-date information on the distribution of income and wealth in Britain is to be found in the Royal Commission on the Distribution of Income and Wealth (Chairman Lord Diamond), *Report*, No. 7, 1979. P. Townsend's *Poverty in the United Kingdom*, Penguin, 1979, is a monumental study. There are also useful essays published in D. Wedderburn (ed.), *Poverty, Inequality, and Class Structure*, Cambridge University Press, 1974. The best recent work is J. Mack and S. Lansley, *Poor Britain*, Allen and Unwin, 1985. J. Hills (ed.), *The State of Welfare 1991*, Oxford University Press, brings together a valuable set of essays on the 1970s and 1980s.

The reconstitution of status

There is no comprehensive modern study of status in British society. There are, however, useful studies of particular groups. Though very different in style, R. Hoggart, *The Uses of Literacy*, Chatto and Windus, 1957, and J. H. Goldthorpe *et al.*, *The Affluent Worker in the Class Structure*, Cambridge University Press, 1969, give authoritative accounts of the status aspects of working-class life in two different times and places. To these two works should be added R. Roberts, *The Classic Slum*, Manchester University Press, 1971, with its graphic description of status distinction within a working-class district of Salford in the first quarter of the century. Two examples of status in more narrowly defined occupational groups are N. Dennis *et al.*, *Coal is our Life*, Eyre and Spottiswoode, 1956, especially ch. 5, and A. H. Halsey, *The Decline of Donnish Dominion: The British Academic Professions in the Twentieth Century*, Oxford University Press, 1992, ch. 10. The status of coloured immigrants in Britain is well treated in the massive sociography by E. J. B. Rose, *Colour and Citizenship: A Report on British Race Relations*, Oxford University Press, 1969. For more recent discussion see J. Benyon (ed.), *Scarman and After: Essays Reflecting on Lord Scarman's Report, The Riots and their Aftermath*, Pergamon, 1984.

The essential source on citizenship as a special form of status is T. H. Marshall, *Citizenship and Social Class*, Cambridge University Press, 1950, and his later work, *Social Policy in the Twentieth Century*, Cambridge University Press, 1967, should also be read, as should Professor T. Jones, *Britain's Ethnic Minorities*, PSI, 1993; J. Solomon, *Race and Racism in Britain*, 2nd edn., Macmillan, 1992; and T. Modood, *Not Easy Being British: Colour, Culture and Citizenship*, Trentham Books, 1992. Professor R. Pinker has put together some of T. H. Marshall's best later essays in *The Right to Welfare*, Heinemann, 1981. W. G. Runciman, op. cit., contains the best general account of changes in status in Britain since the First World War. A new and powerful theoretical development of citizenship theory and social policy is G. Room's *The Sociology of Welfare: Social Policy, Stratification and Political Order*, Martin Robertson, 1979. A further contribution has been made by T. Bottomore in *Citizenship and Social Class*, Pluto Press, 1992.

Reference is made in this chapter to the role of religion in maintaining the status system. For further reading on this question see B. Wilson, *Contemporary Transformations of Religion*, Blackwell, 1976; R. Towler, *The Need For Certainty: A Sociological Study of Conventional Religion*, Routledge and Kegan Paul, 1984; and M.P. Hornsby-Smith, *Roman Catholics in England*, Cambridge University Press, 1987.

The fortunes of party

An illuminating introduction to British twentieth-century politics is S. Beer, *Modern British Politics*, Faber, 2nd edn., 1969, and his *Britain Against Itself*, Faber, 1982, placing politics in 'the age of organization'. The authoritative source on electoral history in Britain in the twentieth century is D. Butler and D. Stokes, *Political Change in Britain*, Macmillan, 1974. C. Crouch, *Class Conflict and the Industrial Relations Crisis*, Humanities Press, 1977, is a difficult but extremely worthwhile book on the relation between government and working-class organization. S. E. Finer, *Anonymous Empire: A Study of the Lobby in Great Britain*, Pall Mall Press, rev. edn., 1966, is indispensable for the further study of 'party' as the term is used in this chapter.

The definitive work on the sociology and history of British industrial relations is A. Fox, *History and Heritage*, Allen and Unwin, 1984. See also C. Crouch, *Trade Unions: The Logic of Collective Action*, Fontana, 1982.

The best account of British political organization from the point of view of electoral behaviour is A. F. Heath, R. Jowell, and J. Curtice, *How Britain Votes*, Pergamon Press, 1985. Heath and his colleagues have since added *Understanding Political Change: The British Voter 1964–1987*, Pergamon, 1991.

Three studies of élites and power may be recommended: J. Fidler, *The British Business Elite*, Routledge and Kegan Paul, 1981; P. Stanworth and A. Giddens, *Elites and Power in British Society*, Cambridge University Press, 1974; and W. Guttsman, *The British Political Elite*, MacGibbon and Kee, 1963. See also J. Scott, *The Upper Classes: Power and Privilege in Britain*, Macmillan, 1982, and J. Scott (ed.), *The Sociology of Elites*, Eldar, Aldershot, 1990.

For the continuing debate on stratification and politics in Britain see R. Rose and J. McAllister, *Voters Begin to Choose: From Closed Class to Open Elections in Britain*, Sage, 1986; I. Crewe and D. Denver (eds.), *Electoral Change in Western Democracies: Pattern and Sources of Electoral Volatility*, Croom Helm, 1985; and P. Dunleavy and C. T. Husbands, *British Democracy at the Cross Roads: Voting and Party Competition in the 1980s*, Allen and Unwin, 1985. See also A. Heath *et al.*, op. cit.

Between the generations

Further exploration of this field might well begin with D. Coleman and J. Salt, *The British Population: Patterns, Trends and Processes*, Oxford

258	*Further reading*

University Press, 1992. The beginnings of the decline in fertility among the upper-middle-class Victorians are well studied in J. A. Banks, *Prosperity and Parenthood*, Routledge and Kegan Paul, 1954. An excellent history of the evolution of the modern family in Europe and North America is E. Shorter, *The Making of the Modern Family*, Collins, 1975. F. Mount, *The Subversive Family*, Jonathan Cape, 1982, is an interesting controversial account. J. R. Goody, *The Development of the Family and Marriage in Europe*, Cambridge University Press, 1983, is an important anthropological account. Two worthwhile empirical studies of the family in Britain are C. Rosser and C. G. Harris, *The Family and Social Change*, Routledge and Kegan Paul, 1965, and M. Young and P. Willmott, *The Symmetrical Family*, Routledge and Kegan Paul, 1973. G. Gorer's *Sex and Marriage in England Today*, Nelson, 1971, is worth reading, and H. Gavron, *The Captive Wife*, Routledge and Kegan Paul, 1966, is a well-known book on the role of the housewife. See also A. Oakley, *Housewife*, Allen Lane, 1974, and E. Roberts, *A Woman's Place*, Blackwell, 1984. Childhood is well treated in M. Pringle, *The Needs of Children*, Hutchinson, 1980, and a modern treatment of the problems of family policy is M. Wynn, *Family Policy*, Penguin, 1972. A collection of essays by S. B. Kumerman and A. J. Kahn, *Family Policy: Government and Families in Fourteen Countries*, Columbia University Press, 1978, includes a study of Britain by R. A. Parker and H. Land which argues that public policies assume and support a traditional form of family organization. A bibliography of recent work is R. Chester, *The Family: A Register of Research in the United Kingdom*, Economic and Social Research Council, 1984. For current controversy on the family and its future see P. Hewitt, *About Time: the revolution in work and family life*, IPPR/Rivers, 1993; A. H. Halsey, 'Changes in the Family', in *Children and Society*, 7/2, 1993, 125–36; K. Kiernan, and V. Estaugh, *Cohabitation: Extra-marital Childbearing and Social Policy*, Family Policy Studies Centre, 1993; N. Dennis and G. Erdos, *Families without Fatherhood*, IEA, London, 1992; J. Bradshaw and J. Miller, *Lone Parent Families in the UK*, DSS Research Report, No. 6, HMSO, 1991; and N. Oldfield and A. C. S. Yu, *The Cost of a Child: Living Standards for the 1990s*, CPAG, 1993.

On old people see P. Laslett, *A Fresh Map of Life*, Macmillan 1989, and M. Young and T. Schuller, *Life After Work: The Arrival of the Ageless Society*, Harper Collins, 1991.

A fascinating account of research on the domestic division of labour is J. Gershuny, 'Changes in the Domestic Division of Labour in the UK,

1975–1987', in N. Abercrombie and A. Warde (eds.), *Social Change in Contemporary Britain*, Polity Press, 1992.

Mobility and education

On meritocracy the indispensable source is M. Young, *The Rise of Meritocracy 1870–2033*, Thames and Hudson, 1958. On comprehensive schools see C. Benn and B. Simon, *Half Way There*, McGraw-Hill, 1970, and S. Ball, *Beachside Comprehensive*, Cambridge University Press, 1941. On educational policy against poverty see H. and P. Silver, *An Educational War on Poverty: American and British Policy Making 1960–80*, Cambridge University Press, 1991.

The classic study of social mobility in Britain is D. V. Glass (ed.), *Social Mobility in Britain*, Routledge and Kegan Paul, 1954. Recent work is reported in J. H. Goldthorpe (in collaboration with C. Llewellyn and C. Payne), *Social Mobility and Class Structure in Modern Britain*, Oxford University Press, 1987; and A. H. Halsey, A. F. Heath, and J. M. Ridge, *Origins and Destinations*, Oxford University Press, 1980. A lucid exposition of the general state of research on mobility is A. F. Heath's *Social Mobility*, Fontana, 1981, rev. edn., 1994. A milestone in advanced method and comparative study is R. Erikson and J. Goldthorpe, *The Constant Flux*, Oxford University Press, 1992.

Order and authority

For an introduction read D. Lockwood, *Solidarity and Schism*, Oxford University Press, 1992. A good general and valuable set of essays on social order is E. Shils, *Tradition*, Faber, 1981. An empirical study of the division of labour in Britain now is R. E. Pahl, *Divisions of Labour*, Blackwell, 1984.

In the literature on problems of devolution and disintegration in the United Kingdom, J. Osmond, *Creative Conflict: The Politics of Welsh Devolution*, Routledge and Kegan Paul, 1977, is outstanding, but see also T. Nairn, *The Break-Up of Britain*, New Left Books, 1977.

Criticism of the traditional British social order and proposals for its reform along egalitarian lines are to be found in R. H. Tawney, *Equality*, Allen and Unwin, 1952, and *The Acquisitive Society*, Bell, 1943. See also R. Williams, *Culture and Society*, Chatto and Windus, 1959, and *The Long Revolution*, Chatto and Windus, 1961; and Julian Le Grand, *The Strategy of Equality*, Allen and Unwin, 1982.

For criticism of the basis of income distribution, a classic source is B. Wootton, *Social Foundations of Wages Policy*, Allen and Unwin,

1955, but see also J. H. Goldthorpe in D. Wedderburn (ed.), *Poverty, Inequality, and Class Structure*, Cambridge University Press, 1974.

Analysis of the social order from a fraternitarian point of view is carried further by A. Vincent and R. Plant, *Philosophy, Politics and Citizenship*, Blackwell, 1984. Also highly relevant is A. MacIntyre, *After Virtue*, Duckworth, 1981. Altruism is analysed in the context of contemporary Britain in M. Ignatieff, *The Needs of Strangers*, Chatto and Windus, 1984; R. M. Titmuss, *The Gift Relationship*, Allen and Unwin, 1971; and also the essay by R. H. S. Crossman in A. H. Halsey (ed.), *Traditions of Social Policy*, Blackwell, 1976. A more general introduction to the study of social policy in Britain is J. Parker, *Social Policy and Citizenship*, Macmillan, 1975.

A powerful study of social integration and anomy in the workplace is A. Fox, *Beyond Contract: Work, Power and Trust Relations*, Faber and Faber, 1974. N. Dennis's analysis of the relation between people, local government bureaucracies, and local politicians may be found in his *People and Planning*, Faber, 1970, and *Public Participation and Planners' Blight*, Faber, 1972. See also D. E. C. Eversley and E. Evans, *The Inner City*, Centre for Environmental Studies, 1980; D. Donnison, *Urban Policies: A New Approach*, Fabian Tract 487, 1984; and J. Seabrook, *What Went Wrong*, Gollancz, 1978.

Three excellent works on social integration in England, Scotland, and Wales are B. H. Harrison, *Peaceable Kingdom: Stability and Change in Modern Society*, Oxford University Press, 1982; C. Harvie, *No Gods and Precious Few Heroes: Scotland 1914–1980*, Edward Arnold, 1981; and K. O. Morgan, *Rebirth of a Nation: Wales 1880–1980*, Oxford University Press, 1981.

On Thatcherism (apart from the account of herself) see R. Skidelsky (ed.), *Thatcherism*, Chatto and Windus, 1988; B. Jessup, 'From Social Democracy to Thatcherism: Twenty Five Years of British Politics', in Abercrombie and Warde, op. cit.; I. Gilmour, *Dancing with Dogma: Britain Under Thatcherism*, Simon and Schuster, 1992; and D. Bell, *Communitarianism and its Critics*, Oxford University Press, 1993.

INDEX

OXFORD

MORE OXFORD PAPERBACKS

This book is just one of nearly 1000 Oxford Paperbacks currently in print. If you would like details of other Oxford Paperbacks, including titles in the World's Classics, Oxford Reference, Oxford Books, OPUS, Past Masters, Oxford Authors, and Oxford Shakespeare series, please write to:

UK and Europe: Oxford Paperbacks Publicity Manager, Arts and Reference Publicity Department, Oxford University Press, Walton Street, Oxford OX2 6DP.

Customers in UK and Europe will find Oxford Paperbacks available in all good bookshops. But in case of difficulty please send orders to the Cash-with-Order Department, Oxford University Press Distribution Services, Saxon Way West, Corby, Northants NN18 9ES. Tel: 01536 741519; Fax: 01536 746337. Please send a cheque for the total cost of the books, plus £1.75 postage and packing for orders under £20; £2.75 for orders over £20. Customers outside the UK should add 10% of the cost of the books for postage and packing.

USA: Oxford Paperbacks Marketing Manager, Oxford University Press, Inc., 200 Madison Avenue, New York, N.Y. 10016.

Canada: Trade Department, Oxford University Press, 70 Wynford Drive, Don Mills, Ontario M3C 1J9.

Australia: Trade Marketing Manager, Oxford University Press, G.P.O. Box 2784Y, Melbourne 3001, Victoria.

South Africa: Oxford University Press, P.O. Box 1141, Cape Town 8000.

Oxford
Paperback
Reference

OXFORD PAPERBACK REFERENCE

From *Art and Artists* to *Zoology*, the Oxford Paperback Reference series offers the very best subject reference books at the most affordable prices.

Authoritative, accessible, and up to date, the series features dictionaries in key student areas, as well as a range of fascinating books for a general readership. Included are such well-established titles as Fowler's *Modern English Usage*, Margaret Drabble's *Concise Companion to English Literature*, and the bestselling science and medical dictionaries.

The series has now been relaunched in handsome new covers. Highlights include new editions of some of the most popular titles, as well as brand new paperback reference books on *Politics*, *Philosophy*, and *Twentieth-Century Poetry*.

With new titles being constantly added, and existing titles regularly updated, Oxford Paperback Reference is unrivalled in its breadth of coverage and expansive publishing programme. New dictionaries of *Film*, *Economics*, *Linguistics*, *Architecture*, *Archaeology*, *Astronomy*, and *The Bible* are just a few of those coming in the future.